DATE DUE

WITSEC

Books by Pete Earley

Family of Spies
Inside the John Walker Spy Ring

Prophet of Death
The Mormon Blood-Atonement Killings

The Hot House
Life Inside Leavenworth Prison

Circumstantial Evidence
Death, Life, and Justice in a Southern Town

Confessions of a Spy
The Real Story of Aldrich Ames

Super Casino
Inside the "New" Las Vegas

WITSEC

*Inside
the Federal
Witness Protection Program*

PETE EARLEY
AND GERALD SHUR

Bantam Books

NEW YORK   TORONTO   LONDON   SYDNEY   AUCKLAND

WITSEC: INSIDE THE FEDERAL WITNESS PROTECTION PROGRAM

A Bantam Book / February 2002

BOOK DESIGN BY ROBERT BULL DESIGN

Library of Congress Cataloging-in-Publication Data

Earley, Pete.
    WITSEC : inside the Federal Witness Protection Program / by Pete Earley and Gerald Shur.
      p.   cm.
    Includes index.
    ISBN 0-553-80145-7
    1. Witnesses—Protection—United States—History.   2. Criminals—United States—History.   I. Shur, Gerald.   II. Title.

KF9672 .E117 2002
345.73'066—dc21

2001043425

Published simultaneously in the United States and Canada

Bantam Books are published by Bantam Books, a division of Random House, Inc. Its trademark, consisting of the words "Bantam Books" and the portrayal of a rooster, is Registered in U.S. Patent and Trademark Office and in other countries. Marca Registrada. Bantam Books, 1540 Broadway, New York, New York 10036.

PRINTED IN THE UNITED STATES OF AMERICA

BVG   10 9 8 7 6 5 4 3 2 1

For Patti Michele
who has made all my dreams come true

—PETE EARLEY

For Miriam
my lover and best friend, who has been my lifelong inspiration

—GERALD SHUR

Start by doing what's necessary,
then what's possible,
and suddenly you are doing the impossible.

—St. Francis of Assisi

CONTENTS

ERALD SHUR thought he was going to vomit. The black-and-white photograph in front of him showed a woman splayed on a tile floor with her throat slit. Not satisfied to simply kill her, the murderer had mutilated her body by cutting her open from throat to navel. He'd then yanked out several of her internal organs, leaving them displayed on her abdomen. The woman had been an informant helping federal agents in a mob case, and the gruesomeness of her murder had been meant as a crude warning: Those who spill their guts to the authorities risk having their own guts literally spilled out by the Mafia.

Shur, a young attorney in the U.S. Department of Justice's Organized Crime and Racketeering Section in Washington, D.C., slid the photograph into a file folder and slipped it into his desk drawer. No need to have his secretary stumble upon it. The murdered woman was the twenty-fifth government informant killed in the past five years. It was October 1961, and Shur was still new at his job. He hadn't yet become accustomed to the viciousness that gangsters could unleash.

An excited Internal Revenue Service agent telephoned him later that day. "We got a promising lead," the agent declared. "How fast can you get here?" Shur caught the next flight to New York City. The IRS had learned that Johnny "Sonny" Franzese, a notorious member of the Colombo crime family, was extorting money from the owner of a trucking company. If the agents and Shur could convince the owner to testify against Franzese, the government would be able to put one of the city's most violent gangsters in prison.

"Two guys showed up at my business one day," the owner explained after he welcomed Shur and the agents into his Long Island home. "These guys tell me Sonny Franzese wants to be my new business partner. I tell them, 'Hey, I don't need a business partner,' and they look at each other and laugh, and say, 'Oh yeah, you do.' I told them to get out of my office."

The next morning, one of his new trucks wouldn't start. Someone had poured sand in the carburetor. Still, he continued to ignore Franzese until four men attacked him with baseball bats. The last thing he remembered before being knocked unconscious was one of them telling him that Sonny wanted to see him. A few weeks after he was released from the hospital, he signed over half of his business to the mobster.

"What happened ain't right," he told Shur. "You guys in the Justice Department should do something."

"If you testify," Shur explained, "we can tie Franzese directly to extortion and send him to prison for a minimum of five to ten years."

"*Testify?*" the owner asked.

Shur was taken aback. "Of course. We'll need you to tell a jury what he did. We can't make the case unless you testify."

"I thought just telling you would be enough," he replied. "The mob will kill me and my entire family if I testify. No way am I speaking out against Sonny Franzese! I'd rather pull up stakes and move to Florida."

"Suppose we put him in jail right away—I mean tonight?"

"What about tomorrow when he gets out?"

"You don't really have a choice," Shur warned. "Sonny Franzese is going to bleed your business to death. He'll destroy it and ruin your reputation."

But nothing Shur or the agents said could sway him. During the car ride back to Manhattan, Shur fumed. "There's got to be a way to get witnesses to testify against the mob."

"Would you?" asked one of the agents in the car.

The question made him think. What if *he* had been the trucking company owner? What if *his* wife and *his* family had been the ones at risk? He thought about the photograph of the dead woman and the frozen look of terror on her face. What would—what could—the government do that would convince him to risk his life and the lives of his wife, his son, and his daughter to testify against the mob?

At exactly 7:30 A.M. on April 19, 1995, a black helicopter swooped over the guard towers at the Federal Correctional Institution in Phoenix, Arizona, and hovered above the Mesa Unit, a two-story concrete structure. The unit was an isolated "prison inside a prison," surrounded by its own fence topped with razor wire. At the same moment the helicopter appeared, an armored personnel carrier roared across the prison yard into the Mesa Unit complex and six burly men wearing black jumpsuits burst out. Each carried an automatic weapon and wore a black hood to conceal his identity. A sharpshooter in the helicopter flying overhead watched as the commandos hustled inside. Ignoring the other inmates locked in their cells, the squad went directly to where a solitary federal prisoner was waiting. They ordered him to put on a bulletproof vest and hustled him outside. Four cars were waiting for the APC after it exited the prison. They raced alongside it toward a heavily guarded military airfield where a Learjet stood ready, its engines already burning. The commandos formed a human shield around the inmate as he stepped from the APC and onto the jet. It lifted off seconds later, its destination a secret so well guarded that only four government officials knew where he was being taken.

The inmate now sitting comfortably in the jet was a cold-blooded killer. By his own admission, he had committed nineteen murders. But the armed guards with him were not there to prevent him from killing again. They were protecting him from harm. Salvatore Gravano, better known as "Sammy the Bull," reportedly had a $2 million price tag on his head. His testimony had helped the Justice Department send thirty-six of his former Mafia pals to prison. The biggest prize had been John Gotti, the "boss of bosses" in New York City. The government had tried twice to convict him, but juries had found the country's best-known racketeer innocent, prompting the media to dub him the "Teflon

Don." He had seemed invincible until his closest friend had betrayed him.

Federal prosecutors had gotten Gravano to testify by making him an offer that he couldn't refuse. They had evidence he had killed a fellow gangster. Gravano could go to trial, be convicted, and spend the rest of his life in a maximum-security penitentiary, or he could testify against Gotti and win himself a reduced sentence: in his case, twenty years. Better yet, he'd only have to actually serve five years of it in prison—the rest would be suspended—and all of his previous crimes, including eighteen other murders, would be forgiven.

John Gotti was convicted in 1992 and sent to the nation's toughest prison for life. Gravano, meanwhile, took up residency in the heavily guarded but much more relaxed Mesa Unit. Just before his release, he was flown to Washington, D.C., for a private meeting at the Justice Department. The government wanted to offer him another deal. He had become too famous for it to risk losing him. If the mob murdered him, other gangsters would be scared to testify. So Gravano was offered lifetime protection in the federal Witness Security Program, commonly called WITSEC. His name would be legally and secretly changed. He'd get a new social security number and other vital documents, and he'd be relocated along with his family in a new community. The government would pay all his moving costs and provide him with a house, a car, and a monthly check for living expenses until he could find a legitimate job. Best of all, if he ever suspected he was in danger, all he would need to do was call a special telephone number and a squad of deputy U.S. marshals would hurry to his front door. Because WITSEC was completely voluntary, Gravano could drop out at any time, no strings attached.

Sammy the Bull signed up.

Gerald Shur was the Justice Department official who made the WITSEC spiel to Gravano. Getting him into the WITSEC program was his last official act before he retired. It seemed fitting. Three decades earlier, Shur had failed to convince the owner of a trucking company to testify against Sonny Franzese. Now he was ending his career by reeling in Gravano, a Mafia underboss, the second in command. What better proof was there that the much-feared Mafia code of *omertà* had been broken?

Gerald Shur, relatively unknown to the public, played a major role in the government's war against organized crime. His official title when he retired was senior associate director of the Office of Enforcement Operations in the Criminal Division of the U.S. Department of Justice, but he was better known as the "father of WITSEC." He was the program's creator and for thirty-four years the driving force behind it. No witnesses got protection in WITSEC without his personal attention. He wrote nearly all of the program's rules, shaped it based on his own personal philosophical views, and guided it with a steady but iron hand. During his tenure, WITSEC protected 6,416 witnesses and 14,468 of their dependents, including wives, children, and lovers. None of the witnesses who followed his rules was murdered. He was involved with *every* major Mafia witness in recent history, starting with Joseph Valachi, considered the first to tell the mob's secrets. The other gangsters form a who's who of organized crime: Joseph "the Animal" Barboza, Vincent "Fat Vinnie" Teresa, Aladena "Jimmy the Weasel" Fratianno, Joseph "Joe Dogs" Iannuzzi, and Henry Hill of the best-selling book *Wiseguy* and the popular movie *Goodfellas*. Name a mafioso who turned against the mob, and in one way or another Shur dealt with him.

He also dealt with their problems. At various times, he served as a mob marriage counselor, substitute father, even priest. He helped create false backgrounds for witnesses, arranged secret weddings, oversaw funerals, and personally persuaded corporate executives to hire former mob hit men as delivery route drivers. Once he arranged for the wife of a Los Angeles killer to have breast enlargement surgery to keep her husband happy. In return, WITSEC witnesses helped topple the heads of *every* major crime family in *every* major city in the nation. Some ten thousand criminals were convicted in large part because of WITSEC witnesses during

Shur's tenure. Today WITSEC is considered one of three tools essential in combating organized crime. The others are federal wiretaps and the Racketeer-Influenced and Corrupt Organization Act, known as RICO. Ask any federal prosecutor and the answer will be the same: A good eyewitness can almost always guarantee a conviction. Fingerprints, murder weapons, forensic findings—all are helpful, but none is as convincing as a credible witness who takes the witness stand and swears under oath: "I was there and I saw the defendant do it."

The John Gottis of the world are not the only criminals whom WITSEC has helped imprison. Colombian drug dealers, outlaw motorcycle gang members, white-collar con men, and, more recently, international terrorists have also been convicted because of WITSEC witnesses. It is difficult to find a major criminal case, whether it be the Watergate scandal or the 1993 World Trade Center bombing, where WITSEC witnesses have not played a pivotal role.

Without the WITSEC program, few witnesses involved in major crimes would step forward. It not only keeps them alive before, during, and after a trial, it gives them a fresh start. A recent Justice Department study found that 82 percent of criminals who entered WITSEC never committed another crime after they were given new identities and relocated. By comparison, only 60 percent of criminals paroled from prison stay out of trouble. That makes WITSEC one of the most successful rehabilitation programs in the country.

Not everyone who enters WITSEC becomes rehabilitated, however, and those who do not are the main reason it remains a controversial and hotly criticized program. In its first decade of operation, witnesses in WITSEC committed twelve murders after they were relocated in unsuspecting towns. Others used their new WITSEC identities to dodge creditors and pilfer millions of dollars by operating new scams. Sammy the Bull was accused of running an illegal drug ring less than five years after he was relocated by WITSEC near Phoenix, Arizona. Witnesses protected by WITSEC are often as vicious and deadly as the defendants whom they help convict. A former U.S. attorney once complained that about half of the witnesses whom Shur put into WITSEC didn't belong there. "They needed protection before and during trials, but after that, they could have been sent home," he explained. "There was no reason for Shur to change their names and unleash them in new communities." A U.S. Senate subcommittee investigator accused Shur's program in the 1980s of being the worst-run in the government, quipping it was "like a body without a brain."

This book has been written jointly, but it began as two completely separate books about WITSEC. After Gerald Shur retired in 1995, he started writing an account of his career for his grandchildren to read. He decided to turn it into a book after several of his former colleagues heard what he was doing and encouraged him to expand it around the same time I was researching my own book about WITSEC, a program that I had first become interested in while writing an earlier book, *The Hot House: Life Inside Leavenworth Prison*, which describes everyday life inside a maximum-security federal penitentiary. Dozens of convicts had told me that WITSEC witnesses had lied about them in court in order to cut themselves sweetheart deals with federal prosecutors. I was told that WITSEC witnesses were rumored to receive special perks in prison, from being allowed to order lobster dinners from local restaurants to conjugal visits with prostitutes. I set out to learn more and immediately began hearing stories about Gerald Shur. Some witnesses described him as a saint who had personally saved them from lives of crime and violence. Others attacked him viciously. In a magazine article published in 1991, a disgruntled WITSEC witness described Shur as a "small man with a small mind and a God complex." In that same story, Shur was called "WITSEC's biggest administrative problem—he is known as something of a monomaniac in the J. Edgar Hoover mold and his decision-making process has been called dictatorial and capricious." A fellow journalist who had written extensively about WITSEC after interviewing more than a hundred relocated witnesses warned me that Shur was a "master bullshitter with an extremely vengeful attitude." Although Shur had granted a few interviews during his career, he'd never really told anyone about his experiences running WITSEC or revealed the behind-the-scenes dramas in the program. When I first asked to interview him, he declined, saying he was busy working on his own book. But after several lengthy conversations, we decided to join forces, and it soon became clear, at least to us, that it was a good merger.

From the start, we agreed this would not be a traditional "as told to" book in which I would simply ghost-write Shur's memoirs. While we both felt that his story needed to be told, we also wanted this book to be a fully documented history of the WITSEC program. The best way to accomplish this, we decided, was for me to interview Shur just as I would any other source and present his statements and thoughts in a third-person narrative. This meant making Shur a character—the central character—of this book, rather than its narrator. This structure allowed us to reach out and include interviews with other key players in WITSEC's development, including persons who had been critical of Shur. We also agreed we needed a first-person account from a WITSEC witness to give readers a full picture of the program. We wanted someone to describe what it felt like when the U.S. government decided to make you disappear. Part Three of this book recounts the story of Witness X. She is not meant to be representative. No single witness can be. All of the thousands of witnesses who have entered WITSEC are individuals with unique stories: some heroic, others tragic, several terrifying. Many of the witnesses who were interviewed for this book adjusted quickly and easily to their new identities. Other witnesses, especially the small number in the program who were not criminals, found this transition overwhelming, even torturous. Having to give up their identity and live a life that to all appearances eradicates one's past was deeply disturbing for them. Many felt themselves trapped in two different worlds. Within the safety of their family, they shared a past—a heritage, memories, actions, relationships—that they were forced to deny every day as they lived a lie at work or with friends and went about their daily routines not only in an alien place but in a totally new guise. Relocation destroyed their sense of self. Witness X captures this anguish as only someone who has lived it can convey.

Dozens of Mafia books have been written since the early 1960s, and while our book discusses many famous organized crime figures, it remains a story about a crime *fighter*, not someone perpetrating it. After spending two years working with Gerald Shur and interviewing dozens of his supporters and critics, I have come to see him as an honorable man who wrestled with the problem of getting into bed with the enemy, but saw in doing that a larger purpose. Over the years, he had to deal with prima donnas who included petty federal marshals, arrogant mob stars, and pompous members of Congress; with bureaucracy and budgets; with infighting and outfighting and betrayals. He had to handle malicious criminals and ordinary citizens who happened to be in the wrong place at the wrong time and desperately needed protection because of what they had seen. At different times, he was both rhapsodized and maligned in the media. Neither the praise nor the condemnation seemed to faze him. He overcame the obstacles before him because he was both realistic and idealistic. Most of all, he succeeded because he believed in principle, had a passionate commitment to justice, and remained dedicated to his beliefs. This book is his story and the story of the program that he launched, and how, together, they helped end the mob's deadly grip and forever changed the face of American justice.

PART ONE
A DEADLY SILENCE

In 1919, the Mafia in Kansas City murdered an eleven-year-old boy whose last name was Carramusa. The hit man was identified as Paul Cantanzaro, but before he could be brought to trial, the witnesses against him were methodically terrorized and the detective who had arrested him was murdered. The judge had no choice but to release Cantanzaro.

Ironically, the murdered boy's brother, Carl, was arrested in 1946 for selling drugs for the Mafia. To avoid prison, Carl agreed to testify. On the morning of the first trial, Paul Cantanzaro, the hit man who had killed Carl's brother, swaggered into the courtroom and began making threatening gestures as soon as Carl took the witness chair.

Carl fled to Chicago with his wife and daughter after the trial. Three years later, he stopped at a traffic light. A car pulled up next to his, and Carl glanced over in time to see a shotgun being aimed at his face. The blast blew off his head. When the police went to tell his wife, they found her dressed in her nicest clothes, waiting for Carl to come home from work. It was their wedding anniversary.

CHAPTER
ONE

GERALD SHUR was fifteen when he came face-to-face with his first gangster. He was eating cheesecake with his father, Abraham Shur, in Lindy's restaurant in Manhattan when two men sauntered by their table.

"Hello, Abe," one said as they passed.

Shur's father nodded at him.

"Who's that?" his curious son asked.

"They're Johnny Dio's bodyguards," his father replied. "I know them from work." Abe Shur was a dress contractor in New York City's mob-infested garment district. His son recognized the name. John "Johnny Dio" Dioguardi was the mob's "labor expert." In the 1950s and early 1960s he controlled several unions for his Mafia boss, crime-family head Tommy "Three Finger Brown" Lucchese. Not long after this chance encounter, Shur read in the newspaper that labor columnist Victor Riesel had been attacked as he was leaving Lindy's by a man who threw sulfuric acid into his face, permanently blinding him. Riesel had been writing columns critical of Johnny Dio's cozy relationship with Teamsters union president Jimmy Hoffa, and although Johnny Dio was the prime suspect behind the attack, he was never prosecuted. Witnesses refused to testify, and Abraham Telvi, the punk who threw the acid, was found dead a few days later. He'd been executed on his knees with his hands and legs tied behind him. He had reportedly tried to blackmail Dio.

When Gerald Shur would later think back about his childhood and try to pinpoint what had influenced him most, he would
find three common strands: his loving parents, his Jewish faith,
and organized crime. From the time he had started reading newspapers, Shur had been captivated by gangsters. No doubt, stories
told by his father around the dinner table and by his favorite uncle,
who was a successful attorney, fueled his interest. "My father
hated the mob and what it did in a community, and he instilled in
me at an early age a determination to become involved somehow
in the fight against it."

As a child, Shur idolized his father. Abraham Shur was a self-
made man. He'd been only six months old in 1903 when he and
his three siblings were brought to America by his parents, Russian
Jews fleeing persecution. Forced to quit school at age eleven to
help support the family, Abe had gone to work delivering dresses
for a manufacturer and had gradually moved up the ranks until he
became the general manager of the United Popular Dress Manu-
facturers' Association, a trade group that represented dressmakers
in contract negotiations with the International Ladies' Garment
Workers' Union. The 1930s were perilous times in labor relations,
especially in Manhattan's steamy garment district. Mobster Louis
Buchalter, better known as Louis Lepke, was at the peak of his
power, having first seized control of the tailors' and cutters'
unions. From there, he and his mobster pals beat and murdered
their way into the bakery drivers' union, where they forced bakers
to pay a penny-a-loaf "tax" if they wanted their products delivered
fresh to stores. Lepke was one of the first mobsters to realize that
if you controlled the trucks that moved goods, you could control
an entire industry, and he put that knowledge to work by demanding extortion payments from hundreds of businesses. Police
would later estimate that Lepke and his partners were collecting
$10 million per year in payoffs from frightened businessmen. It
was in this mob-run climate that Abe Shur cut his teeth as a labor
negotiator.

Gerald was born in 1933, the second son of Abe and Rose. His
mother had been a secretary in a dressmaking company when Abe
met and married her in 1927. Most of Shur's earliest childhood

memories were set in Far Rockaway, then a small town in Queens, where the family moved in 1935. Gerald would recall happy times there playing games with his older brother, Walter, and helping his father pull weeds from the family's wartime victory garden, an acre patch packed with tomatoes, potatoes, watermelons, beans, and peas. At age nine, he'd gone door to door with his little red wagon, collecting tin cans and cigarette and candy wrappers for recycling to help the war effort. Crime in the city seemed far away. Those idyllic days ended in 1943, when Rose was stricken with pneumonia and nearly died. After she recovered, she told Abe that she wanted to move back into Manhattan to be closer to her family. The couple rented an apartment on the middle-class Upper West Side, and Gerald, now ten, got a quick lesson in how tough New York streets could be. On his very first day in his new neighborhood, he was confronted by a gang of teenagers.

"What's your religion?" one asked.

"Jewish," he replied.

"Then you're a Christ-killer," the boy shouted. "You need to pay."

The boys beat him until he collapsed, and it took him a week of bed rest to recover. Ironically, the gang's leader was a police sergeant's son. Shur had never before encountered religious prejudice. "From that point on, I absolutely hated intolerance of any kind. My parents had been ahead of their time when it came to teaching us that prejudice was wrong, regardless of whether it had to do with race, religion, or nationality. That beating made me intolerant of intolerance."

Abe and Rose were keenly aware of what was happening in the city and the world, and they expected their sons to stay informed. At night, the family listened to the news on the radio and discussed current events. "No matter what my answer was to a question, my father would reply with 'Why?' When I explained, I got another 'Why?' and the whys continued until I ran out of answers. This was his way of teaching me. Never did my father give his opinion before he received mine, and never did he tell me my opinion was wrong. I was taught to listen to other people's opinions, to consider them thoughtfully, but also to question them vigorously and be ready to defend my own views under similar grilling."

Shur's parents encouraged him to keep a scrapbook of newspaper clippings, and it soon was stuffed with articles about the mob. There was a lot of news to clip. The Federal Bureau of Narcotics (the predecessor to the Drug Enforcement Administration) had caught Lepke smuggling narcotics into the city, and the gangster had gone into hiding. He agreed to surrender to radio newsman Walter Winchell and FBI director J. Edgar Hoover after a fellow mobster assured him that Hoover would seek only a five-year prison sentence. That turned out to be a lie, and Lepke was sentenced to death on a murder charge and executed. Johnny Dio quickly moved in to fill the void left by Lepke, which is why Abe Shur was familiar with Dio's bodyguards. The mobster and his goons were familiar figures in the garment district.

By this time, Abe had quit his labor-negotiating job and opened his own dress-manufacturing shop. Manhattan was the center of America's dress industry; in the late 1940s and early 1950s nearly every dress sold in the country was manufactured there. Competition was brutal. During the day, Abe oversaw his sewing machine operators. In the evenings, he met with jobbers to find work to keep his employees busy. Profit margins were thin, kickbacks common. Whom you knew mattered.

Abe Shur proved to be a shrewd businessman, his dressmaking shop prospered, and the family decided to give Gerald a splashy bar mitzvah. Two hundred guests were invited. Gerald's initials were carved in four-foot-high blocks of ice. There was a five-piece band. All the attention embarrassed him. "I only danced with my mother, and I was more interested in getting a chance to play the band's drum set than all the festivities." During the party, several guests handed him gift envelopes filled with cash. Years later, he would learn that some of the guests were gangsters.

"Why did you invite them?" he'd ask his father.

"They *had* to be invited," Abe had replied. "They were important people in the industry, and not to invite them would offend them."

Despite his rough start, Shur enjoyed life in the city. He had two best friends, Eddie Schwarzer and Bernie Breslin, and one day he talked them into auditioning with him for Ted Mack's *Original Amateur Hour*, a popular radio and then television show. "Gerry played the drums, and another buddy of ours had an accordion," Breslin recalled. "But Eddie and I didn't even play musical instruments. That didn't stop Gerry. He gave me a set of claves to click together and Eddie a set of maracas, and off we went to this audition. We said we were a band. Of course, we were absolutely terrible and didn't make it." During another outing, the boys spotted a blind man dressed in a homemade robe, sandals, a flowing cape, and a horned Viking helmet standing on Sixth Avenue at Fifty-fourth Street. "Gerry walked right over and introduced himself," said Breslin. The Viking was Louis T. Hardin, who had legally changed his name to Moondog in 1947 out of respect for a former pet that had howled at the moon. He would become famous as the "Viking of Sixth Avenue" and be quoted by Beat Generation poets. "Gerry used to talk to Moondog all the time," said Breslin. "He didn't dismiss people because of the way they looked or acted, and I remember he was very curious about other people and what made them tick."

During the summers, Shur worked for his father as a turner of collars and belts, which were sewn inside out. His job was to reverse them by using a bent coat hanger to pull them right side out. It was hot, tedious work. He never complained. The job showed him a different side of his father's life. One morning Shur saw a city fire inspector push several crates in front of the fire escape exit. The inspector then called Abe over, showed him the crates, and threatened to fine him for having a blocked exit in violation of city codes. As the younger Shur watched in disbelief, Abe led the fire inspector to a rack of new dresses and let him take two. "I'll be sure to pay you the next time I see you," the inspector said, leaving. That afternoon, two more firemen came in and took dresses. Gerald was confused and angry.

"Why didn't you stop them from stealing those dresses?" he demanded during the ride home that night.

"They would have shut me down, and everybody would be out of work for a few days. Once we reopened, they would harass me, I'd lose our operators, and then I'd be out of business."

The answer didn't satisfy the idealistic teenager. "My father insisted he could do more for the garment industry by being accepted in it and by sometimes conforming rather than by taking the stand that his teenage son would have liked to see him take. I eventually came to believe that he really didn't have a choice. On the one hand, he had to deal with and be friendly to those who would exploit, extort, and kill, and on the other hand, he knew this was wrong yet felt powerless to do anything about it. He was convinced somebody, somebody who cared, could and perhaps someday would do something about it. But it wasn't a job that he could take on."

Shur left home in September 1951 to enter The University of Texas at Austin, determined to become a lawyer. However, his interest in school waned as soon as he spotted Miriam Heifetz, a marketing student from Corpus Christi. He asked her to marry him on their second date. She said no, but a month later agreed. They were seventeen, and neither had a job. They didn't care. Texas law required women to be eighteen and men to be twenty-one to marry. Since neither of them was old enough, they rode a bus to a small town where they mistakenly thought they could fool the marriage clerk. Rebuffed and embarrassed, they returned to Austin, where they found a clerk who wasn't as nosy; and after a brief civil ceremony, a friend dropped them off at the McCandless Hotel for a one-night honeymoon. They kept their marriage secret and lived apart on campus. Four months later, both sets of parents agreed to let them marry, and in July 1952 they had a wedding ceremony. "We planned on having a small wedding because we were already married, even though no one knew it. Miriam's mother and the rabbi, who had known Miriam from birth, decided otherwise." Shur knew only a few of the several hundred guests. "The rabbi spoke for several minutes about how wonderful Miriam was, covering all of the high points in her life. When it came time to talk about my life, he simply said, 'And here is Gerald. Isn't he lucky to have found Miriam?' I didn't care because I was truly lucky."

Shur did just enough work to pass his undergraduate courses. He was preoccupied by an event that he considered much more important. In 1950, U.S. Senator Estes Kefauver launched a two-year investigation of the mob. Even though the Mafia had become entrenched as a national syndicate in the United States during Prohibition, no one had ever gone after it the way Kefauver did. The Tennessee Democrat held hearings in eleven cities, and in every one his Senate Special Committee to Investigate Crime in Interstate Commerce, better known as the Kefauver Committee, uncovered evidence of mob corruption. "I respectfully take the Fifth Amendment" became part of the public's vernacular as one mobster after another refused to answer the committee's questions for fear of self-incrimination. "I went to the university library every night, not to study, but to read everything I could about the mob."

Shur graduated and entered the university's law school, but Miriam dropped out to give birth to a daughter, Ilene, and two years later a son, Ron. In 1957, Shur received his law degree and passed the Texas bar. He took out a bank loan and opened his own office in Corpus Christi. "During my first week, I saw no clients—none. The phone never rang." The next week, he got one call. It was from a frantic jail inmate accused of burglarizing a clothing store. "I swear to you on my mother's life, I didn't do it," the man pleaded. Shur took the case, and when the local district attorney offered a plea bargain to avoid a jury trial, Shur refused. His client was innocent, he declared, and he was going to prove it.

The first witness to testify at the trial was the clothing store's owner. "What was stolen from your store, sir?" the prosecutor asked him.

"Well," the witness replied, "one thing is that shirt the defendant's wearing and the pants he has on and the shoes he has on."

Shur requested a short recess. "Are you wearing clothes stolen from the store?" he asked his client.

"You told me to wear something neat," the man replied, "and these are the only decent clothes I own."

When Shur left the courtroom that day, his guilty client's relatives booed. Nevertheless, his practice grew, and he found himself being drawn to underdogs. One client claimed a local deputy had threatened to torture him by putting his penis in a vise if he didn't sign a confession. Another said he had been beaten with a hammer handle by a deputy. "After four years, I had finally reached the point where Miriam and the kids and I could eat regularly," Shur recalled, "but I wasn't satisfied. I was still going to the library, reading about organized crime."

Despite Kefauver's dramatic hearings, the government wasn't doing much to rein in the Mafia. The FBI's J. Edgar Hoover had spent nearly three decades insisting there was no organized crime in the United States. Besides, he was focused on trying to identify Americans who were Communists. It was the Mafia itself that finally forced Hoover and the federal government into action. In 1957, the same year that Shur earned his law degree, police had stumbled upon a summit of mobsters meeting in a summer estate in Apalachin, a secluded town in the mountains of central New York. When a squad car pulled into the estate's driveway to see why the stone house was surrounded by black limousines, dozens of panicked men wearing expensive business suits came running outside. Some dashed across planted fields and into the woods. By nightfall, fifty-eight men had been detained. Most were from New York, New Jersey, and Pennsylvania, but others had come from Florida, Texas, California, Illinois, and Ohio. The government would later learn the so-called Apalachin Conference had been organized by Vito Genovese, who had become the new head of the Gambino crime family in New York City, after its former boss, the much-feared Albert Anastasia, was assassinated in a Manhattan barber shop. Genovese had reportedly called the heads of every major crime family together to pick a new *capo di tutti capi*—boss of bosses.

News about the mob summit sparked national headlines. Under public pressure, Hoover sent seventy-five FBI agents to investigate, and President Dwight D. Eisenhower created a special task force to prosecute the gangsters. There was just one problem: It didn't appear they had broken any laws by meeting. The government charged them with engaging in a "conspiracy to obstruct justice" because they had refused to tell a grand jury why they were meeting in Apalachin. At the end of their trial a jury convicted them, but the Second Circuit Court of Appeals later threw out the conviction. It was out of this public relations disaster that a new mob buster arose: Robert F. Kennedy. As chief counsel for the Senate Select Committee on Improper Activities in the Labor or Management Field, better known as the McClellan Committee, Kennedy set out to outdo Senator Kefauver. During 270 days of hearings, Kennedy interrogated 800 witnesses about the mob, including a belligerent Jimmy Hoffa. Afterward, Kennedy published a best-selling book called *The Enemy Within*, and in it he called for the creation of a national commission to spearhead the government's campaign against the Mafia and oversee the dozens of federal agencies that had jurisdiction over it. The FBI's Hoover was dead set against giving up any of his power, so Kennedy's recommendations didn't get very far until John F. Kennedy was elected president in 1960. When President Kennedy named his brother as the nation's sixty-fourth U.S. attorney general, Robert Kennedy got his chance. Knowing that Hoover would try to stop him if he sought legislation for a national Mafia commission, Robert Kennedy looked inward and decided to turn the Justice Department's Organized Crime and Racketeering Section (OCRS) into a mob command post. The OCRS had been created by President Eisenhower to prosecute organized crime cases, but Hoover had kept it toothless. Kennedy began recruiting new attorneys for the OCRS office. He offered low pay, exhausting hours, dangerous assignments, and the thrill of investigating the biggest and most notorious mobsters in America.

Shur read about Kennedy's call to arms in the *Dallas Morning News*, but he waited several days before mentioning it to Miriam. He assumed she wouldn't want to move to Washington, D.C., because all her relatives lived in Texas and Shur's law practice was finally showing a profit. Miriam surprised him. "Why don't you fly to Washington and apply?" she asked.

He called a friend from law school who knew someone in Vice President Lyndon Johnson's office, and a few days later Shur was in Washington being interviewed by three of Johnson's aides. When Shur said he wanted a job in the OCRS, they began laughing. They assumed Shur had come to town hoping to land a juicy political appointment, not a staff job. They sent Shur to see Edwyn Silberling, the newly hired chief of the OCRS, who had a well-deserved reputation as an anticorruption crusader in New York. He hired Shur that same day and ordered him to report to work ASAP. Back home, Shur closed his law practice, and he and Miriam sold their home, tucked their two children into the backseat of their aging Renault, and set off for Washington, D.C. The *Corpus Christi Times* published a beaming photograph of Shur, then twenty-seven years old, under the headline "Local Attorney Is Hired For Racket-Hunting Job." Halfway to the nation's capital, the Shurs' car broke down. His old friends in New York City were not surprised when they heard that he was joining the Justice Department. Chasing mobsters, they agreed, was just the crazy sort of thing that Shur had always wanted to do.

CHAPTER
TWO

"Gerryshur," said henry petersen, the deputy chief of the Organized Crime and Racketeering Section, running the names together, "tell me your views about organized crime."

Shur began a windy answer based on his years of reading newspaper clippings. When he finished, Petersen said: "I disagree with every word you have just uttered. Now, go pull the files on Profaci, Oddo, and Carlino. We may be meeting with Bobby Kennedy tomorrow, and I want you to be ready to give him a status report on our investigations."

Shur had read about Profaci but didn't have a clue who Oddo and Carlino were. He stopped outside Petersen's office at a pay phone and dialed Miriam. He'd been warned not to make personal calls on government lines. "I've only been at work fifteen minutes," he muttered, "and I think I'm on the brink of being fired!"

Shur was among the first of forty-five new attorneys Robert Kennedy was hiring to revitalize the OCRS. Besides pumping in new blood, Kennedy was taking a fresh look at how the office operated. He asked William Hundley, who had run the office under President Eisenhower, to tell him what sort of problems needed to be fixed. Hundley said the biggest hurdle was getting federal agents to work together. At least twenty-five separate government agencies investigated organized crime, but none shared its information. The FBI was the worst, Hundley warned. Kennedy met immediately with FBI director Hoover and the heads of other agencies and warned them that he expected a change in attitude. The OCRS was going to take charge of *all* organized crime cases. OCRS attorneys, such as Shur, would coordinate and in some cases run critical investigations. Kennedy had handpicked forty racketeers whom he personally wanted targeted. There would be no more bureaucratic nitpicking, no infighting. Everyone was going to be on the same team.

Although Hoover and the others promised to cooperate, Shur got a chilly reception when he flew to New York City to meet with Brooklyn's federal prosecutors and investigators. U.S. attorney Joseph Hoey told aides that Shur wasn't welcome, and the local chiefs of the FBI, the Internal Revenue Service, and the Bureau of Narcotics were just as unfriendly. "None of them really understood what our role in the OCRS was," Shur recalled. "They just wanted me to stay the hell out of their way." Shur had never prosecuted a mobster, overseen an investigation, or worked on the streets. And these were only some of the reasons the investigators didn't want him around. "A lot of the agents in New York couldn't stand one another," Shur recalled. "The head of the U.S. Secret Service would not attend any meetings if the special agent in charge of the FBI office was there, and vice versa. These two men hated each other's guts—and I was supposed to bring them all together."

Shur knew he had to prove himself. When he learned several FBI agents were being pulled off sensitive mob investigations to handle routine matters, he got his bosses in the Justice Department to contact Hoover and free the agents from such chores. "The agents suddenly realized I could be useful to them, so they began working with me." Shur's next challenge was finding a way to maneuver around U.S. attorney Hoey, who was worried that Shur was going to steal the spotlight from him. "Hoey had assigned one of his assistants, Bill Kelly, to accompany me everywhere I went in Brooklyn. The agents working with me didn't feel comfortable with Kelly because he was a political appointee they believed loyal to Hoey, so they wouldn't talk freely about cases if he was around." Shur noticed one afternoon that Kelly left his side promptly at 4:30 P.M. "We simply began holding two sets of meetings." In the morning, Shur and the agents discussed routine problems in front of Kelly. After Kelly had gone, they delved into sensitive matters.

Shur loved what he was doing. At least three days a week he would board a 6 A.M. flight to New York City, where he'd work until ten in the evening. Then he'd fly back to Washington exhausted. He got his first big break when an IRS agent told him an armed robber using the alias Danny wanted to give him information about Sonny Franzese. There was a catch, though. In exchange, Danny, who was accused of committing three armed robberies, wanted the charges against him reduced and a visit with his wife and daughter. Shur agreed to help him but quickly discovered he was being played for a fool. When they met, Danny didn't tell him anything useful. Disgusted, Shur stood up and headed for the door.

"Whatcha doin'?" Danny called after him.

"Something you can't," Shur replied. "Walking out this door."

"You anti-Semites are always picking on us Jews," Danny snarled.

Up to this point, no one had mentioned religion. Shur spun around. "Go to hell!" he spat in Yiddish. "It's Jews like you that make the rest of us look bad!"

Danny hadn't realized Shur was Jewish.

"You tell me something I can sink my teeth into right now," an angry Shur threatened, "or I'm leaving you here to rot in jail."

"How about a murder?" Danny volunteered. In the next few minutes, he revealed that the mob was planning to kill John Mosler, the president of the Mosler Safe Company, and his wife, Sheila. "I was supposed to do it, but since I got pinched, they're looking for someone else."

The Moslers, wealthy New York socialites, had been robbed by three armed men a few weeks earlier. The crime had made a splash in the city's newspapers and the police had arrested the robbers, but they were now free on bond awaiting trial. They had offered Danny $35,000 to kill the couple to keep them from testifying.

Shur hustled Danny into the office of Manhattan assistant district attorney Burton Roberts, but the meeting quickly turned ugly. Roberts wanted Danny to testify in court, a demand that surprised Shur. "Danny had come to me as an informant, and there's a big difference between an informant and a witness," he later explained. "An informant's name always is kept secret. Witnesses are people who testify in public, so everyone knows who they are. Back in the sixties, we had lots of informants, but criminals rarely testified, especially against the Mob." Roberts began yelling profanities at Danny, and the two men were still butting heads when Shur returned to Washington hours later. Around 3 A.M. Shur was jarred awake by his telephone. "Great news, Gerry!" Roberts declared. "Your man has agreed to testify." Shur felt sick.

"What's wrong?" Miriam asked.

"I might just have set a guy up for a beating by the police."

When Shur returned to New York City, he checked on Danny. "I was afraid you'd been beaten," he told him.

"They ain't that stupid," Danny replied. "Besides, they got other ways to make you talk." Danny would later claim that two cops had held him out an upstairs window by his feet and threatened to drop him to his death unless he testified. *The New York Times* published a flattering story that described how prosecutor Roberts, with the help of a Justice Department attorney, had uncovered a plot to kill the Moslers. When the case came to trial, the robbers were sentenced to twenty years in prison and the charges against Danny were dropped.

Shur's education as a Justice Department crime fighter was just beginning. His next big case plunged him into a mob war being fought between Joseph Profaci, the head of a New York crime family, and the Gallo brothers, Albert, Joseph, and Larry, who had once been loyal to Profaci but were now trying to topple him. This was heady stuff for Shur because Profaci was one of the crime bosses on Kennedy's personal hit list for immediate prosecution. He was also one of the richest Mafia godfathers in America. He lived in a mansion on a 328-acre Long Island estate that had its own hunting lodge and private airfield. Kennedy had a personal interest in the Gallo brothers, too. "He had subpoenaed them to testify before the McClellan committee," Shur recalled, "and when they arrived in the Senate committee's offices to meet Kennedy, they began frisking everyone there. As soon as Kennedy heard what they were doing, he rushed into the lobby and stopped them. At that point, one of them mentioned that he was a big fan of John Kennedy and asked if there was anything he and his brothers could do to help get him elected as president. Robert Kennedy replied: 'Campaign for Nixon.' "

Thus far, a half-dozen gangsters had been murdered and ten wounded in what the New York tabloids were calling the Gallo-Profaci "mattress war"—a reference to the mob term "hitting the mattresses." During a gang war, mobsters slept together on mattresses in their hideout at night and stacked them against the doors and windows for protection from bullets during the day. The Gallos were holed up on their home turf in the Red Hook neighborhood of Brooklyn. Early on, Profaci had been forced to flee his mansion during a surprise attack. He'd escaped through a back door still wearing his silk pajamas and was now commanding his troops from a secret hideaway in Florida. The mattress war had started after Profaci had convinced the Gallos to murder one of their closest friends, a Brooklyn bookie. Profaci had promised to cut them in on the bookie's lucrative numbers racket after the killing. Instead, he had kept the racket for himself, sparking the war.

Shur got involved when an IRS agent told him that a gangster wanted to talk in exchange for help. By the time Shur got to the hotel where the gangster was being hidden, the Brooklyn chief of the IRS and his assistant were already interrogating him. He was introduced to Shur only by the initials R.B. He claimed a Profaci capo had offered him $30,000 to murder Larry Gallo, but he had turned down the contract because he was trying to avoid being dragged into the war. The next day, two armed men had grabbed

R.B. and forced him to drive to Staten Island. Along the way they picked up two more goons, and when they reached a beach, the four men began beating him: "They told me Larry Gallo was giving me a present." When the thugs took a heavy chain and several cement blocks from the car trunk, R.B. knew he was about to be killed and dumped in the water, so he broke free. His attackers began shooting, but he ducked under a pier and eluded them. Desperate, he'd called an IRS agent who had investigated him, and asked for help.

For several hours, Shur and several IRS officials questioned R.B. about the maneuvering going on in the mattress war. It was well after midnight by the time they let him go to bed. Although R.B. had contacted the IRS, Shur said he wanted the FBI to take charge of him because its agents were investigating several gang murders and R.B. might be able to help solve them. None of the IRS agents complained, but Shur could tell by their faces that they weren't happy about turning their informant over to another agency. They left the hotel room a few minutes later, leaving Shur and two IRS agents behind to protect R.B. Exhausted, Shur lay down on the other bed. His head had just hit the pillow when someone pounded on the door. The agents sprang toward the door, guns drawn, while Shur hit the floor: "We thought Larry Gallo was going to come busting in, guns blazing." But nothing happened. Finally an agent peeked outside. A drunk had passed out while trying to get into the wrong room. "You know," one of the agents told Shur, "you really need to start carrying a gun."

Early the next morning, Shur walked downstairs to the hotel lobby for a cup of coffee and spotted a fresh copy of a New York tabloid. He turned to Lee Mortimer's gossip column and read, "The IRS has an informant (initials R.B.) stashed in a Manhattan hotel room." Shur was flabbergasted. Mortimer knew nearly everything that had been said in the hotel room. Clearly, one of the IRS officials had leaked the story. "Someone in the IRS wanted to get credit for R.B. before I turned him over to the FBI," Shur recalled. "This was the sort of petty politics I was dealing with. The only thing that some agents cared about was getting credit in the paper."

Because much of the mattress war was being fought in Brooklyn, Shur was responsible for briefing Kennedy. "It was unusual for an attorney general to meet with line attorneys like us," Shur remembered, "yet periodically we'd be called into his office and some of these briefings would go on for hours. Kennedy was really interested in what we were doing, and you couldn't fool him. Once I didn't have anything new to report, so I started repeating information, and Kennedy snapped: 'You've already told me that. Don't waste my time if you don't have anything new!' "

In August 1961, Shur offered Kennedy an especially juicy report. "Joe Profaci tried to have Larry Gallo killed and he almost got away with it," he told Kennedy. The crime boss had secretly contacted Carmine Persico, one of the Gallo brothers' most trusted friends and allies, and had offered him a piece of his criminal empire if he would double-cross the Gallos. "Persico agreed to betray them," said Shur. "He asked Larry Gallo to meet him on August twelfth in a Brooklyn bar on the pretense of strategizing about the war." As soon as Gallo stepped inside the bar, he was overpowered and Persico slung a garrote around his neck. He was being strangled when a policeman happened to walk into the bar. Persico and his men fled out a back door, leaving Gallo gasping for breath on the floor. "The Gallos are now calling Persico 'The Snake,' " Shur reported.

Shur's account intrigued OCRS chief Edwyn Silberling, and in November he gave Shur a special assignment. U.S. attorney Hoey had just convicted Persico of extortion, and he'd been sentenced to prison for fifteen years. "I want you to go see Persico and offer him a deal," Silberling said. "See if you can get him to become an informant in return for us reducing his sentence, but first clear it with Hoey."

As ordered, Shur went to see Hoey. "Do you guys know who Persico is?" the prosecutor asked incredulously. "Persico *is* Profaci. He's not some small-time hood! He's a boss, for God's sake! He's not going to squeal! What's wrong with you guys?" Hoey threatened to call Robert Kennedy personally and complain if Shur tried to talk to Persico. "I'll have your job, Shur!" he yelled.

Silberling told Shur to back off. "Everyone automatically

assumed a gangster like Persico would never talk," Shur said. "Everyone decided it would be a waste of time to even approach him. I disagreed but was overruled."

Robert Kennedy sent a glowing progress report to his brother at the White House near the end of 1961, noting that OCRS attorneys had spent nearly two thousand days in the field, four times more than they had under the Eisenhower administration. Working together, the IRS and FBI under OCRS guidance had cleaned up Newport, Kentucky, a town directly across the Ohio River from Cincinnati that was infamous for its bordellos and gambling dens. "For the first time, federal agencies are cooperating," Kennedy bragged. Shur was not nearly as optimistic. Despite his best efforts, bickering between agents was still rampant, and even though Brooklyn was a hotbed of organized crime, Shur's hard work hadn't led to any major convictions. He decided to step up his efforts, and he chose Larry Gallo as his target.

By this point, Joe Profaci had died of cancer in Florida, but his brother-in-law, Joseph Magliocco, had taken charge of the Profaci crime family, and the mattress war had turned even more violent. Magliocco had increased the killing because he was afraid the other four crime families in New York might try to muscle in on his turf now that Profaci was gone. By mid-1962, five Gallo soldiers had been murdered and three others kidnapped and never seen again. In the midst of all this, an IRS agent casually mentioned to Shur that Larry Gallo had been seen entering a Brooklyn bank.

"Let's find out what he was doing there," Shur suggested.

It turned out Gallo had applied for a Veterans Administration mortgage, and when Shur got a copy of the loan application, he found a letter attached to it written by Gallo's sixty-two-year-old father, Albert. The elder Gallo claimed his son earned $10,000 per year in salary working at the family's Brooklyn restaurant. Shur suspected the old man was lying to help his son qualify for the loan. To be certain, he asked the IRS to pull Larry Gallo's federal income tax returns. "We discovered Gallo had not filed a federal tax return in five years," Shur said. "I knew at that moment we had him cold." Gallo had either lied on the VA application when he wrote that he earned a regular salary or lied to the IRS when he claimed he had not earned enough income to pay federal income taxes. "This was exactly the sort of thing that Bobby Kennedy wanted us to do," Shur said. "We were to look for any and all possible violations, no matter how small, to harass these gangsters."

The IRS wanted to prosecute Gallo for tax fraud, but Shur thought the FBI would have a better chance of sending him to prison if it charged Gallo with "knowingly making a false statement to a federal agency" when he lied to the VA about his income. "The IRS was upset because its agents had done the investigation," said Shur, "and I was tangled up in another interagency squabble, but I got the IRS to go along with me after I assured officials there that I'd make sure they were credited with helping catch Gallo."

Gallo and his father both agreed to plead guilty when they saw the evidence against them. Reporters and photographers swarmed around Larry Gallo when he arrived at the courthouse, surrounded by five bodyguards, for sentencing. The law required that both men be sentenced to a minimum of eighteen months in prison, but the judge suspended all of the elder Gallo's sentence. "I'm not sending you to prison because you were simply trying to help your son," he explained. The judge then suspended all but four months of Larry Gallo's prison sentence. The New York *Daily News* speculated that the four-month prison term "may have saved Gallo's life by giving him sanctuary in a federal prison, away from crime boss Joseph Magliocco's guns."

"Everyone at the Justice Department was thrilled we'd convicted Larry Gallo," Shur recalled, "and then J. Edgar Hoover blew it. He was on Capitol Hill testifying before an appropriations committee, and out of the blue, he brings up the Larry Gallo tax case and cites it as an example of how thorough the FBI is when it investigates mobsters. He tells Congress that it was his FBI agents who had caught Gallo lying on his VA application. I never knew for sure if Hoover was aware he was lying or if some aide had given him false information, but I always suspected he knew exactly what he was doing. Of course, the IRS agents, who had actually done all the work, were livid. They called me and said they would never, ever work again with the FBI. They were furious at me for taking the Gallo case away from them. All I could do was promise that I would set the record straight in my report to Robert Kennedy."

By now, Shur had spent two years traveling back and forth to Brooklyn, and in a memo to his bosses he suggested it was time for the OCRS to change its approach. The problem, he explained, was that the Justice Department was aiming too high. It was trying to bring down New York's top crime bosses. "These figures are simply too well insulated," he wrote. The government needed to lower its sights. "If we could get just one midlevel crime family member convicted of a serious charge that would send him away to prison for life or earn him a death sentence, then we might be able to get him to testify against his master. We have to work from the bottom up, rather than trying to go from the top down."

Shur already had a midlevel gangster in mind. Christopher Furnari had been spotted meeting with one of Magliocco's top lieutenants. Shur knew Furnari was on parole from prison, where he'd been serving a ten-year sentence for rape. Meeting with a known criminal, in this case Magliocco's lieutenant, was a violation of Furnari's parole. "I called the state parole authorities, and they agreed to revoke Furnari's parole and put him back in prison. I told them I wanted to be there when they arrested him. I thought he might be willing to cut a deal." Instead, the gangster pelted Shur with profanities. "The fear of being sent back to prison was simply not enough to make Furnari crack," Shur said. "It was going to take something more."

During a routine search of Furnari's house, agents found photographs of several Gallo gang members hidden in a family Bible. Shur guessed Furnari had been given the pictures because Magliocco wanted the men murdered, a hunch the gangster indirectly confirmed when Shur quizzed him about the photographs.

"I sell life insurance, and my boss gave them pictures to me," he replied sarcastically. "He told me to avoid selling insurance policies to these guys. They might not be living too much longer."

Shur recognized the photographs. They had been taken by the New York City Police Department. "It was obvious to me that a crooked cop had given the photographs to Magliocco's men, who in turn had given them to Furnari."

Shur felt stymied. "The mob had better sources than we did. It wasn't just dirty cops giving the mob police photographs. It was crooked judges, too. The mob was even paying off people in the telephone company. If we learned a telephone number was being used by a bookie, we'd ask the phone company for the address at that number. A few minutes later, our contact at the phone company would call us and tell us the address. But it turned out our contact was being paid by the mob to call them first whenever we asked for an address!"

It wasn't bribes, however, that were keeping mob members' lips sealed. "*Omertà* was very, very real," said Shur, "and we had plenty of photographs of dead bodies in our files to prove it. It didn't take me long, working in Brooklyn, to realize that the only way we would ever be able to cause the mob serious damage was by getting someone from inside its own ranks to testify for us, but *omertà* was simply too strong. Despite all of our best efforts, we rarely learned anything from informants that we could use in court. For instance, an informant would tell us about a mob bookie operation and we'd rush in and bust it, only to discover later that the informant had been using us. He'd send in his own bookies as soon as we locked up his competition. What we needed was a stick and a carrot. We had to find a way to make a midlevel gangster vulnerable, and then we had to offer him a way out. That's what I explained in my memo. But there was another piece to the puzzle. We had to be able to offer a gangster protection. We had to prove we could keep a mobster alive if he testified for us. We had to create some sort of protection program. But how? If we couldn't get federal agencies to share trivial information with each other, how were we ever going to get them to cooperate when it came to protecting a witness? The IRS was not going to trust the FBI to protect an IRS witness, and the FBI wasn't going to trust the IRS to protect an FBI witness, and neither of them was going to trust the Bureau of Narcotics."

CHAPTER
THREE

ERALD SHUR was called into a deputy chief's office in the Organized Crime and Racketeering Section at the Justice Department in March 1963 and given a stunning assignment. A member of the Vito Genovese crime family had been secretly talking to the FBI for nearly a year about his life inside the Mafia, Shur was told. Robert Kennedy wanted to give the president a summary of those private interviews, and Shur had been chosen to write it. "Stop whatever you're doing," he was ordered. "Read the FBI interviews and have a report ready by nine A.M. tomorrow for the attorney general and President Kennedy."

"What's the informant's name?" Shur asked.

"Valachi—Joe Valachi."

Shur had never heard of him. "Because of all the books written about organized crime and the popularity of movies like *The Godfather* and television shows like *The Sopranos*, most people today know how the Mafia operates," Shur recalled. "But Valachi was the first real mafioso to break *omertà*, and before him organized crime in America was very secretive and mysterious. There were still people who didn't believe there really was an American Mafia, and none of us in law enforcement knew how it was structured or understood its rules and rituals. I was handed this huge stack of FBI interviews—more than two feet high—and for the next five hours, I sat at a desk reading what Valachi had said. It was incredible stuff! He was giving up everything he knew."

The fifty-four-year-old Valachi had been a criminal for thirty years, having joined the New York mob in 1930. He'd served as a hit man, robber, numbers operator, enforcer, and drug pusher. Although he was a low-ranking "soldier" or, in mob parlance, a "button man," Valachi was well versed in Mafia gossip. Best of all, he loved to talk. But his interviews with the FBI were difficult to follow because he jumped back and forth between people and events. Valachi would be talking about mobsters in Las Vegas at one moment and the mob's Chicago operations the next. There was no index, no directory that would have helped Shur understand the relationship between the 317 mob members identified by Valachi or why they were important. As he waded through the reams of FBI reports, he realized he'd been given an arduous task. When he read the final interview, he grabbed a blank legal pad and hustled across the street to a pub popular with Justice Department lawyers. He ordered a Jack Daniel's on the rocks and a roast beef sandwich. "My mind was spinning. How was I going to digest all of this information and turn it into a cohesive summary—for the president of the United States, no less?" Shur would later joke that it was the shot of Jack Daniel's that cleared his mind. As soon as he drank it, he began scribbling furiously on the legal pad. Back in his office, he typed nonstop, finishing his summary shortly before dawn. Nearly four decades later, Shur would take a fresh look at the yellowed, thirteen-page, single-spaced memorandum that he prepared that night for President Kennedy and be struck by how rudimentary much of the information in it now seemed. Yet at the time, Valachi's disclosures were considered to be staggering revelations.

"We have achieved what we believe to be a major breakthrough," Shur declared in his opening sentence. "We can now state that a national criminal organization does, in fact, exist. Of this, there can no longer be any doubt." This sentence was aimed directly at J. Edgar Hoover's long-standing claim that there was no organized crime in America. (In one of the slickest public relations moves ever, Hoover would later insist that reporters had misunderstood what he had been saying for thirty years, and he would use Valachi's disclosures as a way to save face. One of Valachi's revelations was that the actual name of organized crime was not the Mafia but La Cosa Nostra [LCN]—meaning "our thing"—and Hoover used this difference in terminology in his defense. He had always known there was a national syndicate, he declared, but it wasn't named the *Mafia*. To this day, FBI agents are taught to call organized crime the LCN, not the Mafia. It is part of Hoover's save-face legacy.)

Continuing with his summary, Shur explained that only Italians could be inducted into the mob.

During a secret ceremony, a boss pricks the new member's trigger finger with a needle, drawing drops of blood, and then has him repeat an oath. A piece of paper, oftentimes a picture of a saint, is placed in the hand of the new member and set on fire . . . as the new member recites, in Italian, the following words: "With this oath I swear that if I ever violate this oath may I burn as this paper is burning." The inductee is then introduced by the boss as a "new friend of ours" and thereafter, if he is ever introduced to someone and told he is a "friend of ours" that means the stranger also is an LCN member.

Shur listed thirteen rules that Valachi said members were required to follow, including six punishable by death if violated.

Executable offenses include:

1. Furnishing information about this organization to any outside person, especially the police.
2. Handling narcotics or deriving a profit from their sale. (Valachi says this rule is most often violated. As long as the boss receives a portion of the money made, there may not be any enforcement.)
3. Engaging in an affair with the wife of another member.
4. Engaging in an affair with the sister or daughter of another member.
5. Stealing from another member.
6. Committing any acts of violence against another member unless approved by the boss.

Shur went on to outline the organizational structure of the LCN and to identify the crime bosses on the mob's "national commission." He was exhausted when he finished, but he was pleased with himself. Only later would he realize that he had misspelled the name of the mob throughout his entire report, writing it as La *Causa* Nostra. His bosses never mentioned it.

Rumors swirled through Washington and New York during the summer of 1963 that a mobster had betrayed *omertà*. When Miriam Ottenberg, a reporter for the *Washington Star*, identified Valachi in a front-page story, the Justice Department moved the mobster from a county jail outside Manhattan to Washington for safekeeping. He was the only inmate on the top floor of the downtown District of Columbia jail. The city's electric chair was located right next to his cell, and Valachi would sit in it as a joke whenever he had a visitor. There weren't many. No one was permitted to talk to the mobster without the permission of William Hundley, who had returned to oversee the OCRS when Edwyn Silberling resigned after spending a year in the job. "Valachi called me his *goombata*," Hundley recalled in an interview. "I've never told anyone about this before, but Jim McShane, the chief marshal in charge of the jail, and I used to sneak Valachi out of his cell at night and take him to Italian restaurants in town to eat. Can you imagine that? The mob has a price on this guy's head and we were taking him out for linguine."

Like most Mafia witnesses who would follow him, Valachi claimed he had not betrayed the mob until it first betrayed him. Valachi's break with the LCN had come on June 22, 1962, when he grabbed a piece of iron pipe in the prison yard at the federal penitentiary in Atlanta, Georgia, and beat another convict to death with it. Fifteen minutes later he discovered he had murdered the wrong man. He had been trying to kill Joseph DiPalermo, a mob hit man. Instead, he murdered Joseph Saupp, a forger with no mob ties who happened to resemble DiPalermo. Valachi was convinced DiPalermo was out to kill him on orders from New York crime boss Vito Genovese, who suspected Valachi of being a police informant. When prosecutors said they were going to seek the death penalty for Saupp's murder, Valachi offered to talk. In return, he was given a life sentence.

"Bobby Kennedy had a special relationship with the McClellan

Committee, and Senator McClellan began pressuring him to have Valachi testify before his committee," Hundley recalled. "This was going to be the first time Valachi had ever appeared in public. I opposed having him testify because I was still hopeful we might be able to make some criminal cases based on what Valachi had told the FBI, but frankly we weren't having much luck. A lot of what Valachi said was hearsay, or we were barred by the statute of limitations from going after people he named."

Kennedy and Hundley met privately with Valachi, and he agreed to testify before the committee. "Kennedy and I cut a deal with Valachi that the press was never told. It was a handshake agreement. Kennedy told Valachi that if he testified before Congress, the government would put him and his girlfriend on a Pacific Island after we were done with him." Kennedy had already picked out an island in the western Pacific that had once been held by the Japanese but was now under U.S. control. "Valachi would be safe there and be able to serve his life sentence."

Valachi's testimony in September and October 1963 was so riveting that crowds gathered on sidewalks outside store windows where merchants put television sets so people who didn't own them could watch the proceedings. A big, hulking figure, Valachi chilled viewers as he matter-of-factly described in his raspy voice cold-blooded murders he had participated in. Hundley believed Valachi had killed at least forty other gangsters. "If Genovese wanted someone knocked off in another crime family, he used Valachi," Hundley said, "but Valachi would never admit it to me because he knew there was no statute of limitations on murder. Instead, he always took the position that he was driving the car and someone else did the actual killing." One morning Hundley took him aside and urged him to confess that he had been a "hitter."

"Joe, under the law, the guy who drives the getaway car is just as guilty as the hit man," Hundley told him, "so why don't you cut out this nonsense about being the driver and tell the public the truth?"

Later that morning, a senator asked Valachi if he was sugarcoating his testimony about the murders he had witnessed. "Senator, it is my understanding that the person driving the car is just as guilty as the one who pulls the trigger," Valachi replied, "so if I were a hit man, there would be no reason for me to hide it. But Senator, I'm telling you, I was only a driver."

Hundley, who was sitting near Valachi, was struck by how convincing he sounded. "This guy had no formal education. But in those few minutes, he had twisted the information I had given him and used it to his advantage to make his claim even stronger. He was incredibly street-smart."

The LCN was not nearly as impressed. When a tabloid reporter asked a known Brooklyn gangster for his opinion of Valachi, the mobster pointed out that Valachi's nickname was "Joe Cago." Valachi claimed he had been given the nickname as a kid because he used to build scooters out of cargo crates. "They called me 'Joe Cargo,' " he said, and when he later joined the mob, Cargo was corrupted to Cago. But the Brooklyn gangster said the word *cago* in Italian meant "shit," and "this is exactly what Joe Valachi is."

A month after Valachi testified, Hundley, Shur, and other OCRS attorneys were briefing Robert Kennedy in his office about ongoing LCN cases when the attorney general excused himself for a lunch meeting. A few minutes later, Shur got a frantic call in his office from Miriam.

"President Kennedy has been shot!" she told him.

A stunned Shur turned on his radio and heard newscasters confirm that John F. Kennedy was dead. "There were rumors the LCN was behind the assassination because Bobby Kennedy was being so tough on the mob," he recalled. "We were ordered to comb through our files right away and look for any possible link. We couldn't find any." When Kennedy's assassin, Lee Harvey Oswald, was gunned down by Jack Ruby two days later, Shur was sent to check the records again. "We found evidence that Ruby had been on the fringes of organized crime, but there was nothing in any of our files of consequence."

Robert Kennedy continued as attorney general through the summer of 1964, but he had lost his zest. Hundley also realized his days were numbered. "Lyndon Johnson's people knew how close I was to Bobby Kennedy, and they wanted me out as soon as Kennedy left. They were going to put their own people in." Hundley asked Shur to take charge of Valachi.

"Hundley didn't want him abandoned," Shur recalled. "Valachi had gotten tremendous public exposure, but Hundley understood all that was coming to an end. He wanted me to hold Valachi's hand, so to speak." But no one warned Valachi that Shur was coming to visit him. "When I introduced myself, he read right away that he was being shuffled off, and he started screaming at me about how much he had done for America. He was flipping out, and then he suddenly stares at me and says, 'You know, if it wasn't for the Jews, there wouldn't be any organized crime because the Jews finance organized crime. The Italians do what the Jews tell them.' I wondered if he knew somehow I was Jewish, if this was a test. I didn't reply, and he changed the subject. I asked if I could come back and see him, and he told me that he wanted to see Hundley, not me." But Shur returned a few days later, bringing several exotic Italian cheeses with him. "Valachi says to me: 'Where's Hundley?' I told him Hundley was tied up but he had sent me over. I gave him the cheeses and said Hundley had sent them. That seemed to mean a lot to him." In return, Valachi gave Shur a recipe for spaghetti sauce. "Everyone in my office wanted a copy." Shur ordered Valachi a subscription to the New York *Daily News* so he could follow the horse races, and Hundley used his own money to buy him a television set.

Shur spent hours questioning Valachi. "Those sessions were literally magical for me because of my lifelong interest in organized crime." Shur never detected any trace of remorse. Valachi could discuss spaghetti sauce and the killing of a close friend with the same lack of emotion. One day Shur introduced him to a delegation of Italian judges who had a list of their countrymen who they suspected were mobsters. "Joe was very careful in picking out only people who he personally knew were in the Cosa Nostra. He didn't want to accuse anyone falsely."

Shur noted a trait when he talked with Valachi that he would see later in other mob witnesses. "Once these guys broke with the mob, they felt isolated and alone. They wanted to be accepted and appreciated for what they were doing, and they turned to the government to give them that support. Valachi had a need for Hundley and me to tell him that he was doing the right thing. One time, he asked me: 'Gerry, what I did was right for America, wasn't it? Didn't I do a lot for America?' He wanted that confirmation because he knew he had betrayed his past."

Valachi grew bored and lonely. "I was so fascinated by what he was telling me, I thought other people would want to learn about it, too. I talked to Hundley, and we decided to give Valachi an assignment. I took over a bunch of legal pads and ballpoint pens and told him that Hundley wanted him to write his life story." Valachi began immediately. "The next time I visited him, I picked up what he had written and it was really interesting stuff. He had an incredible memory. I gave it to Hundley's secretary to type, and every time Valachi saw me after that, he would say, 'Did you show Bill what I had written? Did he think it was good?' "

Valachi labored over his autobiography for months, eventually writing 300,000 words that filled 1,180 typed pages. "Hundley and I both thought it was worth publishing, but the federal Bureau of Prisons had a rule that prohibited convicts from publishing books about their crimes." Hundley got President Johnson's new attorney general, Nicholas deB. Katzenbach, to waive the rule, and then contacted New York writer Peter Maas, a friend of his and Robert Kennedy's, and had Shur introduce Maas to Valachi. The two quickly struck a book deal. But when word leaked out that Valachi was going to publish an autobiography, the Italian American newspaper *Il Progresso* printed a furious editorial denouncing the project. The newspaper claimed that Valachi's revelations had smeared Italian Americans by making it appear as if all of them were criminals. Other Italian American groups joined the protest, and a delegation from Congress protested in person at the White House. "President Johnson caved in," Hundley said. "He told us that Valachi wouldn't be allowed to publish his book. I was horrified because we were doing a complete flip-flop. For God's sake, we had given him the idea and gotten him a writer."

Peter Maas was barred from visiting Valachi, and the Justice

Department filed a motion in federal court to prevent the two men from publishing any pages that they already had written. As further punishment, Valachi was moved out of his top-floor sanctuary at the D.C. jail and to a cell in the federal prison in Milan, Michigan, where he would be less accessible. "Kennedy and I had promised Valachi that he would be taken to an island with his girlfriend, but there was no way the Johnson administration was going to keep that promise," Hundley said, "especially with a delegation of Italian Americans breathing down its neck. Bobby Kennedy tried to intervene, but Johnson wasn't going to help him or Valachi."

Valachi appealed to Shur. "I told Valachi to be patient. I would do my best to get him moved out of Milan as soon as all of this attention blew over." But Valachi couldn't wait. Utterly dejected, he tied the electrical cord from his radio around his neck and hanged himself in his cell's shower stall, but the cord snapped under his weight and a guard found him unconscious but alive. By this point, Hundley had joined a private law firm, but he pulled strings and visited Valachi at the prison. "I apologized to him for what was happening," Hundley said. "The government had double-crossed and betrayed him." Valachi couldn't believe it. He kept saying, "But Bobby Kennedy promised me . . ." Shur arranged his summer vacation trip so he too could visit Valachi. "He truly believed he had redeemed himself by becoming an informant, and he couldn't understand why the government had turned on him. He told me, 'I kept my word, my end of the deal; how can the Justice Department not keep its word?' "

Maas sued the government, and after months of legal wrangling, a federal judge ruled that while the Justice Department could prevent Valachi from publishing his memoirs, it couldn't prohibit Maas from writing a book based on his interviews. *The Valachi Papers* was published in 1968 and became a national best-seller.

After several months in Michigan, Shur arranged for Valachi to be moved to a medium-security prison in La Tuna, Texas, where he was put into two cells that had been converted into a single one on the second floor of the prison hospital. This arrangement gave him a bedroom and living room area. A third cell was made into an exercise room and contained a hot plate, microwave, and refrigerator. "We couldn't risk having him in a cell block with other inmates because they'd have killed him," recalled J. D. Williams, who was Valachi's case manager at the prison. "Sometimes at night, we'd take him up on the hospital roof so he could be outdoors." The guards called his cell "the Valachi Suite"—an ironic description for his bitterly lonely quarters. "I felt sorry for him," said Williams. "He had once lived high on the hog and now he was all alone." Then a prison doctor discovered Valachi had developed testicular cancer. "That bothered him, but not as much as when his girlfriend stopped coming to see him," said Williams. She had been visiting him once a month, but the trip had become too expensive for her. The government turned down Valachi's request for parole. Shur tried to visit Valachi whenever he could, but he was too busy with his career to do this often. "For the rest of us, life continued to move on. Joe's didn't." The last time Shur saw him was in 1971. Valachi, who had spent eight years in prison by then, was now sixty-eight. "I knew something was wrong because his copies of the New York *Daily News* were stacked unopened in a corner of his cell and he didn't pay any attention to the cheeses I brought him." As Shur was leaving, Valachi touched his arm. "I did the right thing, didn't I, Gerry?" he asked.

"You did a great thing," Shur replied.

"You'll tell Hundley, won't you?"

Two months later Valachi died of cancer. A woman who had been writing him for several years arranged to have him buried in an unmarked grave in a cemetery near Niagara Falls. She didn't put a headstone on the grave because she was afraid the mob would destroy it.

"Valachi was a tragic figure," Shur said. "To me, he personified both good and evil, and he gave me my first inkling that a cold-blooded killer could also have a warm heart. There would be others in years to come who would give us better information, but he was the first to open the door."

CHAPTER
FOUR

PRESIDENT LYNDON JOHNSON had his own priorities, and in early 1964 fighting organized crime wasn't at the top of his list. The nation was being torn apart by racial unrest, and he was determined to pass a civil rights bill. Even though it was against the law for federal employees to lobby Congress, Shur and a few of his colleagues were dispatched to the Capitol to give "advice" when the Civil Rights Act of 1964 was ready to be put to a vote. After it squeaked through, Johnson took the unusual step of sending Justice Department attorneys into the South to make certain the new law was followed. Shur stayed behind, continuing to work on the department's now deemphasized fight against organized crime. With the Kennedys gone, federal agencies began feuding again, and several disgruntled U.S. attorneys urged the White House to reel in Shur and his irritating Organized Crime and Racketeering Section comrades. The discovery that the FBI and other federal agencies routinely used illegal wiretaps to eavesdrop on suspected mobsters irked Congress. Morale in OCRS plunged. Within a year, one-fourth of Kennedy's handpicked staff resigned.

In the midst of this turmoil, Shur urged his bosses to start two new programs. "I began writing memos telling people we needed to set up a program to protect government witnesses. I wasn't just thinking about criminals. I was thinking about honest citizens, too, people like the Long Island trucking company owner whom I'd asked to testify against Sonny Franzese. I thought we needed to establish a safe house somewhere—a place where we could hide witnesses so the mob couldn't find them before a trial. Unfortunately, the general feeling was that there simply wasn't much need for a witness protection program because there weren't a lot of mobsters out there willing to testify against the Mafia."

Shur's second idea got an equally tepid response. He wanted the OCRS to automate the old-fashioned index card system it used to keep track of mobsters. For years, Winifred "Win" Willse, a no-nonsense ex–New York City cop who had read every report submitted to OCRS, had had her staff pull out whatever details she thought were important and record them on five-by-eight-inch cards. "If Joe Racketeer owned a funeral home and was visited by Sam Racketeer, Willse's clerks would fill out one index card for Joe, one for Sam, and one for the funeral home; then the cards were cross-referenced," Shur recalled. By 1964, Willse had compiled four hundred thousand cards divided into fifty categories. They contained three hundred thousand names, but much of the information was impossible to access because the index cards were so cumbersome. "It was a database that screamed out for automation," Shur recalled, "but computers were not part of most people's daily lives back then." He had been interested in computers since his college days, and he prodded his bosses to computerize the information. "No one else in the entire federal government is collecting the LCN information we now collect," he explained in a memo, "but this information is useless unless we can process and understand it."

While his bosses at the OCRS were sympathetic, they told Shur there wasn't enough money in their budget to computerize the information. They did toss him a scrap, however. If he could find a way to finance his idea, they would be happy to back it. Shur turned to the FBI for help, but it and the other investigative agencies whose doors he knocked on turned him down. "Most of them didn't want to share the information they had collected about organized crime with us in the first place, and the last thing they wanted us to develop was a centralized, computerized system," he explained. "That would give the OCRS way too much power."

Undeterred, Shur switched tactics. The Justice Department's mainframe computer was being used only by its payroll office, so he suggested the OCRS borrow a programmer from payroll for ninety days. "I thought: 'If I can get at least one programmer interested and some of the information on the cards processed by the mainframe computer, then I can prove just how useful an automated intelligence system can be.'" The department's bean counters said no.

During the next two years, Shur would write countless memos and repeatedly push to get the outdated index card system modernized. It became a personal crusade. Meanwhile, his boss, Henry Petersen, who succeeded Hundley as chief of the OCRS, and another OCRS attorney, Robert Peloquin, came up with a new plan in 1964 to rejuvenate the section's pursuit of the mob. One way to stop the bickering between federal agencies, they decided, was by putting an investigator from each agency onto a special team, called a strike force, and assigning that team to attack a specific target. While this had not been done before, several years earlier Robert Kennedy had put Peloquin in charge of a Justice Department task force whose only assignment was to indict Teamsters president Jimmy Hoffa. It had taken Peloquin's "Hoffa Unit" four years, but it had finally gotten its man. Hoffa was convicted of jury tampering and fraud after he was caught collecting kickbacks from Las Vegas casino owners in return for union loans.

Petersen and Peloquin recruited investigators for the first strike force from six agencies: the Bureau of Narcotics, the Customs Service, the Labor Department, the Secret Service, the Internal Revenue Service, and the Bureau of Alcohol, Tobacco, and Firearms. Hoover's FBI refused to join. Peloquin, who was put in charge, added five OCRS attorneys to the roster. He also decided New York City was too big a target. "We wanted a city small enough so we could tell whether or not the strike force was doing any good," recalled Thomas Kennelly, the OCRS attorney whom Peloquin selected as his second-in-command. "Someone suggested Buffalo, New York, and it seemed perfect." The LCN there was controlled by Stefano Magaddino, who was serving as the boss of bosses while Vito Genovese was in prison. The Magaddino crime family had around 150 members. "That made it a small enough target to be manageable," Kennelly said. There was another reason Buffalo was appealing: Only two mobsters had been prosecuted there in the previous decade. "Anything we did was bound to be an improvement," he pointed out.

Although Magaddino was seventy-five years old in November 1966, when the strike force hit town, he still held a steel grip on the city's throat. He had begun his nearly fifty-year reign during Prohibition, when he used guns and muscle to become Buffalo's biggest bootlegger. Since then, he had murdered several would-be successors and survived two assassination attempts—his sister had been blown to pieces by a bomb in a package delivered by mistake to her house, which was next door to his, and a hand grenade tossed into his kitchen through a window had failed to explode.

Even by the mob's twisted standards, the illiterate Magaddino was considered vicious. The most shocking example the strike force uncovered was the 1961 killing of Albert Agueci, who along with his brother, Vito, was a drug trafficker. The two brothers had been paying Magaddino for protection from the police, but the crime boss turned his back on them when they were arrested for their drug activities. Albert Agueci threatened Magaddino, saying that if he didn't use his connections to free them, Agueci would squeal to the FBI about the crime boss's operations. Magaddino ordered him killed. Albert's badly burned body was found a few days later in a barn. An estimated forty pounds of flesh had been carved from it. His arms and legs had been broken, his jaw shattered, and half of his teeth knocked out. All of this had apparently been done while he was still alive. He had then been strangled with a clothesline and his remains doused with gasoline and set on fire.

The strike force spent its first three months in Buffalo buttering up local agents who resented its intrusion into their jurisdiction. "The local Bureau of Narcotics agent wouldn't even talk to me," recalled Peloquin. The special agent in charge of the FBI's

Buffalo office was more belligerent. "He wrote letters criticizing our every move to Director Hoover, who then sent them to the attorney general, who then sent them to me," said Peloquin. "I adopted a policy: If he wrote ten pages complaining about us, our answer had to be eleven pages long. We always wanted our replies to be one more page than his letters."

Unlike the local agents, the Royal Canadian Mounted Police were eager to cooperate because the Magaddino crime family also operated over the border in Canada. It sent a Mountie to work with the strike force, and one day he volunteered to sweep its offices for electronic bugs. Sure enough, he found a microphone hidden in a conference room, but it hadn't been planted by the Magaddino mob. "It belonged to the FBI," recalled Donald Campbell, another strike force attorney.

With few local sources, the strike force's investigation sputtered and stalled. Then it got a lucky break. Sam Giambrone, a Buffalo police sergeant, told the strike force that a Magaddino crime member might be willing to cooperate, but only if certain conditions were met. Pascal "Paddy" Calabrese, who was serving a five-year prison sentence for a daring daylight robbery in the city hall treasurer's office, wanted out of prison. He also wanted his girlfriend and her children moved out of Buffalo and given new identities so Magaddino couldn't find them. He was willing to deal only with Giambrone and federal agents because he knew Magaddino had several Buffalo cops on his payroll. Initially, Giambrone had taken Calabrese's offer to the FBI, but its agents said their office wasn't equipped to relocate a family. His next try had been the strike force, and Peloquin jumped at the chance.

Calabrese was angry at the mob, he said, because Magaddino had abandoned him as soon as he was arrested, just as he had the dope-dealing Agueci brothers. The difference was that Calabrese was a made LCN member. "A basic tenet of the LCN was that if a member got into trouble, the crime family was supposed to take care of his family while he was doing time in prison," said Peloquin, "but Magaddino was a cheap old man." Sergeant Giambrone had given money from his own pocket to Calabrese's destitute girlfriend, Rochelle, so she could buy food and presents for her children at Christmastime, and it was that generous act that had finally swayed Calabrese.

In a secret meeting on February 27, 1967, Calabrese identified every major criminal in the Magaddino family and told the strike force about numerous crimes the Buffalo LCN had committed. Although he couldn't tie Magaddino directly to these crimes, he was able to implicate his top two underlings: Freddy Randaccio and Patsy Natarelli. Both were juicy targets. Randaccio was believed to be the murderer who had tortured and executed Agueci, and Natarelli was known for sticking an ice pick into the ears of borrowers who had gotten behind in their repayments to Magaddino's loan sharks. Convicting them would deal a major blow to the Magaddino organization. Just as important, it would prove that the strike force concept worked. But first Calabrese's girlfriend and children had to be spirited out of Buffalo.

The strike force moved fast. "We called Attorney General Ramsey Clark, and he got us permission from the Department of Defense to hide the family on a military base," Thomas Kennelly recalled. Racing to Rochelle's apartment, the team hustled her and her children into unmarked black cars and sped away. Their final destination was the tiny Strategic Air Command post outside Presque Isle, Maine, where Rochelle was given an alias and housed in a bungalow usually reserved for married naval officers. Her neighbors were told that her husband was a marine pilot on a secret overseas mission. Even the base commander didn't know the truth. Simultaneously, Calabrese was taken from his cell in the Elmira Reformatory under heavy guard and brought to the "Valachi Suite" inside the federal prison in La Tuna, Texas, for safekeeping. Only the warden knew his true identity.

The strike force was now geared to arrest Randaccio and Natarelli, but on what charge? The most damaging information Calabrese had offered was thin at best. He claimed they had once sent him to California to rob an armored car and steal some precious gems, but neither man had gone with him. In fact, Calabrese himself had been called home before he could commit the robberies. Since the mobsters hadn't gone to California and no one had been robbed, what possible crime had they committed? It was Kennelly who came up with an answer. The armored car that Calabrese had targeted routinely collected a bag of cash and checks from the Beverly Hilton Hotel. Since most of the checks were written by hotel guests on out-of-town banks, Kennelly contended that Randaccio and Natarelli had violated federal interstate commerce laws. According to Section 1951 of Title 18 in the U.S. Code, better known as the Hobbs Act, anyone who "obstructs, delays or affects commerce or the movement of any article or commodity in commerce by robbery or extortion, or conspires to do so" is breaking the law. "Checks are part of commerce," Kennelly reasoned, "and a robbery would have clearly affected their movement." The fact that the armored car was never robbed didn't matter, he explained; it was enough that Randaccio and Natarelli had conspired to rob it. At least that was Kennelly's argument. It was clearly a long shot, but it was the only case the strike force could make. It helped that the Hobbs Act was a federal law. This meant the case would be heard in a federal courtroom before a federal judge, completely bypassing the local district attorney and district court. The mob wouldn't be able to pull strings.

As soon as Randaccio and Natarelli were arrested, the Magaddino family began hunting Calabrese and Rochelle. Rumors surfaced that Magaddino was offering $100,000 to anyone who could find them. Mobsters questioned Rochelle's neighbors, harassed the couple's friends and relatives, even interrogated Calabrese's former barber. No one knew where they were hiding. As the trial date drew closer, the LCN became bolder. "Several of us on the strike force began getting threatening telephone calls," recalled Donald Campbell. "We were shocked because there had always been an understanding that the mob didn't go after federal agents or their families. You just didn't cross that line." Strike force members began traveling in pairs, taking special precautions. Campbell sent his wife out of town. Finally, Giambrone and a Bureau of Narcotics agent took matters into their own hands.

They drove to the Magaddino family estate in Niagara Falls. "Giambrone goes up to the door and knocks, and when Magaddino is summoned and comes to the door, Giambrone whips out his revolver, sticks it in Magaddino's mouth, and says, 'If one more phone call comes in or anyone attempts to do harm to my family or anyone else's on the strike force, we are going to come back and blow your fucking head off,'" Campbell recalled. "I knew Giambrone and this other agent and so did Magaddino, and he knew they meant it. From that moment on, the harassment stopped."

Kennelly personally argued the case against the two mobsters when it finally came to trial in late 1967. "I was worried about two things," he recalled. "Would jurors believe Calabrese—an admitted criminal, scoundrel, and mob member—and if they did, would they buy the conspiracy theory?" Calabrese, who was brought to the courthouse encircled by agents, was grilled for hours by the defense attorneys. They tried to portray him as a hot-tempered thug and pathological liar by dredging up everything they could from his criminal past. But Calabrese proved unflappable, and Kennelly called several witnesses to buttress his testimony. "Everything Paddy Calabrese said—down to details about which hotel he stayed in while he was in California—was corroborated," said Kennelly. "It was clear that Paddy was telling the straight story about the robberies, but I didn't know if that was going to be enough. It all hinged on whether or not jurors accepted our conspiracy theory." They did. Randaccio and Natarelli were found guilty, and each was sentenced to twenty years in prison.

The strike force was so grateful to Calabrese that Kennelly personally appeared on his behalf before the state parole board. It voted him an immediate parole. "Suddenly we had to figure out what to do with him," Kennelly recalled, "and none of us had a clue." Kennelly suggested that Calabrese change his last name to Angelo. "One of our strike force members got a priest in Buffalo to give Paddy and his family new baptismal certificates with their fake names on them." At the time, those were sufficient for the couple to obtain new driver's licenses. Another strike force attorney persuaded a Buffalo school superintendent to change the last names on the children's school records to Angelo so Rochelle could take the records with her. "The hardest job was finding someplace to hide them. One of our guys on the strike force had a brother who ran a manufacturing plant in Jackson, Michigan," Kennelly said, "so we arranged for him to hire Paddy. Everything we did was through strike force members. There was no one else we could ask for help."

Kennelly conjured up $600 to pay three months' rent for Calabrese. Members of the strike force passed around a hat and collected another $500 so the family could buy a used car. That was it. After the "Angelos" were delivered to Michigan, they were on their own. From the start, Kennelly wondered whether they could adjust. "Paddy had been a mob guy all his life, and now he was supposed to work forty hours a week in a manufacturing plant. It was unrealistic. He was supposed to start carrying a lunch bucket to work, but he didn't even know what one was!" Within a week, Calabrese was on the telephone to Kennelly. "We're dying here," he griped. "You got to give us more money." Kennelly suggested he take out a bank loan. That's what legitimate families did. Three months later, Kennelly received a call from Calabrese's boss at the manufacturing plant. The "Angelo" family had taken out a loan and then vanished without repaying a cent, leaving behind a very angry bank manager.

Paddy Calabrese would later be identified as the first mob witness to be given a false background and relocated by the Justice Department. It was not an awe-inspiring beginning.

CHAPTER
FIVE

A T ABOUT THE SAME TIME the strike force was trying to decide what to do about Paddy Calabrese, the FBI was dealing with a mob witness of its own in New England, and its agents, much like their counterparts in Buffalo, were traveling in uncharted waters. Joseph Barboza, nicknamed "the Animal," had agreed to testify against New England crime boss Raymond L. S. Patriarca after he learned Patriarca was trying to kill him. Like Calabrese, the Barboza case would become one of the stepping-stones that was eventually to lead to the creation of WITSEC.

A ruthless contract killer, Barboza was responsible for at least twenty murders, nearly all done at Patriarca's bidding. He was such an important mob witness that J. Edgar Hoover personally called his agents each day when they were interrogating the hit man to hear what he was telling them. There would be speculation later that Hoover was hoping Barboza would somehow link the mob to the Kennedy family, since Patriarca controlled the LCN in Massachusetts, but apparently he didn't know of any ties. The thirty-five-year-old Barboza had been arrested in October 1966 on several minor charges and had assumed Patriarca would post his bail, as he had done before. Instead, the crime boss seized the opportunity to kill three of Barboza's closest friends and put a contract on him in prison. Patriarca had heard gossip that Barboza was secretly plotting to take over his operations, which stretched from the outskirts of New York City to the Canadian border with

Maine. As soon as Barboza agreed to testify, the U.S. Marshals Service sent deputy U.S. marshal John J. Partington to protect the gangster's wife, Janice, and his young daughter, Terri. The Marshals Service is the oldest of all the federal law enforcement agencies, dating back to 1789, when the first Congress created the job of U.S. marshal to oversee federal court proceedings, protect judges in court, and handle witnesses. Partington, who was stationed in Providence, Rhode Island, was chosen for two reasons: He'd guarded witnesses before in local cases, and he was familiar with Patriarca, who operated out of an office in a laundry in Providence. Partington suspected the FBI had another reason for passing him the job—its agents didn't want to be bothered baby-sitting a mobster's family.

As soon as Partington arrived at Barboza's house in Swampscott, Massachusetts, he posted deputies with shotguns at the front and rear doors. "Looking back on it now, I've got to say we were like the Keystone Kops," he later recalled. "Protecting families was new to us. There were no manuals, no instruction books. We were learning as we did things." Partington proved to have good instincts. To this day, he is considered by many to be one of the best deputies the U.S. Marshals Service ever produced when it comes to witness protection. Partington had just turned thirty in 1966, but he looked even younger. He had sandy brown hair, sparkling blue eyes, a lanky frame, and aw-shucks, small-town manners. He'd grown up outside Providence in a tiny hamlet, where he'd gotten his first job as a police officer after a two-year stint in the army. In 1961, he had joined the U.S. Marshals Service, and when Robert Kennedy fingered Patriarca as one of the LCN bosses he wanted to indict, Partington was sent to help two IRS agents nab him. They were not the first to try. As early as 1930, Patriarca had been identified as Providence's "public enemy number one," but he had been sent to prison only once, and that incident had sparked a statewide scandal. Patriarca had been sentenced in 1938 to five years for armed robbery but was paroled by the governor after serving only a few months. It turned out that one of the governor's aides had arranged the release in return for a large campaign contribution.

Partington had first met Patriarca in 1961, when the newly hired deputy was sent to serve a subpoena on the aged mobster in Federal Hill, an Italian American neighborhood that overlooks the state capitol in Providence. A Long Island newspaper reporter described Federal Hill this way back then: "It is Patriarca's stronghold, an armed camp where gnarled old men with undersized fedoras watch suspiciously from their chairs propped against the walls of darkened social clubs, ready to make hand signals whenever a stranger approaches." The moment Partington stepped through the front doors of the Patriarca-owned Nu-Brite Cleaners, two bodyguards stopped him. "Patriarca came out from his office in the back to see who I was," Partington recalled. "He was eating a sandwich." Not knowing any better, Partington started to reach inside his coat jacket for his badge. Patriarca dove behind a door, dropping his sandwich. His bodyguards grabbed Partington's arms and pinned him to the wall. They thought he was reaching for a handgun.

"It's okay!" Partington yelled. "I'm a federal man."

After Partington handed Patriarca the subpoena, the LCN boss lectured him about mob etiquette. "Anytime you want me, kid, I am here. But don't you ever go to my house, you hear? My wife, she don't have nothing to do with my business. *Capisce?*" The FBI, which had an illegal bug planted in the cleaners, overheard Patriarca telling his attorney a few minutes later that he'd been served a subpoena by a "real Boy Scout."

Partington was surprised when he met Barboza's wife. Janice Barboza was not the mob moll he expected. Still in her twenties, she was polite, bright, and beautiful. Her three-year-old daughter reminded him of the child movie star Shirley Temple. "I wanted them to live as normal a life as possible while we were protecting them," Partington recalled, "so I told my men that no one was allowed to use the bathroom in the house. I didn't want her cleaning up after us. I also had the Marshals Service send out a matron to be with us because I didn't want three men alone with this very attractive woman every day and night." Within minutes after Partington arrived, the Barbozas' cat escaped out a back door, and Terri began to cry. The two deputies with Partington were not about to run outside and look for it, but Partington did—much to their irritation. "A lot of deputies didn't like protecting witnesses or their families because they considered them scum, but I didn't feel that way," he recalled. "What had Barboza's little girl ever done? It wasn't my job to judge them. We were there to keep them alive, and I knew it would be easier if they knew I cared enough about them to chase down a family cat."

During the next month, Partington spent sixteen hours a day at Barboza's house, and although he lectured his men not to get personally involved with Janice and Terri, he grew close to both of them. Terri waited in the kitchen each morning for "Uncle John" to arrive. At night, he read her stories before she went to bed. Once a week, deputies took Janice to visit Barboza, who was being hidden under an alias in a jail on Cape Cod. Otherwise she never left the house, and soon she was going stir-crazy. One morning she asked to go to a nearby beach. Partington knew his bosses in Washington would say it was too risky, but he agreed to take her. She came downstairs wearing an eye-popping bikini. A few nights later she asked him to take her dancing at a local nightclub where mobsters sometimes socialized. Partington set it up. "You got to have balls in this business," he said later, "and I wanted Patriarca's men to know we weren't scared of them." Partington also started bringing his wife, Helen, to the house to visit with Janice. "I knew it wasn't professional to involve my wife, but Janice needed someone to talk to besides us men, and I knew my wife would feel better about this situation, too, since I was spending all of my time with another woman."

Meanwhile, the FBI was pumping Barboza for information. He had plenty to tell. The hit man claimed Patriarca had once asked him to kill a gambler named Willie Marfeo. He'd agreed, but said someone else beat him to it. Marfeo had been shot to death after he was lured into a telephone booth. Based on Barboza's claims, the FBI arrested Patriarca in May 1967 on a "conspiracy to commit murder" charge in the Marfeo case. Reporters noted in their front-page stories that Patriarca was rumored to be offering $300,000 to anyone who killed his accuser. Worried that the Cape

Cod jail was no longer safe, the FBI decided to reunite its witness with his family and move them to an island hideout. Barboza thought he was heading for a tropical paradise, but that was not what the government had in mind.

Partington was sent to a private airfield in Cape Cod to pick up Barboza. Even though it was nearly midnight, the gangster arrived wearing black sunglasses when he stepped out of an armored police van. He looked exactly as Partington had imagined. His greasy black hair was tucked under a fedora. He was unshaven. The collar on his trench coat was turned up, and a cigarette was dangling precariously from his lower lip. "There must have been twenty FBI agents carrying machine guns surrounding him," Partington recalled. Strutting toward the waiting seaplane, Barboza yelled to Partington: "Hey you, where are my guards?" There was only one other deputy on the tarmac.

"Lose the cigarette," Partington ordered. Barboza ignored him. "He was testing me," Partington explained later, "so I told him, 'Put out the goddamn cigarette or we're not going anywhere.'" Barboza slowly took it out of his mouth and flipped it onto the runway.

"Who are you, the goddamn warden?" he asked. Partington didn't reply. "I said, which one are you?" Barboza demanded.

"I'm Partington."

"Oh, you're the prick who's been taking my wife to the beach in her bikini. You're the one who's been trying to . . ." The noise of the seaplane drowned out the rest of his sentence as they climbed aboard. They landed at another airport a short time later and boarded a helicopter for the final leg of the trip. The sun was rising by the time Thacher's Island came into view. It was a half-mile-long clump of jagged rocks off the coast of Gloucester, Massachusetts. "You gotta be shitting me," Barboza groaned as the helicopter circled his new home. "You expect me and my family to live on this shithole?"

There were two lighthouses, known as the Twin Lights, on the island. Each was made of granite blocks, stood 124 feet high, and had been built in 1861. There were also two white Cape

Cod–style houses, but they hadn't been occupied since the Coast Guard had modernized the lighthouses several years earlier so that they operated automatically. The island was now inhabited only by bugs, rats, snakes, and seagulls, which survived by feeding off each other. The FBI thought it was perfect. Visitors were rare, and escaping from the island would be foolhardy. The waves crashing against its rocky shoreline were too strong for most swimmers, and landing a boat there would be very risky. Janice and Terri were waiting for Barboza in the smaller of the houses. The other was reserved for the sixteen deputies assigned to guard the family in three round-the-clock shifts. Both houses had been swept clean and painted but were still spartan.

Partington and Barboza locked horns from the start. Later that same day Barboza was outside helping his daughter learn how to ride a bicycle the deputies had gotten for her when Partington heard the child calling him.

"Uncle John," Terri said, dashing up to him, "can I ride my bike some more?"

"Sure, sweetie, ride it all you want," he answered.

Barboza grabbed her as she tried to climb back on the bicycle. Partington hadn't known Terri had been told she was finished with her bicycle lesson and it was time for her to take a nap. "I don't like you!" she screamed at her father. "I want John as my daddy."

An hour later, Partington spotted Barboza walking on the rocks near the shoreline and went out to talk to him about what had happened. Without warning, Barboza sucker-punched him in the chin, knocking him down. At that same moment, a helicopter swooped down. Barboza walked to it nonchalantly and greeted the FBI agents who had come to see him. Striking a federal officer was punishable by ten years in prison, and Partington's lip was bleeding by the time he joined the group.

"Is there a problem, John?" an FBI agent asked.

"No," he replied, shooting a glance at Barboza. "No problem."

From that point on, the two men held each other in grudging

respect. "We spent hours talking. I was fascinated by how he operated, and he was curious about how we did our jobs. He explained to me how he killed people. He was teaching us his tricks as a mob hit man so we could do our job and keep him alive."

When the FBI sent word that two hit men were headed toward the island on a yacht, Partington ordered all sixteen of his deputies to stand along the shoreline with their carbines in full view. He wanted the mobsters to think it was an armed fortress. It worked. The thugs retreated back to Boston. The deputies celebrated that night by giving Terri candy when she knocked repeatedly on their door. It was Halloween.

Some deputies thought Partington was coddling Barboza. When the gangster, who was an avid boxer, complained about being bored, Partington got him two different kinds of workout bags and arranged for a local prizefighter to be flown onto the island to spar with him. "Barboza would come busting into the deputies' quarters foaming at the mouth and raising hell," retired deputy marshal Jesse Grider recalled, "and instead of saying, 'Get your ass out of here and back to your own cabin where you're supposed to be,' Partington would calm him down by saying, 'Joe, let's talk about this.' There were several times when I thought Partington needed to be firmer with him, but Partington said it was important to keep Barboza happy."

The deputies rotated on and off the island every two weeks and most grew to hate their arrogant charge, but Partington lived on the island full time and later defended his actions by saying it was important to keep Barboza in good spirits. "If we simply had wanted to keep him safe, we could have stuck him in federal prison like we did with Joe Valachi," he explained, "but keeping Barboza alive was only part of my job. Most people don't have a clue about the emotional shit a guy like Barboza goes through once he decides to testify. Joe had been a criminal since age fourteen, and now he was turning against his friends and becoming the one thing he hated most—a rat. I had to keep him pumped up, keep his mind sharp so he'd testify. Otherwise we'd lose everything we'd spent months pulling together."

With no television and few amusements, boredom and isolation began taking a toll. After two months, even Partington had had enough. "Barboza couldn't stand losing, and one night we were playing cards and Joe says, 'Whoever has the ace of hearts fucks his mother in the ass.' I was sick of him, his attitude, being on the island, being away from my family—it had gotten to me—so I leaned forward, looked him right in the eye, and said, 'Joe, what if I tell you I have the ace of hearts?' and without flinching, he says, 'Then, John, you fuck your dead mother in the ass, you asshole.' I lunged at him." The other deputies had to separate them. Later that night, they made peace and talked about how their lives might have gone if they'd made different choices. "Joe was as cold as they came, but I discovered another side to him. Here's a guy who would kill you in a heartbeat, but also wrote poetry and adored his daughter."

When a Boston newspaper revealed Barboza was on the island, Partington arranged for a helicopter to ferry the family to a new hiding place. This time it was a seashore estate owned by a multimillionaire. The day after they left, the FBI learned that a hit man had planned on crashing a boat loaded with sixteen hundred pounds of dynamite into the island. During the next thirteen months, more than three hundred deputies served two-week stints under Partington's command protecting Barboza. The Marshals Service had never before undertaken such a complex security operation, and matters were about to become even more dangerous. "When the trial finally began, we had to bring Barboza out of hiding, and that meant the mob would know exactly where he would be and when he would be there," Partington explained.

The FBI would later learn that at least five different hit men were waiting outside the courthouse on the morning Barboza was scheduled to appear. One was hiding in a nearby office building with a high-powered rifle, the others at various entrances. Partington fooled them all. He had smuggled Barboza inside the courthouse three days earlier. The two of them had been sleeping on cots in a basement storeroom. Steel plates had been welded over the storeroom's windows to keep bombs from being tossed inside. But the mob didn't quit. A known LCN killer stole a police officer's uniform and tried to bluff his way past deputies guarding the courtroom. When that didn't work, the mob planted a bomb in a car driven by Barboza's attorney. The blast, which cost the attorney his right leg, was supposed to intimidate Barboza, but it only made him more determined. He testified for three days and kept his cool during intense grilling by defense attorneys. A jury found Patriarca guilty, and he was sentenced to five years in prison.

Patriarca's trial was just the beginning. In the coming months, Barboza testified against a dozen other LCN members. Partington used a variety of schemes to sneak him into Boston for his court appearances. He had a Coast Guard cutter drop him at the Boston docks in the middle of the night, had him ride on a fishing boat to an isolated pier, hid him in the rear of the U.S. Postal Service truck delivering mail to the courthouse, and landed him by helicopter on the roof of a nearby office building. He and Barboza once arrived at the courthouse in a bright red sports car with caps on their heads and mufflers draped around their necks. Another time, Partington had a deputy disguised as Barboza arrive at the courthouse in an armored car with a police escort, complete with wailing sirens and flashing red lights, while Barboza sneaked in through a side door.

His testimony gutted Patriarca's organization. After the last trial, the government decided to send Barboza and his family to live at a military base in Fort Knox, Tennessee, until it could decide what to do with them. Janice and Terri went ahead, but Barboza stayed behind. He was angry. By this time he'd become enamored of all the attention, and he didn't want to be shuffled away. The night before he was scheduled to leave, he began threatening the deputies. He was going to "end it" his way.

"Just wait until tomorrow," he warned. "You're gonna see the real Joe Barboza, not the rat fink. You bring your big shiny badges, bring your big shiny guns, because you're gonna need them."

The next morning, Partington announced he was going in alone. "I'll take my walkie-talkie with me," he explained. "If I click it twice, I want you to come in shooting." Partington walked inside the house. Barboza hadn't slept all night. He'd been exercising, preparing himself, just the way he did before a boxing match. Partington strolled over to the living room couch and stretched out on it lazily, pulling his cap over his eyes.

"Joe, we'll leave here in about ten minutes," he said.

"Where are the others?" Barboza asked.

"Do you think for one minute," Partington replied, "after all you've done, after all we've been through, that I would let this end in a showdown? No way, Joe. We're going out the way we came in. Just you and me. No leg irons. No handcuffs. Just the two of us."

That deflated the crisis. The two men walked outside minutes later and rode to the airport. Waiting for them there was a delegation of U.S. marshals and the same U.S. Coast Guard seaplane that Partington had used to take Barboza to the island. The mobster climbed aboard, took out a pack of cigarettes, lit one, and defiantly blew smoke toward Partington. "It was his way of telling me to get screwed," Partington said. He understood the importance of the moment. "We'd taken on the mob and we'd won. Trust me, there were lots of guys in the mob watching us, and the fact we'd protected Barboza and kept him alive gave them plenty to think about. We'd proved it could be done."

CHAPTER
SIX

GERALD SHUR was lying on the living room couch with his head resting in Miriam's lap one Saturday night in March 1966 when he suddenly felt ill. "As I started to lift my head, I felt dizzy and almost blacked out." A wave of nausea swept over him. He felt jabbing pains in his legs and was wobbly. Miriam called their family doctor, but he was out of town. Another physician, a family friend, hurried over but thought the symptoms would pass. The next morning, Shur's eyesight was blurry and he couldn't move his legs or arms. The bee-sting pains had spread from his legs across his entire body. En route to the hospital in an ambulance, he felt certain he was about to die.

Blood tests, X rays, and a spinal tap revealed he had multiple sclerosis. A doctor told him there was no cure and that the course of the disease was totally unpredictable. Three days later, another ambulance took him home. There was nothing his doctors could do but treat his symptoms. Shur's first thought was of Miriam and their children. "I had been working at the Justice Department slightly less than five years, and five was the magic number I needed to qualify for a pension. How was Miriam going to support the family?" She had returned to college and was about to graduate with a teaching degree, but it would be months before she was working. "I told myself I had to live long enough for her to find a teaching job."

A specialist at the National Institutes of Health told them

that MS attacks the brain and spinal cord. Fifteen percent of MS sufferers show only mild symptoms, others have one or two flare-ups every few years, and still others become permanently disabled. While Miriam was encouraged, the report depressed Shur. "I didn't want to be a burden for her." He had developed quadruple vision, his legs hurt all the time, and he had no energy.

Up until that Saturday night, Shur had thought his life was perfect. He was happy at work and loved his family. He and Miriam had moved into a new four-bedroom house in a booming Maryland suburb. They were both active in community events. Together, they had helped start Temple Solel (*Solel* is a Hebrew word for "paving a new path") as an alternative to the Conservative synagogue in the area. The congregation had held its first services in their living room. Now Shur began to wallow in self-pity and was tormented by self-doubt. "I sat in a chair and spent my days worrying about what was going to go wrong next. I could walk, but only if I was holding on to somebody. I was so afraid, I wouldn't go outside." He sat brooding in his room for two weeks until his twelve-year-old daughter, Ilene, confronted him.

"Daddy," she said, "you've told us how we're supposed to act when we have a problem, but you're not acting that way. Tomorrow when I come home from school, we're going for a walk." All the next morning Shur worried. He didn't want to disappoint Ilene, but he was frightened about going outside. What if he fell? What if he could only take a few steps? He hoped she would forget, but she came hurrying in to see him as soon as she got home. "Okay, Daddy, it's time," she announced.

"My daughter put her arms out," Shur recalled, "but I couldn't see her. She touched me. I touched her. We locked arms and went out of the house and started walking down the block. I'd hear kids saying, 'Hello, Mr. Shur,' and I'd say hello back. Suddenly I'm thinking there's a big world out there where it's still Mr. Shur, it's still Daddy. My daughter told me what the day was like. It was bright. I could feel that it was. The sun was on my face. Neighbors came over to say how nice it was to see me. That walk with my daughter got me going again."

A week later, Shur returned to work. His secretary read his mail aloud to him because his vision was still blurry. Walking was difficult, so his boss and colleagues stopped by his office whenever they wanted to chat with him. After a couple of weeks, Henry Petersen asked Shur to attend a briefing with him at the Capitol. Petersen was a chief and had a government car at his disposal, so they rode to the meeting together. Shur knew, however, that Petersen usually walked between his office and the Capitol, a distance of about eleven blocks. "I wanted people to believe I was no different with MS than I had been before, so I suggested after the briefing that we skip the car ride and walk back." Petersen moved briskly and Shur stayed with him, but a block before they reached the Justice Department his legs were ready to give out. He didn't say a word.

"Nice walk," Petersen said when they reached Shur's second-floor office.

"Sure thing," he replied, collapsing in his chair as soon as Petersen was gone. In the weeks that followed, he developed new symptoms, while others would disappear and then return. "It was a roller-coaster ride. I never knew when I was on the bottom or top of the track." He worried that his MS would flare up without warning and get even worse than it was. Miriam Ottenberg, the *Washington Star* reporter who had been the first to write about Joe Valachi, heard about his medical problems and telephoned to see if he would talk to her about MS for a book she was writing.

"Why are you interested in MS?" he asked.

"Because I have it, too," she replied.

The Pulitzer prize–winning journalist explained that everything she had read about MS was negative. She was interviewing MS patients who were leading productive lives in spite of the disease, and was calling her book *Pursuit of Hope*. Having found himself making it through the physical and mental crisis that MS caused him, Shur was optimistic during their talks. "A good marriage gets better because you can dismiss the unimportant things," Ottenberg quoted Shur as saying. "Miriam and I got over little garbage-type arguments. What was important was that we still loved each other; we still had our children; we could still communicate, could still give and feel love. Whether I was ten minutes late became less important, whether dinner wasn't done well had no importance. We weren't the least bit interested in what a neighbor thought or did—just in what we did and could do together."

Ottenberg's health took a turn for the worse, and when she could no longer drive, the Shurs gave her rides. She died four years later at age sixty-eight. "She inspired me," Shur recalled. "I was damned if I'd surrender to MS. She hadn't. I said to hell with it! And that's how I decided to live my life."

Shur threw himself into his job. There was plenty for him to do. He'd finally found a way to get the cumbersome OCRS index card system modernized. Congress had recently passed the Law Enforcement Assistance Act (LEAA), a law that gave federal funds to police departments to spend on new equipment and training. Shur had asked LEAA officials for money to computerize the index card information, but they'd told him LEAA funds could only be awarded to state and local police departments. However, a sympathetic LEAA administrator had proposed a way for him to circumvent his own agency's rules. With the administrator's help, Shur persuaded officials in six states to hire him, without salary, to develop an "organized-crime intelligence system" for their police departments. The LEAA then awarded those six states a federal grant, and the officials there, in turn, sent the funds to Shur. "My plan was simple: After we got our system going, we would teach the states how to replicate it. This would ensure uniformity and help them avoid costly start-up mistakes. Eventually, I thought, we would have a national network—a computerized intelligence system in every state with information about LCN members."

As soon as the LEAA money started flowing in, Shur told the Civil Service Commission, which helped federal agencies with hiring, that he wanted to find ten women to employ as criminal analysts. "I specifically asked for women because there weren't a lot of them walking police beats back then, and there was a feeling that women couldn't be criminal analysts because they'd never carried guns and therefore didn't understand police work or crime. I thought this attitude was stupid, and I wanted to show that bright people, regardless of their gender, could do this sort of work."

The commission gave Shur one thousand resumés to review. "I spent three days whittling that stack down to sixty. When I interviewed those women, I asked each one: 'Do you like to argue?' Their answer was important. I wanted individually minded analysts, the kind of person who wouldn't hesitate to tell me, 'Hey, Gerry, this is a ridiculous request. I know a better way we can do this.' I believed this free-speaking attitude would result in us coming up with better ideas, and the ten women I eventually hired certainly never had a problem telling me exactly what they thought!"

Shur was following an axiom his father had taught him: Stupid people surround themselves with smart people, and truly smart people surround themselves with smart people who disagree with them. None of the women had any police experience or knew much about organized crime. But Shur didn't care. After some rudimentary training, he put them to work on the index cards and incoming reports. "We had to work fast because the LEAA grant was only good for two years. We had to demonstrate that what we were doing was worth permanent funding."

Shur had been in the midst of getting the intelligence system perfected when he was stricken by MS. By then, his analysts had fed information about four thousand racketeers into a computer. If a U.S. attorney in Chicago wanted to know whether a suspect was connected to the LCN, all the prosecutor had to do was call one of the analysts, who were jokingly known as "Gerry's girls." With a few keyboard strokes, they could provide him with a detailed printout. Their files contained information about LCN members' aliases, home addresses, birthdays, business ventures, criminal records, sentences, prison release dates, marriages, divorces, relatives, best friends, even hobbies. For the first time, OCRS analysts were able to identify patterns in mob activities and links between various crime families. They discovered several mobsters who were related through marriage. "My analysts did such an incredibly good job that the Secret Service and the Bureau of Alcohol, Tobacco, and Firearms began hiring women as criminal analysts, too." His analysts even developed their own computer program, with help from the National Security Agency, called the Organized Crime and Racketeering Intelligence Language, for processing LCN data.

One night while Shur was working late, he noticed that Thomas Kennelly, the Buffalo strike force chief, also was laboring over paperwork in a nearby office. Shur stopped to say hello, and Kennelly mentioned that he was filling out a requisition form so he could give cash to two witnesses stashed in a motel. They had agreed to testify in a Utica, New York, mob case, and they needed to buy groceries.

"Tom," Shur said, "you've got better things to do with your time than to fill out these forms. Why don't you let me handle this for you? I'll take care of them so you can focus on getting ready for the case."

Kennelly was delighted.

"Tom thought I was doing him a favor that night," Shur recalled later, "but it was pure selfishness on my part. I was looking for an excuse to jump in and take charge of his witnesses. I'd been telling people for a long time that we needed a uniform way to protect our witnesses. Otherwise, every U.S. attorney was going to be starting from scratch each time a witness came forward. I had been in the Justice Department long enough to realize that if I could get control of the money, by volunteering to be the person in OCRS who handled the paperwork, I could begin to establish procedures about how our witnesses would be protected."

After Kennelly turned the day-to-day handling of his two witnesses over to him, Shur became the OCRS's de facto witness manager. The Justice Department had a small fund, called Fees and Expenses for Witnesses, that it used whenever a U.S. attorney needed to bring in an expert—usually a psychiatrist or other medical specialist—to testify at a trial or to reimburse witnesses for their travel, meal, and housing expenses. Shur began tapping into that fund to pay the cost of hiding mob witnesses. There weren't many—in 1966, only six in the entire nation—and Shur estimated the number would never total more than ten per year. "I didn't see this as a big operation, but I had been thinking about it for several years and I had developed some ideas about how we needed to proceed, based on my experiences in Brooklyn and the Valachi, Calabrese, and Barboza cases."

Shur was convinced that the most efficient way for the government to protect a mob witness was by giving him a new identity and relocating him to a new community. "Protecting someone with guards, the way the government had done in the Barboza case, was expensive and dangerous," Shur later explained. "It also caused a witness problems in the long run. You couldn't afford to have guards protect him for the rest of his life, so he'd always be looking over his shoulder. During the 1960s, I was also very aware of the threat of assassinations. President Kennedy was on my mind. If we couldn't keep a president alive, with the very best agents in the world and unlimited funds, how were we going to protect a mob witness from assassination? The solution was protection through anonymity. The best way to keep a witness safe was by moving him away from the danger area, moving him to a place where no one knew who he was. We weren't dealing with sophisticated KGB spies here, we were dealing mainly with New York metropolitan area mobsters, and many of them had never stepped outside the city. The United States is a big country with plenty of cities where people could be hidden. Of course, if we were going to relocate someone, we then had to give them a new identity so they couldn't be followed."

At about the same time that Shur took charge of the OCRS's mob witnesses, Charles Rogovin knocked on his office door. Rogovin, a professor at Temple University Law School in Philadelphia, was a member of a blue-ribbon panel that President Johnson had appointed in 1965 after the Republican Party accused him of being soft on crime. The panel, formally known as the President's Commission on Law Enforcement and the Administration of Justice, was in the midst of a two-year nationwide study of crime in America. It planned to conduct five national surveys and had started interviewing thousands of prosecutors, police, attorneys, judges, criminals, and crime victims for their views about how the government could better fight crime. Rogovin had been questioning Justice Department officials, and one of them had suggested he talk to Shur.

"I'm looking for fresh ideas," Rogovin told him, "and I was told that you had some."

Shur described the OCRS's computerized intelligence system for organized crime and how the ten analysts running it were all women. "We need to bring more women into law enforcement," Shur said, "if for no other reason than to perform desk jobs so we can get more gun-carrying officers onto the streets." He talked about the need for more computerization and sharing of information between agencies. Near the end of their meeting, Shur also said the government needed to establish a witness protection program. "We need government safe houses," he explained, "places where we can hide these people temporarily until we can relocate them."

Rogovin was impressed when he left Shur's office. "Here was a man who I thought had a number of very interesting ideas," he said later. "Everyone else seemed to assume that witnesses who testified against organized crime were going to be whacked. But Gerry was saying that it didn't have to be that way. It was clear to Gerry that there was a need to do something in a much more sophisticated way to help witnesses than simply handing them a bus ticket to Toledo."

Rogovin relayed Shur's ideas to Henry Ruth Jr., the presidential commission's deputy director, and Ruth put them into writing for the full panel to review. Its final report was presented to President Johnson at a White House ceremony in February 1967, and two of Shur's ideas were included in it. The panel recommended that local and state police departments begin using computers to collect and share information about the LCN. And then it addressed Shur's idea about witness protection.

No jurisdiction has made adequate provisions for protecting witnesses in organized crime cases from reprisal. In the few instances where guards are provided, resources require their withdrawal shortly after the particular trial terminates. . . . Therefore the commission recommends that the Federal Government should establish residential facilities for the protection of witnesses desiring such assistance. . . . After trial, the witness should be permitted to remain at the facility so long as he needs to be protected. The federal government also should establish regular procedures to help federal and local witnesses who fear organized crime reprisal to find jobs and places to live in other parts of the country, and to preserve their anonymity from organized crime groups.

The panel's endorsement had an immediate impact. "Now it was not just Gerald Shur who was running around the Justice Department talking about how the government needed a formal witness protection program," Shur recalled. "A presidential commission had recommended that we begin protecting witnesses, and this gave the idea credibility and tremendous political clout. I jumped on that report. It was exactly what I needed to really get the ball rolling."

When historians, politicians, journalists, and critics would later set out to find the origins of the Federal Witness Protection Program, the paper trail would lead them back to this moment and the thick, blue-bound presidential commission's recommendations. Those who took the time to look behind the panel's one-paragraph recommendation would find Gerald Shur. But what no one, including Shur, realized in 1967 was the significance of what had been started. Thousands of lives were about to change, many for the better, others for the worse, because of his seemingly straightforward suggestion.

PART TWO
BREAKING *OMERTÀ*

If you have any doubts that the mob's most basic tradition—its code of silence—has broken down, just look at what's happening now. . . . Right this minute, there are more than seven hundred guys under federal protection [in WITSEC]. All of them have squealed on the mob. They're street punks, big money-makers, and made guys. . . . They're talking because the government is providing them with something they can't get anymore from their own: protection, real protection.

Vincent Teresa, mobster
My Life in the Mafia, 1976

CHAPTER
SEVEN

AVING NEVER CREATED a new identity or a false background for anyone, Gerald Shur sought advice from the experts. He contacted the Central Intelligence Agency but decided it did too good a job creating false histories. "I wasn't going to send a witness to penetrate a foreign nation, and I didn't need to give anyone a deep cover," he said. "What I needed was just enough new documentation for someone to get a fresh start in a new community." Shur was worried about helping witnesses too much. "Most of them would be criminals, and I didn't want them using us to get away with new crimes." He asked Marcy Edelman, one of his criminal intelligence analysts, what documents she thought a witness would need to start over. They agreed that each person would need a minimum of three records: a new birth certificate, driver's license, and Social Security card. If the witness had children, school records would need to be produced.

Shur would later marvel at how much simpler it had been in the late 1960s and early 1970s to obtain documents and fabricate a new past than it is today. There were few computerized records and no Internet. Credit-reporting companies were in their infancy. Most birth and death records were kept in city or county courthouses scattered across the country, and there was little or no effort to cross-index them. Many states had laws that prohibited insurance and credit card companies from requiring applicants to provide their Social Security numbers; they were considered private, only for use when filing taxes. This meant there was no standard universal identifier or number that followed a person for life, as there were in some European countries.

Shur turned to people he knew personally and trusted for help in getting documents. Several state's attorneys arranged for him to get new birth certificates. He convinced the director of a motor vehicles department to provide him with new driver's licenses. "Of course, I wouldn't give anyone a driver's license unless he already had a valid one." Obtaining Social Security cards was more complicated. Initially, Shur had witnesses apply for a new number, but this meant each witness then had two different numbers—his original one and his new one. "My plan was that after a witness died, his family would send a letter to Social Security and explain that number A matches number B, and then Social Security would combine the two accounts," Shur said, "but this created all sorts of problems. I eventually got officials at Social Security to create a new account for our witnesses and transfer their funds from their old number into the new one." School officials in a Washington suburb agreed to help him with school transcripts. "We would get a child's school records, black out the child's name, and give those records to a school official. This official would then copy the child's grades off their old transcript and onto a new transcript from a local school in the child's new name. The grades were exactly the same, only the child's name and the name of the school were different. We would even make sure any teachers' comments were faithfully copied. Later, some witnesses asked me to give their kids better grades than they had earned. I said no."

There was one type of record Shur refused to provide witnesses. They were relocated without any financial documentation: no credit report, no prior banking records, nothing. They started clean. This made mundane tasks such as getting a telephone installed difficult because companies wanted to know their new customer's payment history, but Shur felt it was too risky for the government to vouch for any witness's fiscal past.

While he tried to keep rules to a minimum, there were two

he established from the start. Every witness had to undergo a legal name change. "This was no different from what happened when an ordinary citizen petitioned the court to change his name, only we asked the judge to seal the court records so no one would know the witness's old name or his new one." Shur did not want witnesses lying when they signed their new names to legal documents, such as real estate contracts or loan papers. "Over the years, witnesses would complain about how long it took us to get them new documents. They'd tell us they could buy a new driver's license or a fake birth certificate on the street in less than twenty-four hours, but I was not going to be part of any fraud." There proved to be an unexpected psychological advantage to the name change as well. "It was a clear sign that the witness was starting over, getting a fresh start."

For security reasons, Shur also required witnesses to keep their new identity and relocation a secret from their relatives and friends from their past. "We didn't want the mob torturing someone's grandparents to discover where a witness was hiding." This was by far the most difficult rule for witnesses to follow. "They could mail letters to one another and talk on the telephone through calls that we arranged through our switchboard, but that was the only contact we allowed them to have." The criminal intelligence analysts in Shur's office took charge of handling the mail. Witnesses sent their letters to Shur's office, where they were put into new envelopes and forwarded. Relatives wrote back in care of Shur's office, which passed those letters along.

When it came to choosing new names for witnesses, Shur followed advice that he'd been given by an IRS agent who had created fake backgrounds for undercover agents sent to Las Vegas to infiltrate mob-run casinos. "He said I should let witnesses keep their same initials or their same first name. This way, if they had to write their name, they might be able to catch themselves if they started writing their old name by mistake. It was easier on everyone involved, especially family members, if Bob remained Bob and didn't suddenly become Charlie."

There would later be a dispute about who was Shur's first

witness to get a new identity and to be relocated. This is because two big cases landed in his lap almost simultaneously. In his mind, they would come to represent everything that could go right and go wrong.

Paul Rigo was terrified when Shur first saw him fidgeting in a leather chair in a Justice Department office in 1969. The wealthy New Jersey engineer, who was in his late forties, had asked for the meeting, and he got right to the point: He was tangled up with the mob in Newark, and now the IRS was closing in on him. He wanted to cooperate but was afraid he'd be murdered. He was looking to cut a deal.

Rigo gingerly explained that the mob had first contacted him after his engineering company was awarded a lucrative city contract. Two men who represented Anthony "Tony Boy" Boiardo came into his office and demanded a 10 percent kickback for throwing the city contract his way. Rigo knew Tony Boy was the son of Ruggiero "Richie the Boot" Boiardo, one of New Jersey's most feared gangsters, but he'd never met either of the Boiardos or asked for any favors. When he refused to pay, the thugs forced him into a car and drove to the Boiardo family estate, where Tony Boy personally threatened to break both of his legs with a baseball bat.

"You got to understand," Rigo said, "I really didn't have any choice. He was ready to bust my legs right there. He said if I went to the cops, he'd kill my wife and kids."

After Rigo paid the kickback, his engineering firm began getting more and more city contracts, and he learned the Boiardos were bribing city officials to hire his firm. It was at this point in his story that Rigo dropped a big name. "Mayor Addonizio is part of this," he declared, "and I can prove it." Hugh J. Addonizio was a nationally recognized Democratic figure who had served seven terms in Congress. He had given up his seat in 1962 to become Newark's mayor after the city suffered one of the worst race riots in the nation. In the seven years since then, he'd rebuilt Newark, and there were rumors he'd be his party's next vice presidential candidate.

Shur and Thomas Kennelly, who was also in the meeting

with Rigo, hid their excitement. They didn't want to appear overeager because they suspected Rigo was much more involved than he was admitting. They asked him to meet with them again the next morning, and when he arrived, they fell into good cop/bad cop roles.

"You haven't told us anything we didn't already know," Shur snapped. "Why should we help you? You could've stopped taking city contracts if you really didn't want to get into bed with the mob. Instead you got rich, and now the IRS is coming down on you, so you want us to bail you out. Forget it!"

Rigo appeared genuinely shocked. A sympathetic Kennelly quickly offered him an out. "I think we can help," he volunteered, "but you're going to have to help us by testifying against these people."

"Testifying? They'll kill me."

"We can protect you," Shur added, "and we can help you get a new start, but only if you testify."

During the next several hours, Rigo admitted that he'd been the Boiardo crime family's "bag man," responsible for collecting kickbacks from other contractors. He also began naming names. Shur and Kennelly called the U.S. attorney in Newark, who agreed to grant Rigo immunity from prosecution in return for his testimony. Now it was up to Shur to keep him safe. He called the U.S. Marshals Service, and it sent over Deputy Marshal Hugh McDonald, known as "Big Mac" because of his hulking size. "I called the marshals because they protected judges in court and handled witnesses." McDonald and Shur drove to New Jersey a few days later to confer with Rigo and his wife. "I couldn't believe his house when we pulled up," Shur recalled. "It was a mansion. He owned a yacht and his own helicopter. The family had a full-time maid and butler. Rigo and his wife offered us cocktails, which we declined, and then gave us a tour. They had thousands of dollars' worth of antique furniture they wanted us to move. I kept asking myself, 'What in the world have I gotten into here?' "

McDonald arranged for the Rigos to go into hiding just before the FBI swooped into Newark with arrest warrants. The couple lived in hotels for more than three months, moving every few days, while they waited for the trials to begin. "Rigo was impatient because he was used to picking up the telephone and telling someone to have his yacht or his helicopter ready and we just didn't operate that way," said Shur, "but he was always very polite. Deep down, he knew we were keeping him alive, and he appreciated that."

The Rigos' antiques and other household goods were crated by a moving company and delivered to a warehouse on a military base. Several weeks later their belongings were unpacked inside the warehouse and put into new crates by a different moving company. A third company would be hired once the trials ended to deliver the crates to their new home. Deputy McDonald felt confident these precautions would keep the mob from tracking them to the Rigos.

Mayor Addonizio, Tony Boy Boiardo, and thirteen city officials and contractors were convicted because of Rigo's testimony. After the trials, Rigo flew into Washington to receive his new identity and be relocated. "I asked him where he wanted to live," Shur recalled, "and when he told me, I said, 'Well, that's the last place we will be sending you.' If a witness told me he wanted to move to San Diego, California, for instance, there was a good chance he'd mentioned how much he liked that city to someone in his past. We couldn't take a chance and move him there." The Rigos' relocation went smoothly. After he and his wife settled into their new home, he started a new engineering firm. Shur liked him. He reminded Shur of his own father. "He was a decent man who felt he had to do business with the mob in order to survive. I disagreed, but I understood it." Rigo died in the 1980s. "I am convinced people who were close to him knew about his past and knew his old name, but the mob never found him. He was our first real success story."

Witness Gerald Zelmanowitz was not. Flashy, brash, and arrogant, Zelmanowitz would later claim he was the first important witness Shur had ever helped relocate. Like Rigo, Zelmanowitz was granted immunity by federal prosecutors in 1969 after he agreed to testify against a New Jersey crime boss. The defendant

was Angelo "Gyp" DeCarlo and the trial sparked
lines, not because of who DeCarlo was, but becau:
blunder by the defense that inadvertently gave the
before-seen look into Mafia operations. During
phase of the trial, prosecutors revealed the FBI had bugged
DeCarlo's office between 1961 and 1965, transcribing 2,300 pages
of conversations between him and other gangsters. The wiretap
had been ordered by Robert Kennedy but had been discontinued
when President Lyndon Johnson ordered an end to all federal wiretaps. In 1968 Congress passed legislation that permitted federal
agencies to begin using wiretaps once again, but only if they followed rigid guidelines. Meanwhile, all information gleaned from
pre-1968 wiretaps was deemed inadmissible in federal courts.
DeCarlo's defense demanded to see the 2,300 pages of transcripts
because they suspected the FBI had used information from them
to make its case against DeCarlo. If they could prove that, they
could argue the charges against him should be thrown out. But the
defense's legal strategy backfired. It turned out the FBI had not
used any of the earlier information. Even worse for DeCarlo, Judge
Robert Shaw ruled that the 2,300 pages had become part of the
court record once the defense had been given a copy of them, and
that meant the public could now read them, too. Their release set
off a media frenzy. In the transcripts, DeCarlo bragged about having dozens of New Jersey police chiefs, politicians, local judges,
and prosecutors on his payroll. But the juiciest tidbits were about
contract killings. Typical was this brief exchange.

TONY BOY BOIARDO: How about the time we hit the little Jew?
DECARLO: As little as they are, they struggle. (Laughs)
TONY BOY BOIARDO: The Boot [Boiardo's father] hit him with a
hammer. The guy goes down and he comes up. So I got a
crowbar this big. Eight shots in the head. What do you think
he finally did to me? He spit at me and said, "You fuck."
(Laughs)

While shocking, the transcripts actually had little to do with
the charges against DeCarlo. Still, they turned a national spotlight
on his trial, and Zelmanowitz became an instant celebrity.

1thout any hint of remorse, he told jurors that he had found an ingenious way to earn millions of dollars by buying and selling foreign stocks overseas without paying U.S. taxes on his profits. His business partner and good friend, Louis Saperstein, had wanted in on the action and had borrowed $115,000 from DeCarlo to get started. But the IRS had been watching Saperstein and froze his bank accounts before he could make any deals. When Saperstein couldn't repay DeCarlo, the mobster threatened to kill him. For five months Saperstein hid out; then he called Zelmanowitz for help in finding ways to pay off the debt. They agreed to meet in the lobby of a New York hotel, but Zelmanowitz, who was himself involved with DeCarlo in other mob deals, brought along two of DeCarlo's thugs. They hustled a terrified Saperstein off to "the Barn," DeCarlo's term for his office.

"When I walked in," Zelmanowitz testified, "Saperstein was already lying on the floor, purple, bloody, tongue hanging out, spit all over him. I thought he was dead. He was being kicked. Then he was lifted up off the floor, placed in a chair, hit again, knocked off the chair, picked up, and hit again."

DeCarlo announced he was doubling the interest that Saperstein owed him, to $5,000 per week. Then he gave Saperstein two months to repay the entire debt. "If you don't, you'll be dead." A few days before the deadline, Saperstein entered a hospital complaining of stomach cramps. He died the next day. Doctors thought he had suffered a heart attack brought on by gastrointestinal shock, but an autopsy showed he had been poisoned with "enough arsenic to kill a mule."

Because there was no evidence that DeCarlo had poisoned Saperstein, federal prosecutors couldn't charge him with murder. Instead, they accused him and three of his thugs of extortion. Zelmanowitz's testimony helped convict all four, and DeCarlo was sentenced to twelve years in prison. Ironically, after the trial Zelmanowitz told reporters he thought Saperstein actually had committed suicide after taking out a large life insurance policy for his family. The day before he died, he had mailed a letter to the FBI accusing DeCarlo of plotting to kill him. It had been Saperstein's way, Zelmanowitz theorized, of taking revenge.

The Zelmanowitzes turned out to be the family from hell for Shur. Nothing satisfied them. Deputy Marshal McDonald found a spacious apartment in Maryland for them to live in while Shur arranged their new background, but Zelmanowitz's wife, Lillian, rejected it because it was a high-rise and she didn't like elevators. She also threw a fit over the fake history that Shur set up for Zelmanowitz; he was supposed to have retired as a sergeant from army intelligence, but she would *never* have married an enlisted man! This was especially ironic because Zelmanowitz had, in fact, been a private in the Marine Corps, which kicked him out after he punched an officer. When McDonald took the couple on a tour of Bowie, Maryland, to see the house that was supposed to have been their previous address, Lillian exclaimed: "What, me live in a house like that? Never!" McDonald didn't tell them it was Shur's. And it went on and on. Lillian's daughter by a previous marriage, Cynthia, wanted to remain with her boyfriend, Norman, which meant he too would have to be given a new identity. Shur insisted they marry, and this triggered more headaches. Shur assumed he'd hustle the couple in front of a rabbi for a quickie ceremony, but the Zelmanowitzes demanded costly wedding clothes and flowers, a reception at an upscale hotel, the works.

McDonald, who had been assigned to protect the family while they were in Washington, noticed they paid cash with money taken from a safe-deposit box for all of the wedding supplies. This made Shur certain Zelmanowitz had hidden his true assets from the government. "I suddenly found myself facing a dilemma. Zelmanowitz was not like Rigo, who I was confident would do no wrong after he was relocated. With Zelmanowitz I had doubts, real doubts; in fact, I never trusted him." Shur urged the IRS to start a new investigation of Zelmanowitz, and deliberately stalled on relocating him. "I decided that for this program to work, I had to be able to conduct two sometimes competing activities at the same time—protection and investigation. I had him investigated with the same zeal I was using to keep him alive. In doing this I saw no conflict. I had to balance our obligation to keep him alive with our obligation to see that he didn't commit crimes in his new community."

Shur and McDonald were dragged into helping arrange the wedding. Security was a nightmare. Guests were told the wedding would take place in a Virginia hotel, but after they arrived, they were taken out the hotel's back door to buses that carried them to a different hotel, where the bride and groom were waiting. "The rabbi gave me a civil certificate with the couple's new name on it," Shur recalled, "but he refused to put their new name on a religious certificate. He didn't mind fooling civil authorities, but he wasn't going to take any chances with God."

Five months after the family had first arrived in Washington, Shur finally agreed to settle them in San Francisco. No sooner had they arrived there than they complained they had been betrayed. They had been receiving a per diem of $60 for their living expenses, but Shur stopped paying it as soon as they reached San Francisco. The IRS had asked him to cut off the funds so it could see if Zelmanowitz would fly overseas to replenish his cash from money it suspected he had hidden there. Furious that he wasn't receiving any financial support, as he'd been promised, Zelmanowitz complained to the U.S. attorney who had prosecuted DeCarlo, and he in turn protested to the Justice Department. In a memo, Shur defended his actions, noting that the Zelmanowitzes already had received more than their fair share of subsistence pay, $55,000, during the time they had lived in Washington. Yet they had constantly complained they were "penniless," even though the average salary for most couples in 1970 was less than $10,000 per year. Shur added that the Zelmanowitzes were wealthy, owning such extras as a $45,000 Chagall painting, $25,000 in jewelry, and his-and-hers mink coats. Shur didn't mention the ongoing IRS probe, but his memo was enough for the attorney general to go along with the freeze on Zelmanowitz's payments. The bickering over subsistence checks ended when Zelmanowitz called Shur at his home one night and dramatically declared that his rent was two months overdue and he was about to be evicted. "When I informed Mr. Zelmanowitz that I could not give him an answer about his subsistence pay," Shur wrote in a memo the next morning, "he said the government and I could go fuck ourselves, and if

I wanted his identity papers back he would mail them and I could stick them up my fat ass."

A few days later, Shur offered Zelmanowitz a payment of $5,000 if he would sign a statement that "forever released" the government from "any further responsibility" for protecting him. Zelmanowitz agreed, and Shur breathed a huge sigh of relief. He thought he was done with Gerald Zelmanowitz. But he was wrong.

CHAPTER
EIGHT

GERALD SHUR felt like a doctor in an emergency room during a war. By the start of 1970, an average of one mob witness a week was seeking protection. So much for Shur's original estimate of ten witnesses, at most, per year. He and Deputy Marshal Hugh McDonald couldn't keep up, even after Shur waylaid two of the women who worked for him as criminal intelligence analysts and got them to help. Fighting crime was back in fashion. Richard Nixon had made it a major campaign issue in the 1968 presidential race, and his attorney general, John Mitchell, had juiced up the OCRS, doubling the number of attorneys working there to 125. He had also created new strike forces. Based on the success of the Buffalo strike force, the OCRS had already dispatched teams into Philadelphia, Chicago, Brooklyn, Detroit, Miami, and Newark. Mitchell sent new ones after mob targets in Baltimore, Boston, Cleveland, Kansas City, Los Angeles, New Orleans, New York City, Pittsburgh, St. Louis, and San Francisco. (Shur would later recall that the strike force concept was so popular that when President Nixon incorrectly stated in a speech that there were eighteen strike forces—there were only seventeen—the Justice Department created another one instead of correcting him. The new one was based in Washington, D.C.) By 1970, the strike forces had indicted the heads of six crime families, and the number of criminal cases brought against LCN members had jumped from 1,166 indictments in 1968 to 2,122. The mob was under a re-

lentless attack, and a growing number of its deserters were turning to Shur's fledgling operation for protection. Shur was feeling
the pressure, too. He was spending all of his time at work and several hours after he got home dealing with witnesses and their
problems. A late-night telephone call from a panicked witness in
early 1970 was typical of the daily melodramas he faced.

"Mr. Shur, there's a guy holding a gun on me," the witness
declared. "You got to come quick!"

"Why's someone holding a gun on you?" Shur asked.

"He says I was peeping through his window at his wife. I
mean, I was, but I didn't do anything. He's called the cops. They're
on their way!"

Twenty minutes later, Shur and McDonald were in a Maryland police substation. "Are you charging him?" Shur asked the
desk sergeant.

"Naw, this is minor stuff. You can take him."

Shur scolded the Peeping Tom as they rode back to the hotel
they had housed him in. One more screw-up and his parole would
be revoked and he'd be sent back to prison. A few days later, a federal prosecutor in Boston called Shur to ask a favor. The Peeping
Tom's girlfriend wanted to move to Washington from Boston and
live with him. Shur didn't like the idea, but after repeated pleas
from the prosecutor, the girlfriend, and the witness, he paid for her
airplane ticket. "She was one of the most beautiful women I had
ever seen," he recalled, "and I wondered how a creep like this witness could've attracted her." A month later, the girlfriend was
waiting for Shur when he got to work. She had tried to break off
the romance, and now the witness was stalking her. "Please help
me," she begged. "I'm afraid of him!"

Shur called in the witness that same afternoon: "Leave her
alone or you're going back to prison."

"Okay, okay," he replied, "but I can't do anything about the
photographs."

"What photographs?"

He'd taken snapshots of her nude when they were living together and sent them to a friend in Boston to deliver anonymously

to the woman's mother. "I mailed them yesterday." Shur had the photographs intercepted and moved the witness to another city. He also suggested the girlfriend leave Washington.

Helping witnesses was proving to be much more complicated than he had imagined. He found himself making up procedures as he went along. "It was clear that we needed to protect other people besides the witness who was testifying. We had to keep the mob from going after a witness's parents or his brother or sister. My criteria was: Is this person someone whom the mob might try to harm in order to intimidate a witness? If the answer was yes, then we had to protect them." One day, a married mobster said he wanted his girlfriend protected. "A lot of these Mafia guys had mistresses," said Shur. "I couldn't let the mob harm her to retaliate against him, so I gave her a new identity. Then we got a witness who was gay, and she wanted her lover relocated with her. I approved it. The one time I was really concerned was when a witness asked me to protect his mistress but not his wife. I protected his wife anyway."

When the mother-in-law of a protected witness needed a hysterectomy, Shur had to find a surgeon because he couldn't risk sending the woman, who also was under protection, back into her old mob-infested neighborhood. Shur contacted the U.S. surgeon general, and he agreed to provide witnesses with free medical care through Public Health Service hospitals. If a doctor needed to review a witness's medical history, Shur arranged a conference call with the patient's former doctor. The two physicians would discuss the case without mentioning names or locations.

But Shur's biggest headache was finding jobs for witnesses. "I never saw this as a program where a witness received subsistence payments for life," he explained. "This was a protection program, not a welfare program." He gave most of them three months to become self-sufficient after they were relocated. "It was tough because many of them had never worked at legitimate jobs." Shur asked Wayne Hopkins, a U.S. Chamber of Commerce official with an interest in organized crime, for help.

"Do your witnesses have any special skills?" Hopkins asked.

"Well, they can kill, steal, embezzle, and sell drugs, and most of them are members of the Cosa Nostra," Shur replied.

"Is that all?" Hopkins said, laughing.

Hopkins arranged for Shur to have lunch with the heads of seven U.S. corporations. "You should know that I will not tell you the real name of a witness or where he is from if you hire him," Shur warned them, "but I will tell you about his crimes and work skills. Even then, I can't really vouch for what skills he might actually have." He added that his plea for help was one-sided. "I will not tell anyone in the Justice Department that you are helping us, so if you are having troubles with the antitrust division or the IRS, don't think hiring a witness will help you out." Shur was stunned when all seven corporate officials said they were willing to help. Buoyed by that meeting, Shur flew to twenty-five cities and signed up more than two hundred companies. "An executive from a manufacturing company in North Carolina asked me not to send him anyone who had hijacked trucks, so I sent him a counterfeiter," Shur said. A few weeks later, the owner called to say the witness had been arrested for felony theft. "But I have good news," he added. "The stuff he stole wasn't ours, so you can send down another witness to take his place."

On occasion, Shur went with witnesses on job interviews. At one, a corporate president eagerly shook hands with the witness but eyed Shur nervously. "I needed a shave, was overweight, and have never been known as a sharp dresser," Shur said. "The witness was clean-cut, trim, and wearing an expensive suit. The president thought I was the criminal."

In most cases, witnesses and their families were flown to Washington to be briefed by Shur and McDonald about the new background that had been created for them. "We'd meet in room 2730 of the Justice Department, a small office I used near the entrance of a corridor that was closed off from the public and protected by locked doors," Shur recalled. "Big Mac and Betty Cleghorn, my secretary, and I would greet the witnesses there. By this time we had already spent days worrying and working out the logistics about the physical move: How would the family be moved to a new city, what about their furniture, cars, school records? We would have answered all of those questions. My approach in these meetings was completely clinical. I was intent on the process and technique of keeping these people alive. I treated this as if I were a heart surgeon sent in to do a job. There was no room for emotion because it might cloud my judgment. But sometimes the human drama of what I was doing seeped in. I remember talking to a family early on and I turned to the son, who was probably six years old, and said, 'Stephen, your father has done a great thing for his country, and because of that you're going to have to move and you're going to have to change your name. Do you think, if I gave you a new last name, you could remember it?' As soon as the boy nodded, I said, 'Okay, your new name is Stephen Robinson. Robinson. Got that?' I talked awhile to his parents, then turned back to him and said, 'What's your name?' 'Robinson,' he said. 'That's right, good job,' I told him. I did this several times during the next hour, and every time, he said his new name right on cue. During one of our exchanges, I thought, 'I am teaching this child to lie, teaching him that it's okay.' It bothered me but we had no choice. It was for the greater good.

"Now, this boy had an older sister, a teenager, and she told me she wanted to stay in touch with her boyfriend. When I told her she could never see him again, she burst into tears. I explained she could write to him but she would have to let her parents read her letters so they could be sure that she didn't accidentally tell him where she had moved. Again, the magnitude of what I was doing hit me. I was wiping out an entire family here: no more visits with grandparents, no parties with cousins, no contact with old friends. If a relative died, they could not go to the funeral. They would have to celebrate holidays alone. We were taking away their pasts—good and bad. One witness asked, 'Can't we sneak home to attend funerals?' I replied, 'No, I will not be a party to your suicide.' It was a phrase I would use over and over again as different witnesses told me of the risks they were willing to accept to keep their family connections alive.

"I always worried the most about the children. I worried

about them slipping up and telling someone who their father really was, and I worried about what we were doing to them. Later, critics would accuse us of doing too much for the criminals who testified for us. What few realized was there were usually innocent people behind each of these criminals. Their wives, children, parents, and other relatives all suffered, no matter how hard I tried to make them whole. This was a program of last resort. No matter how much we tried to do to make the transition easy, being relocated was always a painful event—a move that you made only because you knew it was the only way to stay alive."

Although Shur was up to his neck in witnesses, there was no law on the books that specifically authorized the government to run a witness protection program. He was still financing the cost of relocating witnesses with cash that he withdrew from the Justice Department's expert witness and witness travel fund. The blue-ribbon panel that President Johnson had created to study crime in America had included Shur's ideas in its final report in 1967, but its findings had been recommendations, nothing more. Shur saw an opportunity to formalize the program when Senator John L. McClellan, of the famed McClellan Committee, introduced a massive crime bill in 1969 that was designed to implement President Nixon's new law-and-order agenda. While McClellan's name was listed as the bill's author, much of it had been drafted by his staff, one of whom, G. Robert Blakey, proved to be a genius at finding effective new ways to assault the mob. His previous job had been working for Johnson's blue-ribbon panel, where he'd helped Henry Ruth Jr. insert Shur's suggestions into its final report. Now Blakey took Shur's ideas about witness protection from the panel's report and inserted them into McClellan's crime bill. He also wrote the bill's language that established the Racketeer-Influenced and Corrupt Organization Act (RICO), another critical tool that would be used to devastate the mob.

As a courtesy, major pieces of legislation are sent for comment to federal agencies that are going to be affected by them. When Attorney General Mitchell received McClellan's bill, he sent the few paragraphs that dealt with protecting witnesses to

Shur for review. In effect, Shur was now being asked to comment on his own ideas. By this point, he had been helping witnesses for almost two years and had refined his thoughts. He suggested that McClellan add another sentence to the wording in the bill. Attorney General Mitchell forwarded the recommendation to Senator McClellan, who sent it, in turn, to Blakey.

On October 15, 1970, the Organized Crime Control Act became law. Tucked deep inside it was a short section entitled "Title V: Protected Facilities for Housing Government Witnesses." Not surprisingly, it spelled out exactly what Shur needed to finally have his program authorized by statute. The key line was the sentence that Shur had added. It read: "The Attorney General shall provide for the care and protection of witnesses in whatever manner is deemed most useful under the special circumstances of each case." That was it. As simple and as vague as it sounds, that sentence was enough to justify the creation of the modern-day witness protection program and everything that came with it: a multimillion-dollar budget, giving witnesses new names, drafting false documents, and relocating known criminals to unsuspecting communities. Now that Shur finally had the legal authority from Congress that he needed, he moved quickly.

"I had serious misgivings about my role in the handling of witnesses," he explained, "especially when it came to my giving them money. Here I was, on the prosecution team, paying their living expenses and helping them go into hiding and get new jobs. It wasn't going to be long before a shrewd defense attorney accused me of buying testimony, which is illegal."

Shur needed someone else to take charge of the day-to-day handling of witnesses, a buffer between federal prosecutors and witnesses. "The U.S. Marshals Service was already protecting and relocating witnesses for me through Hugh McDonald, and it seemed like the perfect agency for the job." Shur proposed in a memo that the Marshals Service take over responsibility for protecting, hiding, documenting, and relocating witnesses and that it begin paying the costs of those tasks from its own budget. Shur would continue on as the witness program's overseer and deal with the U.S. Attorneys and federal investigators when it came to deciding who needed protection. But once a witness was approved, he'd be handed over to the Marshals Service. This way, Shur could argue that federal prosecutors had an arm's-length arrangement with the witnesses. "The Marshals Service's priority would be keeping a witness alive, not rewarding him for his testimony, and this was a distinction I wanted jurors to understand. That was one reason why I was eager for the Marshals Service to handle witnesses: because at that time it wasn't an investigative agency in competition with the FBI, IRS, or DEA. It wouldn't have a stake in getting a conviction. At the same time, I knew once I turned over the relocation functions, I would be giving up some control. The Marshals Service was a separate agency in the Justice Department answerable only to the attorney general. I was working out of the Criminal Division with no line authority over the Marshals Service, so whatever I was to accomplish would have to be solely by persuasion."

Under pressure from Attorney General Mitchell, the director of the Marshals Service agreed to Shur's plan four days after McClellan's crime bill became law. The director's staff estimated that the Marshals Service would need a minimum of a hundred additional deputies to efficiently handle the number of witnesses now pouring into the program, and a hefty increase in its budget. In keeping with the program's secretive nature, neither Shur nor the Marshals Service gave it an official name, although the service toyed with several acronyms, including WISPER, short for Witness Intelligence, Security, Protection, Enforcement, and Regulation. It would eventually become known as witness protection or WITSEC, shorthand for Witness Security.

While Shur was eager to see the Marshals Service take charge of witnesses, its deputies got off to a disastrous start when they were called into New Orleans to handle their first big assignment. Legendary crime boss Carlos Marcello was considered untouchable in Louisiana because of the legions of corrupt public officials on his payroll. So when the IRS recruited an informant in 1970 who said he could prove that famed New Orleans district attorney

James "Big Jim" Garrison was one of Marcello's stooges, Justice Department officials got excited. The informant claimed he delivered a bag of mob cash each month to Garrison, who shared it with nine New Orleans policemen. In return for the bribe, they made certain Marcello's local gambling halls were not raided. Garrison had become a national figure in 1969, when he prosecuted a local businessman on charges that he had helped the CIA arrange the assassination of President Kennedy. While jurors didn't believe this, the trial made Garrison a cult hero among conspiracy buffs.

The IRS turned over its informant, who was known as Witness 14, to the federal strike force in New Orleans, and it began pressuring him to testify against Garrison. He refused, explaining that the mob would kill him if he did. "After all the fanfare and excitement, after all the flags waving and the bugles blowing, after all that is over," Witness 14 said, "I have to go home *alone*." After months of prodding, Witness 14 finally agreed, but only after Shur went to Louisiana for a secret meeting with him to work out a deal. Witness 14 was promised a new identity, guaranteed a job that would allow him "to retain the standard of living to which he is accustomed," and told he would be relocated in a foreign country. "He wanted to move to Australia," Shur recalled, "so I contacted its embassy." It took Shur several weeks to get permission from the Aussies, and as soon as he did, the witness changed his mind. Now he wanted to go to Germany. A few days later, he switched again, this time choosing Canada. Shur got Canadian officials to agree and also lined up a job for him with Gulf Oil in Canada at a salary of $22,000 per year.

"None of us knew how deep the corruption ran in the New Orleans D.A.'s office or the police department, so we had to be extremely careful when it came time to arrest Garrison," Shur remembered. The strike force was worried Garrison might discover what it was planning and have Witness 14 arrested and put in a local jail, where federal agents couldn't protect him. They feared Garrison might have assigned men to watch the strike force offices. "The deputies needed a safe staging area to use on the morning of the arrest," Shur explained, "somewhere they could congregate without drawing attention and tipping off Garrison."

He volunteered his twenty-nine-foot-long Airstream trailer. He was scheduled to drive it to Texas on a family vacation but could easily detour to New Orleans first.

Shur didn't tell Miriam or their children why he was changing their itinerary. "I always thought it would be safer for Miriam if she didn't know any details about my job," he explained, "and she understood this and didn't ask me questions." On the morning of the arrest, Shur towed his trailer to a parking lot outside a shopping center near where Garrison lived, and suggested that Miriam and the children go window-shopping. As soon as they were gone, deputy U.S. marshals began arriving. The strike force's plan was simple: Witness 14 would make the mob payoff to Garrison at his house and then be driven by IRS agents to Shur's trailer, where deputy marshals would be waiting to whisk him to a private airfield. "I thought Garrison would try to have Witness 14 arrested, and if that didn't work, he'd come after us out of spite." Minutes before Witness 14 was scheduled to make the payoff, a nosy shopping center security guard rapped on the trailer door. Why, he asked, were Miriam and the Shur children walking around the shopping center four hours before it opened?

"They wanted some exercise," Shur replied. "We're just taking a break."

The guard tried to peek inside the trailer as the heavily armed deputies ducked for cover, but Shur blocked his view. He was afraid the security guard would call the police, but a few minutes later Witness 14 arrived. Everything had gone according to plan. Witness 14 had handed Garrison the payoff and signaled agents waiting outside. They'd rushed in and arrested him.

"Witness 14 was taken to the airfield where Hugh McDonald was waiting to put him on a private plane. Meanwhile, I began driving with my family toward the Texas border," Shur said. "I kept glancing in my rearview mirror waiting for some corrupt sheriff who'd been tipped off by Garrison to stop us and toss me in jail." Just before they crossed the border, Shur heard over the radio that Garrison had been arrested. Miriam shot her husband a "so that's what was going on" look.

Shur's well-crafted plans for relocating Witness 14, who was identified in the media as Pershing Gervais, a top Garrison aide, started to unravel within days after the arrest. Gulf Oil, fearful of bad publicity, withdrew its job offer as Gervais was en route to Vancouver, sending Shur scrambling to find him another suitable job. This was only the beginning. The Marshals Service had housed show dogs owned by Gervais together in a kennel, and one was killed during a dog fight. A moving truck carrying the family's furniture to Canada was burglarized when its driver stopped overnight at a motel. The sale of Gervais's house in New Orleans was taking longer than expected because potential buyers were scared off by the gun-toting deputy marshals assigned to protect the property. The complaints kept pouring in. Because of delays caused by the Marshals Service, none of the Gervais children could enroll in Canadian schools. Tempers flared. Gervais became so incensed at the Marshals Service that he threatened to change his mind about testifying, and the strike force, afraid that it might lose its case, began firing off heated complaints to Shur. After several frustrating months, Gervais warned Shur, "Get ready for a war!"

Without telling Shur, Gervais returned to New Orleans on his own and called a press conference to announce that the government had forced him to "frame" Garrison and then spirited him off to Canada to keep him quiet. He accused Shur of being "a professional liar" and castigated the deputies who had been assigned to help him, calling them stupid and incompetent. His defection made national headlines, and Shur's uncle Samuel mailed him a clipping with Gervais's accusation circled in ink. "I don't believe this," he wrote. "I know you are a very good boy."

Because of Gervais's flip-flop, the strike force lost its case against Garrison, although voters removed him from office the next year. He resurfaced a few years later when he was named to the state's Fourth Circuit Court of Appeals, where he served until 1991, when he was forced to retire at age seventy. He died a year later of a heart ailment, not long after the release of Oliver Stone's controversial film *JFK*, which was loosely based on one of three books Garrison had written about the Kennedy assassination. In the film, Garrison was portrayed as a hero. Gervais, meanwhile, moved back to New Orleans without incident.

Although Shur was convinced that Gervais had been un-happy in Canada and was simply looking for an excuse to return home, the Marshals Service's bungling of the case made him nervous. "I wondered if the U.S. Marshals Service was really ready for the job I was asking it to take on," he recalled.

CHAPTER
NINE

ECAUSE OF HIS EXPERIENCES safeguarding Joseph Barboza, John Partington was one of the first deputy U.S. marshals to take charge of mob witnesses in WITSEC. Handling them proved to be an interminable task. One afternoon in 1971, Partington found himself running up and down a stairwell in a New York hotel where two different sets of WITSEC charges were stashed. Hidden in one room were a mobster's wife, four children, and mother, all fearful about what was going to happen to them next. Two flights below, a different gangster's girlfriend was sobbing uncontrollably because she was being forced to disappear, thanks to her married lover's decision to testify against his former LCN pals. As Partington tried to calm them all, he got an emergency telephone call from Washington.

"We've got a hot one!" his boss said. "Go over right now and get this woman out."

Partington scribbled down an address. It was a Friday afternoon. It was raining. New York traffic was already logjammed. But he left immediately for an apartment in the Bronx. He knew only the bare essentials: A woman employed at a used-car lot owned by a mobster had overheard her boss bragging about a murder. She had tipped off the FBI, and the mobster was now going to silence her—permanently. Partington glanced at his wristwatch. Minutes mattered. He parked in an alley. He saw nothing suspicious, but if the mob had sent a pro, he wouldn't. There was no backup. He was on his own.

"Who's there?" a voice asked after he knocked on an apartment door.

"John Partington, U.S. deputy marshal," he replied.

"How can I be sure?"

He held his badge up to the apartment's peephole.

A woman cracked open the door. Partington noticed a girl clutching the woman's dress. He guessed the child was ten. "Ready to go?" he asked them.

"We gotta take my daughter's rabbit," the woman replied, nodding toward a wire cage.

There wasn't time to argue. Partington scooped up the cage, checked the hallway, and led the woman and her daughter into the alley. Moments later they were stuck in traffic, and the questions flew at him. "How will I get my furniture? How long will I be gone? What about my daughter's homework? When can I call my parents? How am I going to support myself?"

"I can't answer your questions," Partington said. "What I can promise you is that I will keep you alive and safe. The other stuff will have to wait."

During a recent trip outside New York City, he had spotted a motel that had struck him as a good spot to hide someone. It was a three-hour drive, and both of his passengers were asleep by the time he got there. Partington rented a room, carried the sleeping girl and the rabbit cage inside, and gave the woman a hundred dollars in cash for groceries, along with a list of emergency telephone numbers to call if she needed him. Someone would be in touch with her on Monday, he said. He told her to lock the door after he left, and waited to hear the deadbolt click into place. Rather than leave the area immediately, he stopped across the road at a tavern and ordered a whiskey. Every five minutes or so, he glanced at the motel to make certain no one was bothering the woman. After an hour, he decided it was safe to go. He hadn't been home in Providence for three weeks, so he drove there, hoping to salvage what was left of the weekend. He felt guilty. His son had recently accused him of caring more about mob witnesses than his own family because he was always gone. Partington had missed school events, even birthdays. His wife was beginning to feel as if she were a widow. Partington reached home just before daybreak, un-dressed, and was about to slip into bed when the telephone rang.

"You better get out here fast," the motel owner said. "The woman you checked in woke us up. There's blood everywhere!"

It was a four-hour trip. The woman had a gash on the side of her head. She had slipped in the tub while taking a shower and hit a towel rod. He took her to a local emergency room, where she was treated under a false name. On the ride back to the motel, she complained: "What if it had been a real emergency? Why did it take you so long to get there?" Partington didn't reply.

"The demands placed on the Marshals Service when we began the program were spinning out of control," he said later. "There just wasn't enough time in a twenty-four-hour day to do everything we had to get done."

The U.S. Marshals Service has a history of being stuck with jobs that no one else in the government wants to do, so it was no sur-prise when it was pressured into taking on Shur's mobster wit-nesses. During the two centuries since its creation, the Marshals Service has proven at various times to be both a heroic operation and a horrible embarrassment.

Initially, U.S. marshals were in charge of protecting judges, serving federal warrants, making certain that witnesses and de-fendants showed up in court, keeping order during trials, and pay-ing the prosecuting attorneys, court clerks, jurors, and witnesses. They were personally appointed by the president, and in later years a few presidents would treat them as their own private po-lice force.

The first test of the U.S. marshals' power came in 1791, when Congress imposed a tax on whiskey to raise cash to pay its Revo-lutionary War debts. In Allegheny County, Pennsylvania, sixteen whiskey distillers kidnapped a federal tax collector, tarred and feathered him, and stole his horse. The U.S. marshal in Philadel-phia was ordered to serve warrants on the distillers but didn't want to do it, so he gave the job to a deputy, who hired a dim-witted cattle driver to serve the warrants, without telling him what they were. The distillers beat the cattle driver, tarred and feathered him, stole his horse, and left him tied to a tree. President George Washington replaced the cowardly marshal with a new one: David Lenox, who rode off personally to serve warrants on seventy-five whiskey makers. Lenox got U.S. Army general John Neville to help him, but before they could complete the job, five hundred angry protesters chased them back to Neville's farm, took them hostage, and then looted and burned his house. President Washington sent a thirteen-thousand-man militia, raised by four states, into the county to end the so-called Whiskey Rebellion. Marshal Lenox made the arrests.

Over the coming years, presidents had marshals conduct the national census, catch counterfeiters, return escaped slaves to the South, supervise congressional elections, and track down moonshiners. But it was in the Old West where they became famous. Deputy Marshal Pat Garrett killed Henry McCarty, better known as Billy the Kid. Marshal Wyatt Earp and his brothers, Virgil and Morgan, along with Dr. John "Doc" Holliday, gunned down suspected cattle rustlers and armed robbers Billy Clanton and the McLaury brothers outside the O.K. Corral in Tombstone, Arizona. Between 1872 and 1896, 103 deputy U.S. marshals were murdered in what was known as Indian Territory—present-day Oklahoma—and a northern fifty-mile strip adjacent to it called No Man's Land. Justice was dispensed by Judge Isaac Charles Parker, known as the "hanging judge," in Fort Smith, Arkansas. The gallows he personally designed could accommodate twelve at a time. He depended on two hundred deputy marshals to track down lawbreakers. The most famous was Heck Thomas, who, along with his wife, Matty, was the model for Rooster Cogburn and Little Matty in the book and movie *True Grit*.

With the settling of the frontier came local, county, and state police forces, and the need for marshals and their deputies waned. In the 1890s, the government used them to disperse railroad strikers. In one incident, five thousand thugs, mostly billy-club-swinging ruffians already working for the railroads, were deputized and unleashed on the men, women, and children who were picketing because of unfair working conditions. It was a grim period for the marshals. The FBI was created in 1908 and soon became the country's most prestigious federal law enforcement agency, making the U.S. marshal seem even more of a relic.

One reason federal law enforcement agencies viewed marshals as inferior was because of their political status. There are currently ninety-four judicial districts in the United States, and each has its own marshal. Because they are political appointees, even today no qualifications are necessary. A florist, a funeral director, and even a Baptist preacher have been marshals. For more than 150 years, there was no national headquarters, no training, no uniformity, and few standards. In 1956, the Justice Department tried to professionalize the marshals by making them answer to a newly created executive office in Washington. The attorney general selected its director, but most marshals refused to cooperate. Why did they have to listen to a director who was appointed by the attorney general? As one put it: "The president of the United States appointed me, and I don't have to answer to anyone but him."

President John F. Kennedy turned to James J. P. McShane for help in changing this attitude. A former New York City homicide detective and Golden Gloves boxer, McShane was a tough Irish cop who had first met the Kennedy clan while moonlighting on weekends as a chauffeur for Robert and Ethel Kennedy's children. The Kennedys put McShane in charge of the Marshals Service's executive office, and even though he had no more legal authority than his predecessors, he declared himself chief of all ninety-four marshals and began bullying them into line. He turned to the Kennedys whenever he needed political muscle. Neither John nor Robert Kennedy trusted J. Edgar Hoover or his loyal FBI agents, and McShane used that mistrust to his advantage. The Kennedys, in turn, relied on McShane to enforce federal desegregation laws in the Deep South, where local police often turned a blind eye to racism. Southern states had continued to defy the Supreme Court's 1954 decision that overturned the "separate but equal" doctrine, and tried to bar black students from white-only public schools. In 1957 President Eisenhower had sent paratroopers to

Little Rock to control the rioting that ensued when nine black students tried to enter the high school, and in 1960 he sent federal marshals into New Orleans to protect black students enrolling in previously white-only public schools.

Jesse Grider was one of those deputies. He escorted Ruby Mae Bridges, a black first-grader, into a classroom as angry whites spit racial slurs at her. Norman Rockwell's painting *Problems We All Live With* shows Grider, who was from Kentucky, and three other deputies forming a shield around Bridges, although the deputies' faces are not shown. Grider was later assigned to help protect Martin Luther King Jr. in Montgomery, Alabama, in 1961 when an angry mob circled the Baptist church where he was preaching. "You could see pickup trucks arriving loaded with pieces of concrete for the demonstrators to throw at us," he later recalled. The deputies wore surplus World War II steel helmets painted white, with the words "U.S. Marshal" stenciled on the front. Each deputy supplied his own riot baton; many were homemade. Few had any training in crowd control. Nearly all the deputies guarding King were from other states. McShane had brought them into Alabama because he wasn't confident the local deputies would protect civil rights leaders. When the mob began throwing rocks, the deputies charged, swinging their batons. One protestor slashed at Grider's throat with a knife. Grider whacked him hard with a nightstick. Afterward, a deputy from Mississippi berated Grider. "You shouldn't hit a white man over a nigger," he said.

"Hey," replied Grider, "I'm hitting him over me."

The showdown for Chief McShane and a pivotal moment for the Marshals Service came in September 1962, when James Meredith, a black man, was refused entry to the University of Mississippi at Oxford. Robert Kennedy ordered McShane to seize control of the Lyceum, the university's antebellum administration building, where the school's registrar was housed. McShane's force, which included 123 deputies augmented by 316 border patrolmen and 97 prison guards, moved onto the campus late on a Sunday night, taking control of the Lyceum without incident. But the next morning, three thousand protesters gathered outside and began throwing rocks and acid stolen from the university's chemistry lab. McShane had his men spray the crowd with tear gas. Gunshots broke out. One deputy was hit in the neck, but there was no way for an ambulance to pass through the mob. The deputies would crouch behind the white bullet-marked columns of the Lyceum, fire a volley of tear gas grenades, and rush into the mob swinging nightsticks. A French news reporter was murdered by the demonstrators; another man was killed by a stray bullet. McShane asked the Kennedys for permission to let his men draw their weapons, but they refused. By ten o'clock the next morning, with the situation still out of control, the president sent in U.S. Army troops. One hundred sixty deputies had been injured during the fighting, twenty-eight seriously. McShane took a brick in the head; his dented helmet later rested on Robert Kennedy's desk as a reminder of the confrontation.

The deputies' courage won the Marshals Service new respect, and McShane quickly capitalized on it. He convinced the Justice Department to remove the authority to hire and fire deputies from the politically appointed marshals and to make the deputies federal civil service employees, a move that required them to meet minimal standards. This created an awkward chain of command. The deputies still reported to individual U.S. marshals, but because they were federal employees, they were obligated to answer to McShane, too.

McShane lost his White House backing following Robert Kennedy's resignation after JFK's assassination. Although he stayed on as chief until his death in 1968, the Marshals Service floundered. Matters did not improve under Nixon's choice to replace him. The tenure of retired army general Carl C. Turner was brief. He had seen the job as a stepping-stone that would allow him to eventually replace the FBI's aging Hoover, but soon after he took charge, he was accused of stealing government firearms and forced to resign. Nixon appointed an interim director until January 1970, when Wayne B. Colburn, the U.S. marshal from San Diego and a veteran police officer popular with California Republicans, was named director.

Colburn hit the ground running. A series of hijackings of commercial airliners and armed conflicts with the American Indian Movement, known as AIM, had pushed the marshals back onto the front pages. Colburn resolved the air piracy threat by assigning armed "sky marshals" to ride on key flights disguised as passengers, but his battles with AIM were not so easy to fix. They would continue for three years, climaxing in a deadly armed standoff at Wounded Knee, a village on the Lakota reservation in South Dakota that AIM militants seized in February 1973. During the seventy-one-day confrontation, two Indians were killed and a deputy marshal was paralyzed in gun battles. Colburn eventually negotiated a peaceful end to the uprising. Not surprisingly, he had little time for or interest in WITSEC during those early years.

William Hall, who was Colburn's deputy director, would later recall his boss's reaction when he was given the WITSEC assignment. "Colburn returned from a meeting at the Justice Department and told me, 'I think this whole protection program is a mistake and I don't want to do it, but no one else wants to do it, either, so it is going to be our baby.' We all knew it was going to be a can of worms, and we had absolutely no training or extra money. It was like asking lawyers to perform brain surgery with a can opener."

Colburn assigned the task of overseeing WITSEC to one of his top aides, Reis Kash, a newcomer to the Marshals Service with an impressive military past and an impeccable reputation for honesty. He had become a deputy less than two years earlier after a twenty-year stint in the army, where he had risen through the ranks to become the service's top criminal investigator. Besides being the first criminal investigator sent to interview soldiers involved in the controversial My Lai massacre during the Vietnam War, Kash had gained national attention by unmasking a gang of ruthless army officials who were operating an international crime ring. He had become suspicious of them and had just launched his own investigation when he was ordered by his commanding officer to drop the potentially embarrassing probe. Ignoring the order, he kept digging, at great risk to his career and at times his own life, and his findings eventually led to a congressional hearing and the arrest of the gang, which the media dubbed the Khaki Mafia.

Kash had been brought on board at the Marshals Service to investigate the death of a witness in a Baltimore case, not involving WITSEC, after the witness was fatally shot while duck hunting with the deputy in charge of guarding him. He had been shocked to discover how far behind the Marshals Service was when compared to the military police and the army's criminal investigators. "Not much had changed from the old Wild West days," said Kash. "The deputies had simply substituted automobiles for horses. It was a very politically driven operation and a scandalously cheap one." Marshals used their personal automobiles to transport federal prisoners so they could collect mileage payments from the government as well as a per diem payment for food. One deputy was notorious for buying cans of chili and heating them on the manifold of his car so he could pocket the entire per diem when he traveled. In the Baltimore case, Kash had decided in the end that there was no evidence that the deputy had intentionally shot the witness. However, the incident prompted him to write an instructional manual for deputies, based on his military training, that explained some basic dos and don'ts for guarding witnesses and prisoners. When Colburn looked around at his small headquarters staff, Kash seemed the obvious choice to become the service's first WITSEC chief.

"I was delighted when Kash was put in charge," Shur recalled, "because I knew he was a no-nonsense, take-charge administrator, but it quickly became clear to me that he was not going to be given the support that he needed." The Marshals Service had estimated it would need to hire a hundred deputies to run WITSEC efficiently, but Kash got none—not a single new deputy was hired. Nor did he receive a penny more to handle the additional costs of protecting and relocating witnesses.

"Director Colburn never wanted the Marshal's Service to be in charge of WITSEC, so it was simply not a high priority with us or with the top brass at the Justice Department," deputy director

William Hall later candidly recalled. "Yes, it was a high priority to Gerald Shur, but whenever Colburn met with the attorney general and his people to ask for money and more manpower, they told him that our first job was to protect federal judges, then deal with AIM, and then, after a dozen other assignments, at the very bottom of the list, came protecting witnesses. It was *always* at the very bottom."

Despite a lack of staff and money, Kash safely relocated 92 witnesses and 156 of their dependents during 1971, the first full year the program was under his direction. He did it by demanding, cajoling, and sometimes begging deputies and U.S. marshals for help. He also tried to create guidelines for the program. He asked the ninety-four U.S. marshals to contact state offices in their judicial districts so deputies there could obtain driver's licenses and other documents for witnesses. Kash also asked marshals to contact local chambers of commerce to develop area job banks. Few marshals, however, followed through with his requests, in part because they were afraid Kash would relocate witnesses in their jurisdictions. "They didn't want any mobsters put into their districts," Kash said, "and I couldn't really blame them."

Shur realized this. "There was a lot of resistance by marshals and deputies to what I was doing," he later recalled. "Most deputies had joined the Marshals Service because they wanted to catch criminals, and now we were sending them out to buy groceries for the crooks." During a meeting with Kash, one deputy had declared that he was not going to die by "stopping a bullet for some scumbag witness."

"If you take the government's dollar to protect a witness, you have to be prepared to take the bullet whether it is for a scumbag or the president of the United States," Kash told him. "You don't take a bullet for the mafioso, you take it because you are a professional." These were gallant words, but many deputies remained unconvinced. Deputy director Hall would later recall that it wasn't just deputies who felt uneasy about WITSEC. "A lot of judges called me with questions about the morality of using mobsters to testify against other mobsters and then relocating them in communities with new names and identities," Hall said. "They considered it buying testimony, which was illegal, and they really didn't like us rewarding these guys."

Nonetheless, such obstacles did not stop Shur's program from booming. Its first mob star was Vincent Charles Teresa, better known as "Fat Vinnie" because he weighed more than three hundred pounds. Although he was not a made member of the LCN, he had grown up in a Mafia family and had spent twenty-eight years working for New England crime boss Raymond Patriarca. Teresa claimed he had stolen more than $10 million for himself and another $150 million for his mob buddies by dealing in stolen and forged Wall Street securities.

Kash assigned John Partington to keep Teresa alive. It was an ironic assignment because Teresa had been one of the hit men who had been sent four years earlier to kill Joe Barboza while Partington was shielding him on Thacher's Island. "I had you in my rifle sights once," Teresa boasted to the deputy. With Partington now watching his back, Teresa crisscrossed the country testifying in nineteen different mob trials, helping convict fifty gangsters. He also made a special appearance before the McClellan Committee in Washington and during a televised hearing entertained the senators with his quirky sense of humor. At one point he was asked about a loan shark company that he ran called Piranha Inc.

"Why did you call it by that name?" a senator asked.

"Because if youse was late in paying me, I stuck your hand in a tank of piranhas I kept in my office," Teresa said, deadpan.

Between trials, Partington often hid Teresa inside a safe house that the deputy had established in Smithfield, a suburb of Providence. The Victorian house had been equipped with closed-circuit television cameras and electronic sensors that would trigger alarms if anyone entered the yard. "John Partington is the closest thing the federal government has to a thug on the right side of the law," Teresa told reporters after one trial. "He knows everybody who is anybody in the mob and he knows their habits, where they are, what they do, and how they think." Partington managed to foil several attempts to kill Teresa, including a plot that involved dropping sticks of dynamite down a chimney at the courthouse while he was testifying.

Teresa relished his mob star status. In 1972, he invited Kash to a Christmas party at a house outside Washington. "We were hiding Teresa there with his family, and when I arrived, I was stunned to find thirty people at this party," Kash recalled. "Vinnie began introducing me around, and every one of these guys was connected somehow to the mob! Here this guy is with a price on his head and he's throwing a mob party! It was nuts! Vinnie served lobsters that the superintendent of the state police in Massachusetts had gotten flown in for him. He had a Christmas tree that cost seventy bucks, which was almost half of what many deputies earned each week. Everyone was suspicious of my wife and me—we stuck out—until Vinnie says, 'Hey everyone, this is my protector, my witness protection guy,' and then everyone relaxed. It was surreal. All the men talked about what federal prisons served the best food and which prisons they liked the best, and then a few of them got up and started singing arias from Italian operas."

By 1973, Teresa had run out of stories to tell. Prosecutors no longer needed him to testify, but he didn't want to leave the spotlight. "All of our mob witnesses loved the attention they got," said Kash. "They were celebrities but only for a moment, and that was something they didn't understand." When Kash began making plans to relocate Teresa, the mobster decided to up the ante. He told prosecutors that he could deliver a prize that none of them had been able to grab: the legendary Meyer Lansky, who along with Salvatore Lucania—better known as Charles "Lucky" Luciano—was credited with creating the American Mafia. Teresa claimed he had personally delivered bags of mob cash to Lansky in person at his Miami home. Teresa's word was good enough to get the seventy-two-year-old gangster indicted in Florida. The trial attracted international coverage and quickly proved to be an embarrassment for federal prosecutors and Teresa. When the government's star witness was called to testify, he couldn't remember Lansky's Miami address or describe his house. Even more humiliating, Lansky had proof that he was in Boston recovering from a double hernia operation on the day Teresa swore he met with him. Lansky was acquitted and Teresa's credibility was shot. He was finished as a witness.

Because Teresa had testified in public so many times, Shur suggested the Marshals Service alter his appearance by sending him to a hospital to lose weight. "The forced diet worked and he looked like a different person after he shed the pounds," said Shur, "but as soon as the deputies picked him up at the hospital, Teresa had them stop at the first doughnut shop he saw so he could buy a couple of dozen to eat. He was soon back to his old size."

Teresa was forty-three years old and needed a job to support his wife and children, but no one had a clue what to do with him. "Vinnie had held only one legitimate job in his life," Kash said. "He had been hired by an uncle to drive a grocery truck, and he had hijacked that truck." A staff member on the McClellan Committee came to WITSEC's rescue by introducing Teresa to Thomas C. Renner, a reporter for the Long Island newspaper *Newsday*. Together, they sold the rights to Teresa's autobiography to Doubleday. The mobster's cut was $175,000, a significant sum at the time. His story, *My Life in the Mafia*, was published shortly after the release of Francis Ford Coppola's movie *The Godfather*, and the book became a best-seller.

Shur was against allowing witnesses to appear on television shows because it made them more recognizable and therefore more difficult to hide, but Partington ignored him and took Teresa to Los Angeles so he could publicize his book on a nationally televised talk show. During the flight, an excited admirer approached Teresa.

"I know you!" she exclaimed. "I saw you on television!"

Partington grimaced. The last thing he wanted was for everyone on the aircraft to know Teresa was on board.

"You're Minnesota Fats, the pool player," the woman continued. "Can I have your autograph?"

Teresa, whose bulk filled two airplane seats, signed a slip of paper. By the time the flight landed, he had given autographs to nearly every passenger on board and regretfully turned down a request by the flight crew to give a demonstration of his pool skills in the airport's recreation room. Partington kept quiet during the charade.

Kash relocated Teresa in a seaport town, where the government bought him a fish store to run. "Within a few weeks, other fish dealers were complaining because someone was breaking their store windows and doing other nasty tricks to slow down their businesses," said Kash. "We had to move him." Before leaving town, Teresa sold the refrigeration units in his store and pocketed the cash even though the machines were rented. The government next helped Teresa buy a motel and bar in El Paso, Texas, but that didn't last long either, because he got drunk one night, climbed on the bar, and started telling everyone who he really was.

"Teresa used to call me all the time," said Shur, "always begging for money. He was like a kid in college who calls home every week asking for a check. He reinforced my view that we shouldn't give complete backgrounds to witnesses, that is, supply them with false financial pasts, because he just couldn't stop conning people."

In yet another stunt, deputies told Teresa that he couldn't take his car with him when he left El Paso for security reasons— he would be given a different one after he was relocated. "Teresa waited until there weren't any deputies watching him and then he drove his car up the ramp into the moving truck," said Shur. "He'd filled the car with bottles of liquor he had apparently bought on credit, and hid everything under blankets to fool the deputies. When he got to his new relocation spot, he sold the car and all the liquor."

Teresa's final move was to Maple Valley, Washington, outside Seattle, but he got into trouble there, too. In 1981, his son was arrested on a murder charge, and the FBI claimed Teresa had threatened to kill two local prosecutors. A short while later, Teresa was convicted in a conspiracy to burglarize and torch a dentist's office and collect insurance on the loss. He got off with a light sentence but in 1985 was sent to prison after he was caught smuggling hundreds of exotic and expensive birds and reptiles into the country for sale. Most were endangered species.

"Teresa made great use of the word *but*," Shur recalled. "He would say, 'Yeah, I got caught, but . . .' I learned that with certain witnesses, you had to heighten your guard. I could trust some, but with others, I had to double- and triple-check everything, as well as look for corroborating evidence to make sure they were telling the truth."

After he was paroled, Teresa returned to Maple Valley, where he died in obscurity in February 1990 at age sixty-one. The local newspaper noted that Teresa had been living under the alias Charles A. Cantino. The Marshals Service sent a deputy to pay for his funeral.

"Vinnie was an extremely likable guy," recalled Kash, "but I never thought he could go straight. He simply didn't know the direction, and as much as I liked him—and I did like him—I knew he was going to victimize someone after we gave him a new identity. That bothered me."

Teresa was not the only colorful witness to frustrate Shur and Kash. Another early troublemaker was Hugh E. Wuensche, who was given a new identity in 1971 after he testified against the mob and explained to the McClellan Committee how he had laundered more than $50 million in stolen securities for gangsters. "He had a British wife, and all he wanted from us was a new name, some cash, a passport, and an airplane ticket," Kash recalled. "That was a low bid from one of these guys." A year after Wuensche had boarded a flight to England, Kash received a Christmas card from him. "He said he was living in a seventeenth-century mansion, had a chauffeur-driven Bentley, and owned his own bank. I didn't know whether or not he was telling the truth, but he appeared to be fabulously wealthy." A year later, Kash received another Christmas letter from Wuensche, this time begging for help. He was in prison. It turned out that he had been paid some $250,000 in rewards from federal agencies for helping agents recover several million dollars' worth of stolen stock certificates. No one had informed Shur or Kash. He had used his new WITSEC identity to hide his criminal past from British authorities and had bought a controlling interest in a failing London bank with his reward money. He then contacted several gangsters back home and had them send him forged stocks and bonds, which he used as collateral in England to buy an even larger British financial company. By the time he was caught, he had looted more than $2 million from depositors. Furious that they had been hoodwinked, British authorities filed a formal complaint with the State Department and accused Shur of trying to solve the United States' crime problem by sending felons to England under new names. "I got a letter from Wuensche that looked as if it was written on toilet paper," recalled Kash. "He offered to testify against the mobsters who had helped him run his bank scam if I helped him return to the United States. I didn't." Wuensche then called Shur, but he also refused.

Shur noticed that every time a high-profile witness such as Teresa testified in court against the mob, other criminals would step forward and ask to enter WITSEC. "Word was spreading that we could keep witnesses safe and give them a fresh start," he said. By 1972, the number of witnesses entering the program had doubled to about two hundred per year. In 1973, 338 new witnesses entered WITSEC, and by 1974 the number topped 400. By this point, Kash had gotten some help in the Marshals Service's headquarters, but not much. Only ten new deputies had been hired to handle logistics, obtain documents, and help witnesses find jobs. Meanwhile, Kash's WITSEC operation was responsible for overseeing what now was a total of a thousand witnesses and nearly twice that number of dependents. The program was growing at the rate of one new witness a day, and the Marshals Service simply couldn't keep up. "Our success in attracting mob witnesses was choking the marshals," said Shur.

After three years, Kash had had enough, but it wasn't the lack of resources and overwhelming demands that had finally gotten to him. "I was having serious doubts about the wisdom of relocating some of these criminals in new communities," he explained. "I knew we were sending them out to victimize people." While Shur empathized with Kash, he also disagreed with his viewpoint. "This program was much too important to abandon, regardless of how horrible some of our witnesses were," he said. "There is an old tort adage that says 'You take the actor as you find him,' and that applied to witnesses. We were not going to get witnesses to testify against the mob who were priests and rabbis, and they weren't going to testify unless we protected and helped them."

The breaking point for Kash came when he was asked to relocate a pornographic bookstore operator named James Kelly. Kelly had testified against a major New York City crime family and had initially refused protection. Instead, he had moved to Baltimore on his own and opened a striptease club and porno bookstore in the city's notorious "Block," a seedy downtown area. One morning a mechanic doing a routine check on Kelly's car switched on the headlights, and a blasting cap hidden near the engine blew up. It apparently had jiggled loose from the three sticks of dynamite it was meant to detonate. The Baltimore strike force asked Shur to accept Kelly into WITSEC because he had been secretly providing it with information about mob activities on the Block. Shur agreed, but almost immediately Kelly and Kash began butting heads.

At one point Kelly asked the Marshals Service for help cashing an $85,000 certified check—proceeds from the sale of his Baltimore strip club and bookstore. Kelly had just undergone a legal name change, so he couldn't cash the check, which was made payable to him under his old name. Kash refused. An outraged Kelly telephoned the Baltimore strike force chief. The chief sent Shur an angry seven-page letter accusing Kash of being rude, arrogant, and contemptuous. Shur urged Kash to reconsider, but he refused. Kash didn't like the pornographer, didn't think the government should be paying him monthly subsistence, and didn't want to be part of his taking the money from the sale of his businesses and then disappearing. A short time later, Kash was promoted to a different job that took him away from the day-to-day handling of WITSEC. Shur got Kelly the cash that he wanted.

"Organized crime was suffering severely at the hands of the witness program, but we couldn't keep putting some of these people out there and not get burned," said Kash. "Someone innocent was going to get hurt someday because of these witnesses."

Kash's fears had not yet dawned on the public. In fact, WIT-SEC was riding a wave of favorable publicity. A newspaper column by Victor Riesel, the labor writer blinded by the mob outside Lindy's restaurant, was typical. Printed in 1972 under the headline "*Omertà* Dead: Mafia Being Cracked by Hundreds of Informants Now Protected by Special Unit," Riesel boasted about Shur's program. "It works! No witness has gone bad after relocation. Some have been so successful, they are now executives in corporations and fear only their new prominence will expose them. It can be authentically reported that *Omertà* is dead, the Mafia's lethal code of silence has been smashed." *Reader's Digest* weighed in later with a heart-tugging story about a small-time bookie who had been ready to kill himself because of his debts to the mob. Instead, he contacted federal agents and with Shur's help got a fresh start. The magazine noted that Shur received a Christmas card every year from the bookie, thanking him for saving his life.

Favorable news accounts like these, however, were soon to end. Three ghosts from the past were about to visit Shur and cause havoc to his program.

CHAPTER
TEN

THE TELEPHONE CALL took Buffalo strike force chief Thomas Kennelly completely by surprise. A lawyer was on the line asking where former mobster Pascal "Paddy" Calabrese was hiding. It was early 1970, two years since Calabrese had testified against the Stefano Magaddino crime family and gone into hiding with Rochelle and her children. Buffalo attorney Salvatore R. Martoche got right to the point. "I represent Thomas Leonhard, who is Rochelle's husband and the father of their three children. He says the government kidnapped his kids."

Kennelly's mind shot back to late 1967, when he had arranged for Rochelle and her children to be hustled out of Buffalo and hidden at a military base in Maine to protect them from the mob. "We knew Rochelle had a former husband," Kennelly recalled later. "I mean, we knew she was separated or divorced, so there had to be a husband out there, but it really hadn't occurred to any of us that he had visitation rights with the kids. We were busy trying to protect Paddy and Rochelle, and Tom Leonhard wasn't pounding on our door, so quite frankly, no one really ever thought about him." Kennelly was suspicious of Leonhard's motives. Why hadn't he complained earlier?

"He has," said Martoche. "He's been trying to find his children since they disappeared, but no one will tell him where they are." Martoche recited the facts as he knew them. Leonhard and Rochelle were still married in 1967, but they didn't live together because she had moved in with Calabrese. The couple had, however, signed a legal separation agreement that gave Leonhard visitation rights with their three children one day each week. He had driven over on a Sunday morning to pick them up, only this time the kids weren't there. When Leonhard rousted out the landlady, she told him several men riding in two cars had come that Tuesday and taken them away. That was all she knew. Leonhard had gone to the police, but they didn't know anything about Rochelle. It had taken him three weeks to discover that the Buffalo strike force was behind his children's disappearance. But federal prosecutors refused to tell him anything about what had happened to them. Leonhard was a mild-mannered blue-collar worker without much money, Martoche explained, and he didn't have a clue how to weave through the federal bureaucracy. He had tried to hire lawyers several times, but none would take the case. Until now.

"This has to be some sort of mistake, right?" Martoche asked Kennelly. "I mean, in Russia, maybe the government can snatch up a man's kids without telling him, but that just doesn't happen here. That's why I am calling you. My client wants to be reunited with his children."

Kennelly remained wary. "I didn't know Martoche and my first concern was for Paddy Calabrese and his family," he explained. "I knew the mob still wanted Paddy dead, and I was worried that this was some sort of ruse."

Kennelly knew where Calabrese and Rochelle were in hiding. After the couple's failed start in Jackson, Michigan, Calabrese had telephoned him periodically. But Kennelly didn't tell Martoche anything when they first talked about the children's whereabouts in 1970. "I had promised Calabrese in my official capacity as the head of the strike force that the government would never reveal where he was hiding, and that was not a promise I was going to break."

Kennelly stalled for several weeks, but Martoche was persistent, and after repeated telephone calls, he got Kennelly to agree to contact Calabrese and Rochelle and tell them that Leonhard was asking about his children. "Paddy and Rochelle screamed and carried on when I finally reached them," Kennelly said later. "Paddy said to me, 'Don't you dare tell. If you do, we will move and you will never hear from us again. We'll disappear.' "

Kennelly felt trapped. As a father, he understood how horrible it must feel to have your children vanish without warning. But he was convinced that if he broke his promise to Calabrese, he would be putting a witness's life in danger and undermining WITSEC by sending potential witnesses a chilling message—the government can't be trusted to keep your new identity and location a secret.

Kennelly told Martoche about Calabrese and Rochelle's adamant stance, but the young attorney refused to give up. He persuaded Kennelly to forward letters to Rochelle from Leonhard. He wrote three times in late 1970, begging for a chance to be reunited with his children. "I love them dearly and do miss them so much," he pleaded. "The years are slipping by faster and faster. I would like to see them a little before they grow up." Rochelle didn't respond for six months, and when she did, her answer was terse: "In no way shall I ever allow [you] to see them. Calabrese is the only father the children will ever know." She misspelled her husband's name in the letter, adding further insult to her reply.

Martoche decided it was time to take Leonhard's fight into court. He had his client file for a divorce from Rochelle and seek full custody. When she failed to appear at the hearing, the judge awarded the children to him. Armed with the judge's custody order, Martoche marched into the federal court in Buffalo and demanded that the Justice Department reveal where Leonhard's children were hiding. By now it was late 1971. Kennelly had resigned from the government to practice law privately in Washington and Shur was told to handle the dispute. In a letter that he would later deeply regret having written, Shur urged Leonhard to stop trying to find his children. He wrote that Leonhard should be proud of himself for allowing the United States to take them as a "sacrifice in our war against organized crime." Shur's letter infuriated Martoche. "I cannot help but wonder," he replied, "if Mr. Shur would also like to sacrifice his children involuntarily in this undeclared war."

Shur thought the best way to resolve the dispute was by requiring Rochelle to hire an attorney and face Leonhard in a domestic relations court. That way, a judge used to handling custody complaints could decide what was in the best interest of the children. But when a hearing was held in Buffalo on Martoche's motion, the Justice Department elected to take a hard-line, no-cooperation approach. In an affidavit given to the court, Kennelly wrote: "It is my professional and personal judgment . . . that to divulge the whereabouts of the aforesaid children to anyone in Buffalo would seriously jeopardize their personal safety." While the judge hearing the case said he felt sympathetic toward Leonhard, he ruled against him. He explained that Kennelly had not "abused his power as the strike force chief" when he promised Calabrese anonymity, and since Kennelly had not done anything illegal, there was no reason for the court to require him to reveal where the children were being hidden.

Martoche and Leonhard had lost in court, but they were winning in the public arena. Lee Coppola, an investigative reporter for the *Buffalo Evening News* and a former high school friend of Martoche's, had taken up Leonhard's cause, and angry letters denouncing the government began appearing in the newspaper.

Martoche appealed the Buffalo judge's decision to the U.S. Circuit Court of Appeals, but it too ruled against him. "Kennelly acted in good faith," the New York–based court wrote, "and having found no violation of federal law, we need not attempt to indicate how we might have resolved this difficult problem . . . the solution of which calls for the wisdom of Solomon."

By now it was 1973 and Leonhard had not seen his children for six years. Martoche, meanwhile, had incurred thousands of dollars' worth of unpaid legal bills. Nonetheless, he appealed the case to the U.S. Supreme Court. "This is why I had gone to law school," Martoche recalled, "to argue a case that would make a difference." The court declined to hear the case. Having exhausted his appeals, Martoche tried other tactics. He filed a civil suit against Kennelly, Shur, and the Justice Department seeking $40 million in damages for Leonhard's loss. He also persuaded

Congressman Jack Kemp, who represented Buffalo, to introduce a private bill in Congress on Leonhard's behalf. If passed, it would require the Justice Department to tell Leonhard the location of his children or pay him a million dollars in compensation for his heartache. Continuing to turn up the heat, Martoche had Leonhard write to the White House after reading that President Gerald Ford was an adopted child who had never seen his real father while growing up. "Mr. President, you must know how I feel," Leonhard wrote. "I worry about my children very much, their being with this man who gangsters want to kill. Plus, what about me? Don't I have any rights?" Lee Coppola published a copy of Leonhard's letter, whipping up still more public support for Leonhard.

While Shur was aware of the growing public pressure, it was the private bill that Kemp had introduced that worried him. "I did not want someone to get their congressman to pass a private bill saying that we had to do this or that every time we relocated a witness." Just when the dispute seemed deadlocked, Rochelle telephoned Martoche in 1975. "It was the fourth of July and I was having an outdoor barbeque," Martoche recalled. "I answered the phone and she said, 'Hello, this is Rochelle. Tom can see the kids.' I was stunned." She was willing to send the children to visit him in Buffalo if he would pay for their tickets. Martoche assumed the growing public pressure had gotten to her. Coppola's newspaper stories had been distributed by the wire services across the country, and a Hollywood packager had put together a book-and-movie deal for Leonhard. Author Leslie Waller had been hired to write a book, and MGM had cast James Caan to play Leonhard in a movie. Both were titled *Hide in Plain Sight*. Martoche suspected Rochelle was worried about how she was going to be portrayed.

Leonhard quickly arranged for his children to fly to Buffalo. He invited Coppola to be there when they arrived. The children said their mother had called them into her kitchen five months earlier, opened a shoebox filled with newspaper clippings, and revealed to them for the first time that Leonhard was their biological father. "I didn't want to believe her," Karen, age fourteen, told Coppola. "I wrote my real name—Karen Leonhard—for the first time the other day." Incredibly, Rochelle had managed to wipe out much of what both children remembered about their father. Mike, who was fifteen but had been seven when the family had fled Buffalo, said he only remembered "a man who used to come and pick us up and take us places, but every time I asked Mother about him, she said he was just a friend." The children returned home to their mother a few days later, and although they kept in contact periodically with their father after that first reunion, Martoche recalled later that the parental bond between them had been so badly fractured that it never healed.

After the reunion, Coppola wrote a five-part newspaper series that described what had happened to Calabrese and Rochelle after they fled Buffalo and then Michigan. Rochelle had gotten a job in a Reno bank and Calabrese was working as a security guard at a casino, a job that required him to carry a gun. He had gotten a permit without difficulty by using false credentials. Martoche was incensed when he was told the couple lived in Reno. "I would bet that every gangster from western New York has been to Reno, Lake Tahoe, and Las Vegas in the last couple of years," he complained. "Yet the U.S. government insisted that telling Tom Leonhard where his children were would put Calabrese in mortal danger! What crap!"

The fact that it was the Buffalo strike force that had hidden Rochelle and her children without telling Leonhard didn't seem to matter when Waller's book was released in 1976 and the movie began playing in theaters. The government's witness program was cast as a heartless bureaucratic operation run amok.

"Privately, I felt what had happened to Leonhard was absolutely terrible," Shur recalled, "and I was determined that it wouldn't happen again, so I insisted that we begin notifying noncustodial parents whenever their children entered WITSEC. I wanted these parents to have an opportunity to visit their children in a safe place arranged by the marshals." Years later, Sal Martoche became a federal prosecutor, and when he attended a meeting at the Justice Department, Shur sought him out. "I told Martoche," he recalled, "that I had changed our policy because of the Leonhard case, and he was surprised. Up until that moment, he hadn't realized that he actually had won his point."

At the same time Shur was coming under fire from the public because of the Leonhard case, a second ghost from the past materialized. Gerald Zelmanowitz, the demanding witness who had testified against New Jersey gangster Angelo "Gyp" DeCarlo, had done quite well in California on his own after leaving WITSEC. Within two years, he had become president of a small dress manufacturing company in San Francisco, where he was known by his WITSEC alias, Paul Maris. Sales zoomed from $1.5 million to $8 million a year after he launched a daring ad campaign in *Glamour* and *Mademoiselle* magazines that caught the spirit of the early 1970s and turned his company into the hottest label in women's knitted tops and clingy dresses. One ad showed a couple bragging about how they were living together without being married. "We do not have affairs nor are we adulterers," the caption read. Maris rewarded himself with a new Rolls-Royce and his wife, Lillian, with a Mercedes. They moved into an elaborate rural retreat, filled it with antiques, and socialized with San Francisco's elite. When asked about his past, Maris bragged that he had once owned a manufacturing firm in Kobe, Japan, and radio stations in Cincinnati and Cleveland, "facts" that he had added to the fake background the government had created for him.

Had Maris been willing to live a less flashy lifestyle, his past might have remained secret, but that was not to be. Although the clothing company's sales were firecracker hot, its financial backers were not earning the sort of profit they had anticipated, and they suspected that Maris was squandering profits on unnecessary perks. They decided to remove him as president but keep him in charge of sales and promotions. Maris refused to step down, and the company's three hundred employees threatened to strike if he was fired. Eventually the investors sent in twenty off-duty police officers under the command of Hal Lipset, a well-known local private detective, to forcibly evict Maris from the company's manufacturing plant. When the investors went through Maris's books, they discovered he had put thirteen members of his wife's family on the company payroll. But what really stumped them were records that revealed that Maris, Lillian, her parents, Lillian's daughter, Cynthia, and her husband, Norman, had consecutive Social Security numbers. How could six members of the same family, each a different age, have sequential numbers?

Unaware that the investors had found a clue to his past, Maris filed a face-saving $5 million lawsuit against them for besmirching his name. This prompted private investigator Lipset to dig deeper into Maris's past and to discover that his resumé was fake. There was no record of a Paul J. Maris being born in Philadelphia or attending high school there. He was not on the roster of retired army officers. Still, Lipset didn't know what Maris was concealing until an ex-cop read about the $5 million lawsuit and offered to sell the detective information for $2,000. The ex-cop said he had overheard a deputy marshal bragging at a cocktail party that socialite Paul Maris was actually a relocated federal witness who had testified against the mob in New Jersey. His real name was something like "Manlowitz." A search of back issues of *The New York Times* for New Jersey Mafia trials led Lipset to Zelmanowitz. It was at this point in 1973 that he and the investors warned Maris that they were about to put out a press release exposing his past life as Gerald Zelmanowitz.

"It was a Saturday when Zelmanowitz called me at home," said Shur. "He wanted protection, so I called the Marshals Service as soon as he told me what was happening." Deputies arrived within the hour to protect him. Shur also informed the IRS that Zelmanowitz's cover was about to be blown. Although Zelmanowitz did not know this at the time, Shur had been helping the IRS keep tabs on him the entire time he had been rebuilding his life in San Francisco. Its agents were tracking him because they still believed he had millions in cash stashed in Europe. The IRS now decided to file a $1.7 million lien against him for back taxes that it claimed he owed on profits he had earned years earlier as a criminal. It froze all his bank accounts and seized his home, furniture, cars, and other possessions.

Zelmanowitz was outraged that the IRS was choosing his

weakest moment to "hound him" about unpaid taxes, especially since he claimed the Justice Department had agreed to wipe out any tax debts he had owed in return for his testimony against the mob. He also found himself in the awkward position of having to trust Shur to protect him, having now learned that Shur was helping the IRS in its investigation. He demanded that the Marshals Service not tell Shur or the IRS where he was being hidden. Shur had no objection, so deputies flew Zelmanowitz, his wife, and her parents to Rhode Island, where deputy John Partington took charge of creating new aliases for them and finding a different city where they could live.

Through his attorneys, Zelmanowitz then filed a $12.5 million suit against Shur and WITSEC on the grounds that he had been given a faulty alias. "I came home," recalled Shur, "and told Miriam I was being sued. She asked me how much and when I told her she broke out laughing. She said, 'If it was for three thousand dollars or even three hundred, I'd be concerned, but this is ridiculous.'

"I didn't have much sympathy for Zelmanowitz," Shur said. "We'd told him to keep a low profile, and instead he named a company after himself and embellished his resumé, adding a number of conspicuously inflated claims, such as owning radio stations and a manufacturing plant in Japan. What I didn't like was his blaming us." Shur said they had given the family consecutive Social Security numbers because Zelmanowitz had assured them that the only family members who would be working were he and his daughter and son-in-law, and they wouldn't be working together. Social Security numbers were used much less widely then, so there was no reason to think this would matter. In fact, Shur noted, "Zelmanowitz had set himself up for being exposed."

After months of bitter legal wrangling, a judge concluded that the amount of taxes that Zelmanowitz owed the IRS roughly canceled out the value of the property that it had seized from him. Meanwhile, a federal judge threw out his lawsuit against Shur, ruling that WITSEC couldn't be held legally responsible if a witness's past was inadvertently revealed.

But this was far from the end of the problems. Before Zelmanowitz was relocated again, he signed a contract with CBS news reporter Fred Graham, who wanted to write a book about WITSEC. *The Alias Program*, which was published in 1976, focused on the Zelmanowitz case and his charges, and it blistered Shur and his program. Its publisher billed it as a "remarkable exposé of an all but unknown government program conceived in duplicity, contemptuous of Congress, rife with bureaucratic arrogance and bungling." Dozens of newspapers published flattering reviews, and several openly criticized Shur. The *Washington Star* noted sharply that "the Justice Department official in charge, whom Graham portrays as the villain of the book, is still running the program today."

"I genuinely like and respect Fred Graham," Shur recalled later, "and I thought he tried to do a credible job writing about WITSEC. But I also knew his book was seriously flawed because I could not allow myself to discuss individual cases with him, especially cases that involved witnesses we still were protecting. Because of these constraints, I hurt myself and Graham by not giving him all the facts. This also gave Zelmanowitz an advantage, because he could make statements without my challenging them or explaining why we had done what we did. Fred and I also disagreed philosophically about WITSEC and how much help the government should give witnesses after they testify. He wrote in the copy of the book that he gave me this inscription: 'To Gerry—good man, wrong program?' "

Graham's reputation gave his book instant credibility, and—coming as it did shortly after *Washington Post* reporters Bob Woodward and Carl Bernstein's best-selling exposé of Watergate—the book hit the stores at a time when the public's distrust of the government was at a high. In the book, Graham questioned whether the government really needed a WITSEC program, and if so, whether it really needed to be giving criminals new identities. "Should the government officially adopt a program dedicated to telling lies?" he asked.

Graham also accused Shur of overstepping his bounds. He

noted that the Nixon administration's Organized Crime Control Act of 1970 had called only for the creation of safe houses where witnesses could be protected temporarily. It was Shur who had championed the extra wording added by the McClellan Committee that gave the Justice Department permission to spend funds "for the care and protection of such witnesses in whatever manner is deemed most useful under the special circumstances of each case." He charged that Shur had used that vague language to justify relocations, aliases, and virtually anything else he wanted. Congress had been hoodwinked, Graham wrote, because it had never been told that the government was "getting involved in the wholesale business of creating false identities. Thus, there was never any debate on the legal and moral problems that might arise as the government undertook to wash away the past lives of hundreds of people—many of them hoodlums—and to infiltrate them back into society under false names."

It was this revelation—that the government was hiding killers and crooks under false names in unsuspecting neighborhoods—that rattled the public. Graham's book prompted dozens of reporters to write stories about WITSEC. Most were critical, and nearly every one began by warning readers that they might have a Gerald Zelmanowitz living next door to them.

The third ghost from WITSEC's past appeared in February 1976 on the streets of San Francisco, when Joseph Donait was killed by a shotgun blast in broad daylight while unlocking the door of his car on a public street. The killer fired from a passing van. The police found it abandoned a block away with the murder weapon on the backseat. The shotgun's serial number had been burned off with acid, and detectives suspected the murder was a mob hit. What no one knew was why the mob would want to kill Donait, a man with no known police record. The answer came as soon as the FBI examined his fingerprints. They matched those of Joseph "the Animal" Barboza, the hit man who had been hidden on Thacher's Island. The San Francisco detectives called deputy John Partington for help. "I know it sounds odd, but I felt funny as soon as the phone rang," Partington said later, "as though I knew just then, for no reason, that Joe was dead. I just felt it." He had mixed emotions. "I had a love-hate feeling for the guy. He was a killer, but still, we had gotten close."

The recap of Barboza's recent history Partington gave the detectives was a checkered one. In the six years since Barboza had been given a new identity, he had left a merchant marine job the Marshals Service had gotten him, after a fall that brought him $18,500 in workman's compensation; used the money to traffic in drugs; been divorced from his wife, who took their daughter with her; and tried unsuccessfully to fence $300,000 in stolen securities to, of all people, the Patriarca crime family in Providence. A few weeks later he killed a fellow drug dealer in what he claimed was self-defense, but there were witnesses to the killing, and Barboza was sentenced to five years in prison. But even from his cell, he managed to pull off a slick con, charging that he had proof Frank Sinatra was a puppet for the mob. He was persuasive enough to appear before a special House committee investigating organized crime in May 1972. Partington refused to protect him, telling him, " 'Shit, Joe, you don't know nothing about Sinatra, you're just making that shit up!' But he just laughed. 'It gets me out of the joint for a while, don't it?' he tells me."

Barboza appeared before the committee wearing a disguise and accused Sinatra of being a front man for Patriarca in the ownership of the Sands casino in Las Vegas and the glitzy Fontainebleau hotel in Miami Beach. His charges, which were widely reported by the media, gave Sinatra no choice but to appear before the committee to defend himself. He accused Barboza of "character assassination" and called him a "bum . . . running off at the mouth." When reporters revealed that Barboza's accusations were based entirely on hearsay and rumors, a red-faced Congress refused to renew the committee's funding, and it disbanded.

Federal agents urged Barboza to leave California when he was paroled from prison in 1976, but he began shaking down San Francisco bookmakers instead. "He was going around saying, 'You know who I am? I'm Joe Barboza, the mob hit man you've read about in the newspapers. You'd better pay me or else,' " Partington recalled. The police later determined that Barboza had just finished extorting cash from a bookie when he was gunned down. Although his killers were never caught, they were believed to be mobsters from Providence.

The bad publicity caused by the Leonhard child custody dispute, the Zelmanowitz case, and the Barboza murder raised eyebrows in Congress about WITSEC. And then, just when it looked as if things couldn't get worse for Shur, they did.

CHAPTER
ELEVEN

LIKE MANY TEENAGE GIRLS, the Shurs' daughter, Ilene, scrambled to grab the telephone when it rang one evening, thinking it was one of her pals. But the menacing voice on the line was anything but friendly. "Have you ever thought about death?" a man asked. "It's about time you did. Be sure to tell your father I called." Then the line went dead.

The next morning Shur confronted the most likely suspect. "Congratulations," he said when the witness entered his office. "You have just become my family's personal insurer. If anything— and I do mean anything—happens to a member of my family, the entire weight of the Justice Department is going to come crashing down on you and everyone you know. There will be a hundred federal agents investigating your every move and they will make your life miserable." Of course, the witness denied placing the phone call, but the more he talked, the guiltier he sounded.

Shur already carried a gun. An IRS agent had suggested he get one when he first began dealing with mob witnesses. "If you aren't armed," the agent explained, "then we have to worry about protecting you as well as the witness." The U.S. Marshals Service had deputized him with limited authority, which meant he could carry a concealed weapon but could not make arrests. After the scary phone call, Shur had his telephone number unlisted and an alarm system installed in his house. "Intellectually, I knew my job might put Miriam and the kids in danger, but I had been in emotional self-denial until Ilene got that call," he said later. "For the first time, I felt real fear. People I loved were being put at risk because of me. That worried me, but I was not going to be intimidated. Instead I focused on the best way to eliminate the threats."

Shur had lectured Miriam and his children for years about the need to be aware of what was happening around them. When they were riding in the car, Shur would often ask what the color and make of the car behind them was. Miriam and the kids were not allowed to glance back. They were supposed to already know.

Besides frightening telephone calls, Shur was dealing with another personal difficulty. His multiple sclerosis was becoming worse. Almost daily, he was experiencing painful attacks that would come on without warning. His legs would feel as if they were being jabbed by hundreds of sharp needles, his face would burn, and his skin would become so taut, it felt as if it might rip open. Along with these sensations would come an overwhelming feeling of fatigue. He had described it once to Miriam as water rushing down a bathtub drain. That's how quickly the energy in his body seemed to be sucked away. "It was so overpowering that if there had been a fire in the Justice Department, I would not have been able to leave my chair," he said later. Despite this, few of his colleagues ever knew when he was having an MS attack. "I never wanted them focusing on me or being concerned that I wasn't up to doing my job," he explained. "They all knew I had MS. I told them because I wanted them to understand that a person with MS could keep on working. But I hid my attacks from them, mostly because I didn't want any pity." Still, there would be occasional signs. One day, a co-worker asked him why he was limping. Another time, Shur called several members of his staff into his office during the day to ask them questions; he normally walked down to their offices. But usually only his special assistant, Diane Reid, who had worked closely with him for more than a decade, could tell when he was being hit by a severe attack. She would look for simple ways to help him without making a display of it. She'd also try to boost his ego. At home, Shur tried to disguise the attacks, too, but Miriam knew him too well to be fooled.

Miriam Ottenberg's book about MS, *Pursuit of Hope*, was popular with members of MS support groups, and because Shur was quoted throughout it, he soon was being asked to speak at local MS gatherings. Even though he was hard-pressed for time, he rarely refused. When he saw how MS had ravaged others, he realized he was lucky. He began his speeches by removing his jacket so everyone could see the semiautomatic attached to his belt. "You think you've got problems," he'd declare. "Just think about the guy on the opposite end of this gun. How's he going to feel when he learns the man with his finger on the trigger is suffering from MS?"

Shur discovered the best way for him to endure MS attacks was by focusing on his job. "On my worst days, I couldn't wait to get to work because it took my mind off the pain." WITSEC provided him with plenty of distractions.

By the mid-1970s prosecutors, federal investigators, and witnesses were inundating him with complaints about how the Marshals Service was handling—most would say mishandling—WITSEC cases. In its defense, the service insisted it was being unfairly blamed because it had never been given the staff or the funding it needed to do the job right. In 1976 alone, Shur sent the Marshals Service 486 new witnesses to relocate, the highest number ever admitted in a single year.

While Shur sympathized with its difficulties, he knew the program was being undercut by problems other than growing numbers and a dearth of resources. Simply put, WITSEC was still not a priority in the Marshals Service. The job of WITSEC chief had become a revolving door in the four years since Reis Kash had stepped aside. Fourteen different deputies had been put in charge of the program, some lasting less than two months. Morale was terrible. Being assigned to WITSEC was akin to being banished to Siberia. A frustrated Shur found himself writing memos almost daily to the marshals' WITSEC chief of the moment about careless blunders. A typical November 1975 memo listed nine complaints. In one instance, a deputy had "terminated" a witness from the program because the former mobster hadn't landed a legitimate job within six months after relocation. That was the maximum time Shur felt a witness needed to become self-supporting, and the deputy stopped paying the witness's rent and per diem allowance. But when Shur inquired, he discovered the witness hadn't been able to apply for jobs because the Marshals Service had never given him a new Social Security card, and without it, no one would hire him. In another case, Shur discovered that deputies in Newark, New Jersey, had delivered the wrong witness to a trial to testify.

"A witness called me upset by how he was being protected," Shur recalled. "The deputies guarding him kept their guns in holsters hidden under their suit coats, which they kept buttoned. It was winter, so they were wearing heavy overcoats, which they also kept buttoned, and some were wearing gloves. By the time these deputies got their gloves off and undid their coats and suit jackets to reach for their guns, the witness said he'd be dead."

The mistakes overshadowed the times when the Marshals Service did an exceptional job. When prosecutors in Milwaukee, Wisconsin, warned Shur at the last minute that the FBI was about to arrest members of a Mafia-run drug and prostitution ring, he told the Marshals Service that it had only forty-eight hours to locate and protect thirty-five persons, mostly pimps, prostitutes, and local bar owners. "They sent in extra deputies and got the job done," Shur recalled. "It was an incredible feat because they had to grab all thirty-five witnesses at the same moment to keep from tipping off the mob."

But for every success story, there were a dozen tales about botched jobs. It didn't help that several federal investigators and prosecutors frequently made outlandish promises to witnesses that the deputies couldn't fulfill. The handling of Richard J. Blake Sr. and his family was an example of a case gone shockingly bad.

In 1970 Blake and his partner in a landscaping business bid on a lucrative contract to remove dead trees from public parks in the Chicago suburbs. After they agreed to pay kickbacks to a gaggle of corrupt city managers and council members, they were awarded the job. A year later, an IRS auditor discovered the payoffs. To save themselves, Blake and his partner went to work as "IRS confidential sources," which meant that they helped IRS agents gather evidence in return for a promise that their role in the investigation would never be revealed and they would not be charged with any crimes. When the IRS turned its findings over to the U.S. attorney's office in Chicago for prosecution, both men assumed their obligation had been fulfilled. But the assistant U.S. attorney prosecuting the case thought otherwise. He insisted that Blake and his partner tell a federal grand jury how the scam worked. When they reminded him that the IRS had promised them anonymity, he replied that grand jury testimony was secret, so technically he was not breaking the IRS's confidentiality promise. Terrified that they would be killed if they testified, Blake and his partner hired attorneys and threatened to plead the Fifth Amendment if they were subpoenaed. That prompted the prosecutor to ask a federal judge to give both men limited immunity. This meant nothing they said in front of the grand jury could be used to incriminate them, so they could no longer hide behind the Fifth Amendment. If they didn't testify, they would be held in contempt and tossed in jail.

And that is exactly what happened to Blake's partner when he refused to answer the grand jury's questions. He was locked up. The prosecutor then cut a deal with Blake. Like many elements in this case, there would later be an angry dispute about what was said during the meeting between Blake, two prosecutors, and two IRS agents, but this is how Blake recalled that meeting. The prosecutors and IRS agents promised him that he and his family would be enrolled in the WITSEC program. They said the Marshals Service would relocate him to a new community, pay all his living expenses until he got on his feet, reimburse him for any out-of-pocket expenses he incurred, buy him a house, and set him up in another landscaping business comparable to the one he owned.

Blake signed up and testified before the grand jury. His partner, meanwhile, was released from jail and fled town after selling his share of the landscaping business to Blake. The *Chicago Tribune* somehow learned about Blake's testimony and disclosed in a front-page story that forty contractors and more than a dozen corrupt politicians were about to be arrested. While the newspaper didn't name him, it gave enough hints for death threats to begin arriving that same day. When he called federal prosecutors and the IRS for advice about what to do, they urged him to get out of Chicago as fast as he could.

Blake, his wife, and their five children drove to Bozeman, Montana, a town they chose at random, and checked into a motel. They expected WITSEC to call them within a few days, but no one did. After waiting for two weeks, they decided to put down a $2,000 deposit on a house and look for a landscaping business to buy. A month later, two IRS agents and a deputy marshal contacted them and confirmed that the family had been accepted into WITSEC. However, the deputy said that they had to leave Bozeman immediately; since they had moved there on their own, the Marshals Service couldn't be sure they hadn't been followed. Then he dropped another bomb. There would be no reimbursement for their expenses or for the $2,000 down payment on the house because they had gone to Bozeman before being accepted into WITSEC. Protests to the IRS agents and prosecutors in Chicago who had urged Blake to leave town were unavailing. He was out more than $4,000.

More bad news followed. By now Chicago newspapers had identified him as the IRS's chief informant, and prospective buyers of his landscaping business pulled out for fear of mob retribution. The business folded, and he lost another $300,000.

Relocated to Spokane, Washington, the family lodged for six weeks in a motel waiting to hear from the Marshals Service—seven people in two rooms with nothing to do. Finally a frustrated Blake rented a house, paying the first six months' rent in advance because he had no references. At last he called the U.S. Marshals Service office in Spokane. No one knew anything about him. The Chicago deputy had failed to notify them the family was being relocated there.

It got worse. A Spokane deputy told them to choose between the motel or the rented house; WITSEC rules forbade paying for both. But Blake pointed out they were still waiting for their furniture to arrive from Chicago, and they couldn't live in an empty house. "You should have thought of that when you rented the house without checking with us," the deputy replied. For almost a month, which included Christmas and New Year's, the Blakes and their children slept on the floor of the rented house until their furniture arrived—some pieces missing, others damaged.

The disasters kept piling up. The Marshals Service refused to set Blake up in a new business, despite the promises made by the IRS and federal prosecutors in Chicago. "If they made you those promises, then it's up to them to buy you a business, not us," said the deputy. Even the monthly subsistence of $1,300 the family was entitled to under WITSEC rules stopped after two months; the deputy blamed it on a paperwork glitch. The children couldn't enter school because the Marshals Service hadn't given them records with their new names on them, and there was such a huge backlog of such requests that it could take as long as a year for Washington, D.C., to produce them. Even a new Social Security card for Blake would take another six months—if he was lucky. Since he could not look for a job without it, the family survived on their dwindling savings until, four months later, they were broke. Then Blake discovered that back in Chicago, the IRS had put a lien on the money from the sale of his house there for back taxes it claimed he owed. The tax agents had tried to notify him, but the Marshals Service refused to reveal where he was being hidden. He now owed nearly eight months' worth of fines and penalties. The IRS suggested he fly to Chicago to resolve the dispute, but the Marshals Service threatened to boot him out of WITSEC if he returned to "the danger area." In the course of their heated argument, Blake brought up the subject of his subsistence pay.

He would later claim he was told that his monthly stipend had been stopped two months after he arrived in Spokane because of all the complaints he had made about the way he was being treated. He was then offered a thousand dollars in cash to voluntarily drop out of WITSEC. Blake agreed, and in April 1974 used part of the money to fly to Chicago to meet with the IRS. He was there only briefly before he was arrested and jailed. One of the local officials indicted by the grand jury because of Blake's testimony had been tipped off that he was back in town. He accused Blake of making a threatening phone call, and the judge, a friend of the official, set bail at $100,000. Terrified that he was being set up to be murdered in the Cook County jail, the frantic Blake telephoned his wife. She went to the Marshals Service in Spokane, but officials there professed to be helpless because Blake had dropped out of WITSEC voluntarily.

"We're starving," she said.

They suggested she apply for welfare.

"I've tried," she replied, "but they turned me down because you've never given me a Social Security card, so I don't qualify."

Two months later, a different Chicago judge lowered Blake's bail to $5,000, and his wife sold all their furniture and their car to post it. It had been nearly two years since he had testified before the grand jury, and during that time he had lost his landscaping business, been slapped with an IRS tax lien, depleted his savings, been jailed for sixty-three days, and was now unemployed and humiliated. With money borrowed from relatives, he hired a lawyer and threatened to sue the government. It was at this point that the IRS sent William J. DePugh, an assistant chief from its Chicago office, to investigate. In his August 1974 final report, DePugh confirmed that Blake's complaints, in his opinion, were factual and accurate. The government's actions, DePugh wrote, had been "unconscionable."

"It will be very hard to convince anyone that the Blake family situation could be used by the government as an example of how we take care of people who cooperate with us," he wrote.

The Marshals Service objected to DePugh's findings, and federal prosecutors in Chicago also denied that they had ever misled Blake. "This was a case where everyone, and I mean everyone—the federal prosecutors, the IRS agents, the Marshals Service, and the Blakes—each had their own version of what had happened and who was to blame," Shur recalled. "It was a mess. What happened in cases such as this, when I wasn't certain whom to believe, was that I said, 'Okay, it's time to make things right. Let's forget about what has happened and start over. Let's give the witness exactly what he would be due if he were entering the program for the first time. Nothing more, nothing less.' "

The IRS, however, rebuffed Shur's solution. Instead, it worked out a deal completely on its own with Blake and his attorney. Under it, Blake was relocated by the IRS to a new community and reimbursed several thousand dollars for his earlier expenses. Although Shur couldn't prevent the IRS from relocating Blake, he was afraid its actions would set a dangerous precedent. And he was correct. Tired of the deplorable way the Marshals Service was handling witnesses, DEA and FBI agents in the field began lobbying their bosses for permission to relocate witnesses on their own, without help from the Marshals Service. Shur moved quickly to stop the coup. "We couldn't have agencies acting independently," he explained later. "What if the DEA gave their witnesses more than the FBI gave theirs? Not only would that look suspicious in court, it would lead to witnesses shopping around for the best offers. It was a horrible idea."

Shur urged his bosses to give him more time to make WITSEC work, and they backed him. "It was decided that agencies could relocate their own informants," he said later, "but only the Marshals Service could relocate government witnesses."

Incredibly, Shur found that he was defending an agency that didn't want or appreciate his efforts. "Most deputies wanted nothing to do with witnesses," Shur said. "They didn't like WITSEC, and several of them really didn't want the program to succeed."

Shur decided it was time to confront the Marshals Service's director, Wayne Colburn, who had been busy dealing with other programs besides WITSEC. In a long memo, Shur summarized the major complaints that he had heard. Not wanting to be completely negative, he ended his memo by complimenting Hugh "Big Mac" McDonald, the deputy who had been the liaison between the Justice Department's OCRS office and the Marshals Service since WITSEC's start.

"Right after I sent that memo," Shur recalled, "Big Mac told me that he was being assigned to a job in Puerto Rico. The Marshals Service knew Mac's extended family all lived in the Washington metropolitan area, and an assignment to Puerto Rico would be devastating to his wife and family. It was clear to me this was simply a matter of petty politics. I suspected that Colburn had sent my memo down the chain of command, and someone there had decided that McDonald had sold out the Marshals Service and joined my side. That was ridiculous. If anything, McDonald was the linchpin who was helping keep the witness program going. But they wanted to punish him. It made me furious."

Shur protested to Colburn's deputy, William Hall, who assured him that McDonald would not be reassigned. "I trusted Bill Hall. He was an honorable man, so I knew McDonald was safe." Still, the transfer attempt sent Shur a chilling message. "It was clear to me that in some circles inside the Marshals Service, I was the enemy."

Shur decided to try a different approach to getting Colburn to make WITSEC a higher priority inside the Marshals Service. He asked Kenneth W. Rath, who was in charge of the Justice Department's management and budget office, to launch a departmental review of the WITSEC program. Shur rode in the same carpool as Rath, and they were friends. Departmental reviews were done to pick apart a program's weaknesses. This was information Shur already had, but he felt a formal review would send Colburn and his staff a message: The Justice Department is concerned about WITSEC. No federal bureaucrat would want his career linked to a troubled program.

Shur's plan worked. Shortly after Rath's office announced it was going to investigate WITSEC, Colburn sent out a memo that said he "had not been aware of the gravity of the problems in WITSEC." He told Shur that the Marshals Service would seek an additional $3.76 million in its next budget request specifically for WITSEC, to pay for new equipment and to hire two hundred more deputies.

But Shur's delight didn't last long. Colburn's budget request didn't make it through the Justice Department's review process.

"The sad truth is that witness security was about as important as a mosquito on a gnat's ass when it came to getting money in the federal budget," WITSEC's deputy director, William Hall, recalled later. "Gerry Shur cared about this program, but no one else in the Justice Department really did."

Shur began snooping around to find out exactly who in the Justice Department had killed Colburn's request. "I learned there was a very strong feeling in the department's hierarchy that the Marshals Service was an inefficient operation," Shur said later. "There was a strong feeling that enough deputies were already on board to handle the WITSEC caseload. I wrote a number of memos challenging this view, but I couldn't change this negative attitude." It was now painfully obvious that Shur had to gain support from within his own ranks for WITSEC if he hoped to win it more money. He decided that Benjamin Civiletti, then an assistant attorney general in charge of the Justice Department's Criminal Division, was the most likely to listen to his plea. In a twenty-two-page memo, Shur warned Civiletti that WITSEC was on the verge of collapsing. "I cannot conceive that seven years after WITSEC began, we would be less organized than at any time in our program's operation," Shur wrote, "but simply put, the current system doesn't work."

Shur cited examples of dangerous situations that had happened because of a lack of funds, deputies, and shoddy work.

• To save money, deputies were dropping off witnesses at airports and sending them unaccompanied on flights back to "danger areas" to testify. They were supposed to be met by another deputy when they arrived, but often no one was there. In one instance, a late-arriving deputy had a mob witness paged over the airport intercom under his true name. In another, a witness stepped off a flight and bumped into one of the Mafia thugs he had come to testify against. "It is not uncommon for witnesses to have to hail airport taxis to get to the federal courthouse on time for a trial," Shur noted. "After they get to the courthouse, they have to hunt down deputies to protect them."

• Weeks' worth of mail for witnesses was left in stacks at Marshals Service headquarters because no one there had time to forward it. Some of the letters that were forwarded arrived at the witnesses' new homes in envelopes that had the words "U.S. Marshals Service/Witness Security" as the return address. The postal carrier who delivered them and anyone else who saw them would be able to guess the recipients were protected witnesses.

• A known mob hit man had knocked on the door of an apartment one night looking for Vincent Teresa. The terrified occupant had explained that Teresa had moved. Luckily, the hit man didn't recognize the tenant, who was also a WITSEC witness. To save money and avoid the hassle of having to keep renting new apartments to hide witnesses in, the Marshals Service was using the same apartment over and over again. Worse, the landlord in this case was a convicted bookmaker with known mob ties.

• The Marshals Service's headquarters was so far behind in providing new documents for witnesses that deputies in the field were creating their own. The fake credentials were not "backstopped," which meant a quick check would reveal they were phonies. One ingenious deputy blotted out his name on a copy of his own birth certificate and used it to make dozens of copies of birth certificates for witnesses. Naturally, all of them were given certificates that showed they had been born at the same hospital. To make them look official, the deputy had rubbed one corner over a half-dollar coin to give it a "seal."

Shur's memo to Civiletti ended with an ominous warning: "WITSEC is being so poorly run that it is amazing no government witness has been killed. This success should not lead to the conclusion that we have been skillful at concealment. Instead it is the result of dumb luck and the savvy of the witnesses themselves."

One of Civiletti's special assistants, William J. Brady, reviewed Shur's memo before it was given to Civiletti and attached a short summary to it, as well as his own recommendation. He proposed taking WITSEC away from the Marshals Service. "The marshals were never set up to care for people such as these witnesses," Brady noted. "The very education of a deputy marshal is repugnant to being kind and helpful to one who is an admitted accomplice in an organized crime case. Up to now, the program has survived *solely* because of the work of Gerry Shur." Brady urged Civiletti to create a new office within the Justice Department exclusively for witness protection. It would have its own budget and own WITSEC officers, and would act independently of other federal law enforcement agencies to guarantee that all federal witnesses were treated equally. He recommended that Shur be put in charge.

Shur was flattered but dead set against Brady's proposal. Instead, he urged Civiletti to appoint a panel of outside experts to review the WITSEC program. "No one was simply going to hand over more funds to the marshals," Shur recalled, "but if a panel of experts said, 'Okay, here is a problem, this is how we can fix it, and one of the solutions is that we need more money,' then I felt the Justice Department hierarchy would give the Marshals Service the funding it needed to make WITSEC work."

Civiletti backed Shur's idea, and a panel of managers from other divisions inside the Justice Department began a two-year review of WITSEC. One of its recommendations was the creation of the Memorandum of Understanding (MOU), a document given to every WITSEC witness. It spelled out exactly what the Marshals Service would and wouldn't do. "One of the key questions on the MOU was: 'Have any promises been made to you?' " Shur recalled. "A witness would then write down exactly what he had been promised—maybe by a federal prosecutor or a federal agent— and either a deputy or I would read it and say, 'Hey, no one is going to do this for you' or 'Sure, we can do this for you.' The MOU was designed to ensure that every witness had in writing exactly what he was getting into. We didn't want another Blake case. Once we began using them, the number of witness complaints coming into my offices dropped dramatically."

In appealing to Civiletti, Shur had unknowingly pinned his hopes on a rising star. By the time the panel of experts had finished writing its final report, Civiletti had been promoted to the job of deputy attorney general. "He was now the person to whom the panel was required to give its findings," said Shur. "It was up to him to decide which of its recommendations would be forwarded to the attorney general." Then, while his aides were scrutinizing the report, Civiletti was named U.S. attorney general. "All of this couldn't have worked out better for me," said Shur. "Civiletti was now the top guy, and he was reviewing recommendations that he himself had set in motion. I had someone in power who was keenly aware of the problems that WITSEC faced."

Shur felt confident Civiletti would get WITSEC the money and manpower it needed, but that was still not going to be enough. The U.S. Marshals Service's long-standing attitude of indifference had to be changed. The question now for Shur was how to pull that off.

CHAPTER
TWELVE

I N MARCH 1978, Congress decided to jump in. Enough horror stories had surfaced about government witnesses being abandoned by the Marshals Service that a Senate Judiciary subcommittee decided to conduct three days of public hearings to investigate WITSEC. "I know some managers would have circled the wagons, thrown up their defenses, and tried to paint a rosy picture," said Shur, "but I felt strongly that if the subcommittee truly understood the problems I was facing, then it could become my ally. I began meeting privately with the subcommittee staff and furnished them with detailed information about all the problems we faced. I was frank. It may sound strange, but by the time the hearings were scheduled to start, I was actually looking forward to the criticism that I knew we were going to get because I believed those criticisms would ultimately help me move WITSEC forward."

Senator James Abourezk, the subcommittee chair, began by saying he had never heard of WITSEC until he read Fred Graham's book, *The Alias Program*, published two years earlier. "Fred's revelations prompted this subcommittee to launch an intensive nine-month investigation," Abourezk declared. "Sadly, our investigators found the problems in this program are as bad or even worse than what Mr. Graham suspected."

Congressional hearings, like television talk shows, thrive on drama, and Senator Abourezk began with a juicy case. He said the subcommittee had met the day before behind closed doors with a protected mob witness named Gerald Festa, who had almost been murdered because of bumbling by deputies. Senator Abourezk blamed the Marshals Service's office in Newark, New Jersey, for mishandling Festa's case from the start. After the gangster was hurried out of town, it had forgotten to protect his house and a Chicken Delight restaurant he owned. The house was looted, and vandals sprayed the words "Canary Delight" in yellow paint across the front windows of his fast-food restaurant. But it was what happened next that worried Abourezk.

Festa was being hidden by the FBI in a rural jail under an alias when two deputy marshals from Newark showed up unexpectedly and took him with them without notifying the FBI. They drove Festa to a jail in Newark where several mobsters who wanted him dead were being housed. When the deputies started to check Festa into the facility under his real name, he smelled a setup and began protesting. A sympathetic guard called the FBI, which quickly intervened, hustling Festa off to a new hiding spot—this time, an even more remote rural jail. The next day, two men dressed in hunting clothes and carrying shotguns arrived at the jail, claiming to be prison guards from another state. They tried to talk their way inside by asking questions about the jail's kitchen facilities, which they asked to see, but the jailer refused to open the front door and spoke to them only through an intercom. When the men persisted, the jailer called the local sheriff's office and they fled.

Worried that someone inside the Newark Marshals Service's office had leaked information about Festa to the mob, the FBI contacted William Hall, who had replaced Wayne Colburn in May 1976 as the Marshals Service's director. A former FBI agent himself, Hall asked the FBI to investigate. Its probe failed to find sufficient evidence to make arrests, but several deputies abruptly resigned amid rumors they had been paid $5,000 each by the Mafia to locate Festa.

In his secret appearance before the subcommittee, Festa said he didn't trust anyone in the Marshals Service except deputy John Partington. "Them others," he testified, "can be bought off!"

When Senator Abourezk asked the subcommittee's first public witness, Thomas C. Renner, what the biggest problem plaguing WITSEC was, the *Newsday* crime reporter, who had co-authored Vincent "Fat Vinnie" Teresa's best-selling memoir, said it was the Marshals Service's openly hostile attitude. "One deputy called witnesses 'animals who should be chained and locked up.' . . . Another bitterly complained to me that 'these hoods are getting more from the government than I do,' " Renner testified. "Of the twenty WITSEC witnesses I have interviewed, not one would tell a friend to enter this program."

Next, Senator Abourezk asked John Partington for his advice. "First of all, Senator," the blunt deputy told him, "you got to understand we're not dealing with Billy Graham churchgoers here. You're talking about witnesses who are professional criminals. They know their business. We should know our business. I have handled over five hundred witnesses personally since 1967 and I can tell you that these witnesses look at us like we're airline pilots. If we make a mistake, they die." Partington blamed the "suits" at headquarters for WITSEC's problems. Most just didn't give a damn about the program, he testified, so mob witnesses were being dumped in cities without new documents and somehow being expected to survive on their own.

Abourezk's hearing didn't lead to any new laws, but it accomplished what Shur had hoped. Faced with an ongoing internal Justice Department review and three days of criticism before a Senate subcommittee, Hall and his deputy director, John Twomey, began scouring their ranks to find someone who could clean up the Marshals Service's WITSEC operations. When they couldn't find anyone they believed could handle the job, Twomey called Peter Bensinger, the head of the Drug Enforcement Administration, who was a close friend. Bensinger had been director of the Illinois Department of Public Safety when Twomey was the warden at the state prison in Joliet. "We need a tough, solid manager," Twomey told him. Bensinger had just the man. He called Howard Safir, one of his assistants, into his office.

"How'd you like to go to the Marshals Service for a year?" Bensinger asked.

"What'd I do wrong?" Safir answered, grinning.

Bensinger offered Safir a promotion and a pay raise if he
would agree to spend one year on loan to the Marshals Service. A
few days later, Safir reported to work at his new job. The Marshals
Service's WITSEC operations office, which was located in a suite
above a grocery store in downtown Washington, D.C., was so
messy, it looked to him as if "someone had set off a bomb inside
it." Security was appalling. Anyone could have walked inside
from the street. Desks were left at night stacked with confidential
reports about mob witnesses. The office files didn't have locks on
them. "Most of the employees didn't want to be there," Safir recalled. "One told me, 'I hate baby-sitting these goddamn criminals.' I said to myself, 'How in the hell can you operate a program
with people who don't want to be here and don't like their
clients?' It was clear to me that if you screwed up in the Marshals,
this is where they sent you."

Safir was so embarrassed by his new assignment that he wore
his DEA identification badge to work. He didn't want anyone he
met to think he was employed by the Marshals Service. During his
first day on the job, he asked his secretary what he thought was a
routine question: How much subsistence was WITSEC paying a
specific witness each month?

"I can have that information for you in about a week," she
replied.

"A week? Can't you just look it up on your computer?"

"Sir, I have trouble getting ribbons for our manual typewrit-
ers. No one here has a computer."

Safir marched in to see Hall and Twomey. "I can fix this program," he said, "but I am going to need money and I am going to
have to get rid of nearly every deputy assigned to the office." A
few days later Safir returned to the director's office and outlined
his plans. "I intend to transform the witness protection unit into
an elite squad of deputies capable of protecting not only mob witnesses, but foreign dignitaries and government officials as well. To
start, I want to create a new job classification inside the Marshals
Service. I want to call it 'witness security inspectors,' and I want
them to be paid more than other deputies. This will be a way for

us to begin attracting the best rather than the worst deputies into this program."

Not only was Safir the right man for the job, but he came at the right time. Weary of complaints, Hall and Twomey were eager to back him up inside the Marshals Service, and he had the immediate support of Shur in the Organized Crime and Racketeering Section of the Justice Department and the backing of U.S. attorney general Civiletti. "Howard Safir was the first real advocate the witness program ever had inside the Marshals Service," Shur recalled. "He didn't mind pounding on people's desks, making demands, shaking things up. He was a determined Mr. Fix-it, and once he put his mind to it, he was impossible to stop."

Safir was given a free hand, and he immediately got rid of almost every deputy assigned to WITSEC, replacing them with fifty-three new hires, most of whom he handpicked. Several were Vietnam veterans eager to prove themselves. "I wanted young people who could be good cops, but who also could say, 'Okay, yesterday you were a scumbag criminal but today you are a witness, so we are going to treat you the way a human being should be treated.' " As part of his plan to turn the Marshals Service's WITSEC operations into an exclusive unit, he stopped the agency's practice of having deputies rotate in and out of witness protection details—a move the deputies' union unsuccessfully tried to block because it meant less overtime pay. In the coming months, Safir hired secretarial staff and replaced the old training manual that Reis Kash had drafted with a more modern and demanding one that spelled out exactly how Safir expected his new witness security inspectors to operate. He began upgrading training, too. He even designed several specialized training courses exclusively for his inspectors. "Most witnesses can never be happy in this program," he told them, "but we can make them content. There is a difference. You must learn to do what's reasonable, compassionate, and right. The witness himself may have been an ax murderer, but his wife and children weren't."

Under Safir, no one got inside the Marshals Service's WITSEC operations office without first being cleared by a uniformed guard. Information about witnesses was shared on a need-to-know basis. Files were kept locked. Safir got the DEA to set up a computer system in the operations office. He didn't tolerate sloppy desks, poorly written reports, screw-ups with witnesses.

Safir would later recall that he succeeded where others had failed because he established a "winner's attitude" in his troops. He told his inspectors that he was going to mold them into "the best personal protective service in the world, with a reputation for never losing anyone." Any deputies who didn't measure up would be booted out. He arranged for the best among them to be sent to New York City each year to help protect foreign diplomats when the United Nations General Assembly was in session, an assignment that helped instill pride and gave them experience working with other agencies, as well as bonus pay.

A short time after he became the Marshals Service's WITSEC chief, Safir announced that he no longer wanted his inspectors answering to the country's ninety-four politically appointed U.S. marshals, many of whom he considered to be partisan hacks. He wanted the marshals cut out of the loop when it came to every aspect of WITSEC. His inspectors would be stationed in several key cities and would work in the U.S. Marshals Service offices there alongside other deputies, but they would answer only to Safir. They would not be sent to serve arrest warrants or to fetch some judge's laundry. He also declared that in the future, neither he nor his inspectors would inform the U.S. marshals when a mob witness was being relocated in their jurisdictions.

Safir's declarations set off a firestorm. Dozens of U.S. marshals complained to Hall. They accused Safir of being arrogant and overstepping his bounds. But Hall backed up his feisty WITSEC chief, and Safir continued his reforms. "By cutting the U.S. marshals out of the process, Safir ended a lot of the politics when it came to where witnesses were being sent," a deputy assigned to headquarters later recalled. "A marshal could no longer call up and tell the WITSEC chief not to put anyone from the LCN in his town." Safir matched his inspectors with individual witnesses and their families. Witnesses no longer had to depend on local deputies, many of whom had never dealt with a mob witness, when they arrived in a new town. Now they dealt with trained WITSEC inspectors who oversaw their case from the moment they were accepted into the program until they left it. This made it difficult for them to con the Marshals Service, and it provided them with better support because the inspectors got to know them personally. "Howard was amazing to watch," said Shur. "He made my job much easier. A U.S. attorney would call and say a witness needed protection. My staff at the OCRS would review the case and give me a recommendation. Then I would call Safir at the Marshals Service and tell him the witness had been approved. He then took care of everything—protecting the witness, giving him a new identity, and relocating him."

Not surprisingly, Safir's curt, ramrod style ruffled feathers. He didn't suffer fools, had little patience, and barked orders as if he were a general. He didn't seem to care whose toes he stepped on. "What was the Marshals Service going to do to me?" he recalled later. "All anyone could do was send me back to the DEA, which would have been fine with me." Ironically, the fact he was an outsider gave him more rather than less clout.

"Some people didn't like Howard's strong ego," said Shur, "but he also had a very strong desire to be perceived as someone who was turning the Marshals Service's WITSEC operations around and really doing a good job, and that combination worked wonders." Shur finally had a strong ally rather than an opponent as WITSEC chief, and the two men became a team. Safir could count on Shur to push WITSEC's cause inside the rest of the Justice Department, and Shur could count on Safir to push it inside the Marshals Service. Their working relationship became even closer after Safir hired Marilyn Mode as his special assistant. She had started her government career working for Shur and both men trusted her judgment.

Safir and Shur shared similar backgrounds. Like Shur, Safir's parents were Jewish immigrants who had settled in New York City and ingrained in their son an intense desire not only to succeed but to do something important with his life. Safir's father had been a presser in the garment district, his mother a switchboard operator. His father had helped unionize the sweatshops of the Lower East Side of Manhattan, a dangerous cause at the time. As a child, Safir had sat mesmerized at the family table listening to stories told by his uncle, Louis Weiner, a famed New York City detective who had helped arrest notorious bank robber Willie Sutton. After completing college in 1963, Safir joined the New York State Police, but he quickly moved to the federal Bureau of Narcotics, which later became the DEA. At age twenty-three, during a time when some his age were demonstrating against the Vietnam War and experimenting with illegal drugs, Safir went undercover, posing as a hairy, toga-wearing, drug-buying hippie in San Francisco's Haight-Ashbury district. From there, he served stints in Southeast Asia, Mexico, France, and Turkey.

At Marshals Service headquarters, Safir gained a reputation for rewarding loyalists and crushing dissent. To the surprise of no one, he and John Partington clashed. As capable as he was, Partington had never been a team player, nor had he ever paid much attention to his bosses in headquarters. "John Partington was a cowboy and exactly what this program needed in its early days," said a friend of both men. "With the help of a handful of other cowboy deputies, Partington literally held WITSEC together, flying across the country putting out fires, handling all of the most important witnesses. He did things his way, by the seat of his pants, because he had to. No one in headquarters really wanted to know what was going on; they just wanted John to handle it. When Safir came in, the entire playing field changed. Howard was intent on building a well-disciplined, well-trained squad of inspectors who answered to him and him alone. There wasn't a place in WITSEC any longer for the cowboys."

After Partington testified before Abourezk's subcommittee, he was transferred from Providence to Washington headquarters. Senator Abourezk had warned him that his candor might get him in trouble, but Partington had shrugged it off. "Director Bill Hall called me in after the hearing," Partington recalled later, "and told me: 'Partington, you're always coming down here to Washington complaining; it's time that you paid your dues. Let's see if you can do things better.' I went stir-crazy the first week in Washington because I was used to being on the street, not sitting shuffling papers. It was horrible."

Partington had been at his new desk job for only a few weeks when Safir took charge. "There was an immediate rivalry," Partington remembered. Deputies began identifying themselves as "Partingtonites" and "Safirites." One of Safir's first acts was to review the status of every witness in the program, and he discovered that several mobsters were still being paid monthly subsistence even though they were no longer testifying for the government and had been told months before that they needed to find legitimate jobs and begin supporting themselves. Safir ordered an end to their monthly checks. Several called Partington, who already had a reputation inside the Marshals Service for being too close to witnesses, and he confronted his new boss. "I have lived with many of these wiseguys," he declared. "I know everything about them, their wives, their kids, and these are good guys who have done a lot for this government. You can't just terminate them like this. It's disrespectful." Safir, who wasn't about to receive a lecture from Partington, was irked. *He* was running WITSEC, he declared, not Partington. While the mobsters were entitled to lifetime protection, which meant they could call at any time and ask for deputies to come and protect them, they'd never been promised a free ride on the government's back. Despite Partington's outburst, the mobsters were booted off the subsistence rolls.

"Safir saw these witnesses as old cases," Partington said later. "He was focusing on the dollars. I saw them as people. You know, I didn't spend Christmas and New Year's at my home with my family; I spent those holidays with wiseguys. I stayed up all night one New Year's Eve keeping a witness from killing himself because he was so depressed because now he saw himself as a rat. This had never been just a job to me. People said I had gotten too close to witnesses, and they were right. I cared about these wiseguys. They were my friends."

One afternoon Partington got a call from a WITSEC inspector who was bringing a gangster into town to testify before a congressional hearing. The mobster, who had been relocated by Partington a few years earlier, had specifically asked to have Partington at his side when he testified. The day after the hearing, newspapers printed photographs of the witness wearing a black hood over his face to conceal his identity as he testified. Sitting nearby was Partington, watching the crowd for trouble. Neither the inspector nor Partington had told Safir about the hearing. He was furious. He had the inspector transferred out of WITSEC operations, and he had Partington sent back to the Providence office. "I was told I would never handle another witness," Partington said later. "I was given a desk and I sat there and sat there and sat there with nothing to do. I had wiseguys from all over the country calling me. 'John, what's happening? We need you.' I told them I was being terminated from the program—just like they had been."

Partington called in several favors, and in 1979 President Jimmy Carter appointed him the U.S. marshal in Providence. He was now in charge of that office, but his career as a presidential appointee was short-lived. Although he had been assured by one of Rhode Island's U.S. senators that his job would be protected, he was replaced when Ronald Reagan was elected in 1980. After nineteen years in the Marshals Service, he was out. "I was determined not to be bitter, but I was hurt. I had given my life to my job, and I felt the way witnesses did when the government didn't need them anymore: thrown away like garbage." Partington went to work as a police officer in his hometown and then later became the public safety commissioner in Providence.

At headquarters, his departure barely caused a ripple. In less than a year, Safir had restructured and energized its WITSEC operations. The inspectors working there were loyal to him. Their focus was on the future, not Partington and past wiseguys. None of them had to wait long to cut their teeth. The highest-ranking Mafia witness ever to testify for the government was entering WITSEC. His name was Aladena Fratianno, better known as "Jimmy the Weasel," and the mob wanted him dead.

CHAPTER
THIRTEEN

THE STRIKE FORCE CHIEF asked Shur to personally fly to California to explain WITSEC to Aladena Fratianno. During the flight, he thought about what he would say. "Jimmy the Weasel was precisely the sort of mob witness I hoped we could get when we first created WITSEC," he recalled. "He knew it all. He'd been a made member more than thirty years, knew every crime boss in the country, and had the potential to be the most important witness we had ever recruited. But I had had enough experience to know I had to be tough; otherwise a wiseguy like Fratianno would eat me alive. The trick was making him understand that I was there to help him, that I had something he desperately needed, that he was going to be a dead man unless I saved him. Then I would have the upper hand in our talks, not him."

The sixty-three-year-old mobster looked like someone from central casting when Shur met him in a San Diego prison. With his dyed pompadour, cigar clenched in his teeth, and scrambled syntax punctuated by profanity and mob lingo, he could change in a heartbeat from a charming rogue into a stone-cold killer. Fratianno had contacted the FBI on his own several months earlier, in August 1977, after he had gotten into a tough predicament with the cops and the mob. He was being indicted for murder and was convinced that Los Angeles crime boss Dominic Brooklier had put a contract out on him. Brooklier had named Fratianno as his temporary replacement when he was sent to prison for a short stint, and Fratianno had used the opportunity to make several lucrative deals with other crime families back east for himself. That had made Brooklier suspect that Fratianno might attempt to take over the L.A. mob permanently. At least that was the reason why Fratianno believed Brooklier was trying to have him killed. Only later would he discover that the FBI had deliberately stirred up the mistrust between him and Brooklier, at one point making Fratianno believe he was being pursued by a Las Vegas hit man when, in fact, he was being followed by an FBI agent.

Fratianno knew all about mob hits. He was known in the media as the "Mafia's executioner on the West Coast" even though no one had ever been able to make a murder case against him stick. He'd later admit he had killed five mobsters with his own hands and helped murder six others. His specialty was the "Italian rope trick," which he used to silence fellow gangster Frank Niccoli one afternoon when the two of them were sipping beers in Fratianno's living room. After four men burst in and overpowered Niccoli, Fratianno looped a rope around his guest's neck and announced matter-of-factly, "Frankie, your time's up." He handed one end of the rope to one of his goons and began pulling on the other end, choking Niccoli to death.

Fratianno was currently negotiating a plea agreement with FBI agents and federal prosecutors, but he had not yet signed anything. Shur was being brought in to help persuade Fratianno that he should become a witness and enter WITSEC. While he was eager to cooperate, Shur was against using WITSEC as a reward program, and he didn't think Fratianno was entitled to any special favors.

"We will keep you alive and see to it that you do your sentence in a safe prison atmosphere," Shur told the mobster. Fratianno's attorney, Dennis McDonald, quickly interrupted. Why would Fratianno need to be sent to a federal prison? he asked. Since he was such an important witness, couldn't he be confined by WITSEC deputies in a hotel or on a military base?

"Mr. Fratianno is going to prison," Shur replied firmly. "That is not negotiable." Years later, he would recall why he had been so adamant. "I knew that each time Fratianno testified in court, some defense attorney was going to suggest he had gotten a sweetheart deal. So I took the exact opposite position that his attorney took: I felt it was crucial that Fratianno go to prison because he *was* so important. I wanted juries to know he was being punished."

Continuing, Shur told Fratianno that even after he was paroled, he wouldn't have an easy time in WITSEC. "We're not offering you a glamorous life and certainly nothing compared to what you're used to. The only thing we're guaranteeing is to keep you alive on our terms. That means we'll choose a place to relocate you, feed you, and cover your basic needs until you start making a living. That's it."

"Are you kidding?" Fratianno snapped. "You're going to stick me in some town I've never seen before, and then put me to work? At my age? With all that I'm going to give you guys? Fuck that!"

"I think you have to understand something," Shur said. "You're not giving *us* anything. You may be helping the U.S. attorneys and the FBI, but those are other parts of the Justice Department. I'm not here to cut any deals. I'm just telling you what's going to be. If you don't like what we're offering, well, I can walk out of here today without a second thought about you."

Shur's hard-line stance flustered Fratianno, and his attorney suggested they take a short break.

"I felt Fratianno really didn't have much of a choice but to say yes to our program," Shur said later, "because he was already too far committed to turn back. No one in the mob was going to believe that he hadn't talked to us. So I wasn't really too worried. I also wanted to keep the upper hand."

When the meeting reconvened, Fratianno explained that he had several girlfriends in California and didn't want to be relocated out of state. Shur said he'd have to cut off all ties with the women and leave the state. "Listen," said Shur, "you need to join the program for your own protection, but there is more at stake here. You need to testify because it is the right thing to do. You need to do it for your country and your family, to have something your grandkids can point to with pride."

Donald "Bud" McPherson, a deputy marshal from Los Angeles sitting across the table from Fratianno, fought back a grin. "Gerry Shur was a great con man when it came to dealing with witnesses," McPherson said later. "I had heard him sweet-talk people into WITSEC for years with his Kennedyesque 'ask not what the country can do for you' speech. But Jimmy the Weasel didn't give a shit about his country or anything else that Shur was trying to move him with. It was the first time I ever saw Shur fail in trying to con a con."

"Get out of my fucking life," Fratianno snapped. "The question is not what I am going to do for my country, it is what is the fucking country going to do for me?"

Shur and Fratianno continued at each other for nearly an hour. Fratianno would make a demand. Shur would reject it. When they took another break, Fratianno approached McPherson.

"Listen, this Shur character, now he's the big boss in Washington, right, but you're the guy who actually does the legwork," Fratianno said, "so maybe you can help me out here?" McPherson knew Fratianno was trying to hustle him, but he, too, refused to promise the gangster any special favors through WITSEC. Finally, Fratianno asked: "Where you from?"

"Brooklyn," McPherson replied. "I grew up with a lot of guys you probably know." He mentioned several gangsters from his old neighborhood.

"You're shitting me," Fratianno replied. "You knew them guys?"

"I used to play football with 'em," McPherson said, "and during the war, we stole ration stamps and sold them to neighborhood wiseguys."

Fratianno laughed. "Hey, I didn't know there were guys like you out here in California. I want you to be *my* guy in this program."

McPherson told him the Marshals Service didn't allow witnesses to choose who was going to protect them. "Sure they don't," Fratianno retorted sarcastically. "We'll see about that, okay? Just remember: You're gonna be my guy!"

Later that day, Fratianno agreed to enter WITSEC. Shur flew back to Washington. "I was exhausted. I hadn't really given Fratianno anything he had demanded, but we had spent the entire day going back and forth while he tried every possible angle." Shur still needed to tie up one loose end. He had to convince Fratianno's wife, Jean Bodul, to enter WITSEC. She had been the gangster's longtime mistress until four years before, when they had married, but theirs was such an explosive relationship that they rarely lived together. "I contacted Jean by phone, and when I explained the rules to her—about how she would have to be relocated and given a new identity—she told me she wasn't interested," Shur recalled. "She said she was going to begin driving south. She wasn't sure where she was going. I asked her to call me every day so we could be certain the mob hadn't killed her. For several weeks she called and told me every day where she was. And then finally she agreed to enter the program."

Back in L.A., McPherson got a phone call from WITSEC chief Howard Safir. "I want you to personally handle Fratianno," he announced. "I'm not putting you in charge of him just because he asked for you. I think you're the only guy who can handle him."

One of McPherson's first assignments was to sneak Fratianno into New York City so he could help federal prosecutors there decipher some twelve thousand wiretapped conversations between mobsters. Their bantering was confusing because they referred to each other by nicknames and frequently used unfamiliar mob terms or spoke in Italian. McPherson hid Fratianno in a mothballed World War II women's barracks at Fort Hamilton, an army base on the Brooklyn waterfront. It was only a short distance from where crime bosses Joseph Colombo and Frank "Funzi" Tieri lived. "Don't you know there are twenty-five hundred made guys in New York?" Fratianno asked the deputy. "We're sitting right in the center of their camp!" McPherson wasn't worried.

"I knew wiseguys," he said later, "and I knew they were not going to come onto a military installation and whack a guy. Terrorists might, but not wiseguys—at least not back in 1978."

When Safir sent word that he was flying up from Washington

to personally meet Fratianno, McPherson decided to run a scam of his own. He attached empty beer cans to wire coat hangers and then looped them over the doorknobs in the barracks so the cans rattled each time someone opened a door.

"What the hell is this?" Safir asked when he walked inside.

"That's our alarm system," McPherson replied. "We don't have any electronic anti-intrusion equipment, so we rigged up these beer cans."

Two days later McPherson received a crate filled with infrared alarm sensors, motion detectors, and video surveillance cameras. "I had been reaching a bit with the beer can stunt," McPherson remembered, "but we were desperate for equipment back in those days. We never got anything in WITSEC operations until Howard Safir became chief."

Fratianno spent his free time in the barracks cooking for McPherson and the other deputies assigned to protect him. They pooled the per diem the government paid them, and Fratianno sent McPherson to buy groceries. "I went to shops owned by mobsters and brought back cheeses and meats for Fratianno to eat. These mobsters didn't know it, but they were feeding the very guy who was going to destroy them."

Months later, when it finally came time for Fratianno to testify in a case for the first time, he stayed up all night, pacing, smoking cigars, and talking to McPherson. "All of his life, Jimmy had hated rats, and now he was going to walk into a courtroom and be one," McPherson remembered. "It was incredibly difficult for him, but I kept reminding him of how many times the mob had screwed him, and he would pause and then tell me about some other incident where he'd been screwed. That night, and for many more nights that followed, he talked to me about his past and the things he'd done, the people he'd known. He told me his life story so many times that later, when he began giving interviews to the media, the two of us used to joke that I could have traded places with him."

Fratianno had arrived in America from Italy in 1913, when he was only four months old. His parents settled in a tough section of

Cleveland called Little Italy. At age three, he saw three men murdered in his neighborhood by gangsters wielding machine guns. When he was six, he hit a policeman with a rotten tomato and then darted between people and cars to escape. An onlooker yelled, "Look at that weasel run!" The policeman noted in his report that the suspect was nicknamed "the Weasel," and it stuck. Fratianno became a waiter in a speakeasy at age twelve. By the time he was seventeen, he was robbing illegal gambling joints. He turned twenty-three in prison, where he was serving time for beating up a bookie. After he was paroled in the 1940s, he moved to Los Angeles, where he fell under the spell of John Roselli, who was Chicago crime boss Sam Giancana's man in Hollywood and Las Vegas. Had Roselli been given a choice, he probably would have been a movie producer. He made several Hollywood B movies, but none was memorable. Still, in Fratianno's eyes, Roselli epitomized the successful wiseguy. He had style, a code of honor, respect from gangsters and movie stars. It was Roselli who sponsored Fratianno in 1946 when, at the age of thirty-three, he became a made member of the Los Angeles crime family then being run by Jack Dragna.

During the next three decades, Fratianno established his reputation as a hit man and rose through the ranks. Casino skimming in Las Vegas; President John Kennedy's sexual trysts with Judith Campbell Exner, who also happened to be Chicago mobster Sam Giancana's mistress; the CIA's attempt in the 1960s to hire the Mafia to assassinate Cuban dictator Fidel Castro—Fratianno gossiped with other mobsters about hundreds of such mob schemes. But in the early 1970s, he started to become disillusioned with the mob after he was sent to prison on an extortion charge and a fellow wiseguy tried unsuccessfully to rape his first wife, Jewel Switzer. He became even more embittered in 1975, after John Roselli's body was discovered inside a fifty-five-gallon oil drum bobbing in Miami's Biscayne Bay. Roselli was seventy-one years old and had been living in retirement in Florida when he was choked to death. By the time his killers got his body on board a boat, rigor mortis had set in, so they had to cut the corpse in half to make it fit into the drum. They weighted it down with heavy chains, but it floated to the surface anyway. He had been murdered shortly after he testified before a U.S. Senate subcommittee investigating Operation Mongoose, the CIA's reputed covert attempt to kill Fidel Castro, but he hadn't really revealed anything new, and Fratianno felt the hit was unnecessary. His relationship with the mob continued to go downhill after that.

The pretrial jitters that had kept Fratianno awake all night before his first trial vanished as soon as he was seated in the witness chair. "Jimmy had an incredible memory," McPherson recalled. "He could remember times, dates, names, and details. He never finished high school, but I saw him outsmart dozens of brilliant defense attorneys. I remember one attorney shouted, 'Isn't it true you are a proven liar?' And Jimmy replied, 'Yes, I've lied all of my life and done a lot worse, but if I lie about your client, my deal with the government is off and I will be out on the street and I will be murdered. If I tell the truth, nothing can happen to me.' He would make defense attorneys regret they questioned his integrity. He had a way of talking to a jury and connecting with them."

As part of his plea agreement, Fratianno had to serve nineteen months in prison. He spent several weeks in the notorious Valachi Suite, but most of the time he was on the road with McPherson, living in motels while he was being interviewed by various prosecutors. The pairing of Fratianno and McPherson was a brilliant stroke. Rude, pushy, and often arrogant, Fratianno was considered "a royal pain in the ass" within the Marshals Service's WITSEC operations branch. He would strut back and forth filling the air with vulgarities, all the while threatening to drop out of WITSEC and disappear unless his demands were met. It was McPherson's job to calm him down. "I never forgot who Jimmy was," McPherson said. "I showed him respect, but I was firm. I told him what I could and couldn't do for him, and I never broke a promise. That was important. He respected that."

McPherson was forty-five years old and had been a deputy for six years when he was assigned to protect Fratianno. "I think the fact I had grown up in a tough Brooklyn neighborhood gave me an edge with Jimmy. Everyone was either Italian or Jewish back home. I was neither, so I had to get along with both to survive." McPherson had gone straight from high school into the army, where he served in Korea, and then returned home to become a New York City cop. But he hated the politics. "On my first day at work, I was told never to give anyone connected to Joe Profaci or Frank Tieri a hassle—not even a traffic ticket. I said, 'Are you kidding? What the fuck makes these mobsters so special?' But that was how it was. The higher-ups didn't want to bother the wiseguys."

McPherson switched to the city's fire department, got married and then divorced, and was injured on the job. He remarried and headed to Los Angeles to make a fresh start. Warner Brothers hired him to work as both a fireman and a policeman on movie sets, but he lost the job when the studio changed hands. He and his wife sold everything, bought a tractor-trailer rig, and spent two years delivering furniture for Global Van Lines, living in the truck cab and motels. One morning he read that the government was hiring "sky marshals" to prevent airplane skyjackings, so he applied and was hired. "I'd sit in first class flying from Los Angeles to Hawaii, where I kept a set of golf clubs in a locker. I'd play a few rounds and then return home to L.A. just in time to catch a flight to New York City, where I visited my parents." When the hijacking threat lessened, the government grounded the sky marshals and had them begin inspecting luggage. "I didn't want to spend my life looking through people's skivvies, so I became a deputy U.S. marshal." He finished first in his training class, something no deputy from Los Angeles had ever done. As a reward, he was put in charge of protecting witnesses—a job no one else in the office wanted. He'd been at work for only a few weeks in 1973 when he was told to meet a witness at the airport.

"Who is he?" McPherson asked.

"You'll recognize him when he lands."

Passenger "John West" turned out to be ex–White House counselor John Dean, who had just turned against President

Richard Nixon. The Watergate scandal was starting to unfold, and Dean was the only witness at the time who could tie the White House to the break-in at Democratic National Committee headquarters. "The U.S. marshal in Los Angeles had been appointed by Nixon and was loyal to him. He told me: 'I don't want to know anything about what you are doing with John Dean. Just handle it and keep me out of it.' I figured I was the fall guy. If something happened to Dean, my boss would say, 'Hey, McPherson finished first in his training class. Don't blame me, we put our best guy on it.' "

Events heated up quickly. In October 1973, Nixon ordered Attorney General Elliot Richardson and his deputy to fire Archibald Cox, the special prosecutor investigating the Watergate scandal. Rather than comply, both resigned. Nixon had Richardson's replacement, Robert Bork, fire Cox and ordered the FBI to seal off his office. The media called it the "Saturday Night Massacre." "The country was in turmoil, and everyone was afraid Dean was going to get whacked," McPherson said. "There were whispers that Nixon was going to send the CIA out to silence him. There were deputies who were afraid to help guard him." Dean and his wife, Maureen (Mo), hadn't wanted to use aliases or go undercover with new identities, so McPherson personally protected them. He and the couple flew to Nashville at one point so Dean could go over his Watergate testimony with federal prosecutors. "The Deans were getting cabin fever, so Dean asked if he and his wife, Mo, could take a break and visit the Grand Ole Opry," McPherson recalled. He hid them under floppy hats and sunglasses, but he couldn't conceal the fact that Mo was a shapely blonde. As they were walking through the Opryland amusement park, Dean became nervous. "Those guys are staring at me," he whispered to McPherson. Four men standing a few feet away were clearly gawking.

"Okay, let's go," McPherson replied, hustling them off.

"Those guys *were* staring," he recalled later, "but not at Dean. They were staring at Mo, who was wearing a tight sweater. I just didn't have the heart to tell him."

At another point, Dean happened to cross paths with Vinnie Teresa, who was in California and also being protected by McPherson. "You look a little wet behind the ears to be the president's lawyer," Teresa told Dean. "How'd you get there so young? Your old man put in the fix?"

"No," Dean replied. "I just kissed a lot of ass, Vinnie, a lot of it."

During the next five years, McPherson relocated more than three hundred witnesses. They were usually sent to him by John Partington. "John would snatch up these guys in New York and New England and protect them while they testified. Then he would send them out to me and I would find them a place to live and help them adjust. I ended up buying furniture out of my own pocket and keeping it in storage so when a family got here, I had something to loan them until their furniture was shipped out here. They knew I'd do things like that to help them. I became 'Uncle Bud' to their kids, the best man at their weddings."

If McPherson got into a pinch, he skipped over Marshals Service headquarters and spoke directly to Shur at the Criminal Division in the Justice Department. "My private line would ring," Shur recalled, "and Bud would say, 'This is a noncall,' meaning that he didn't want anyone to know he was calling me directly. He'd describe a witness problem that needed fixing, and I'd do what I could to resolve it. It was his way to get around red tape, and I came to trust him completely."

Relocating gangsters was difficult. "Italians are clannish," McPherson said. "Families are very important to them. Nearly every wife who was relocated was angry because her husband was responsible for taking her away from her family and the neighborhood where she had grown up. In Brooklyn, she had her mother, her sisters, her brothers, her friends, her priest, whom she could turn to for support and help. Out here, there was only me. I'd get a call at two A.M. from a hysterical wife saying her husband was chasing other women or beating up one of their kids. I'd drive over and take the wiseguy into another room, because you never wanted to belittle him in front of his family, where his ego would be on the line. I'd say, 'Listen, you're in the fucking program now, and there are rules. You aren't on the streets anymore. I'm running this show, and if you don't like it, get the fuck out of here. You'll be dead in twenty-four hours. You need this fucking program to stay alive, and I'm going to throw your ass out of it if you don't straighten up and play by the rules.' My lecture usually worked. What was difficult was when the wife and kids would get into a fight or the son would have a drug problem or get into trouble at school. I couldn't threaten to throw *them* out of the program."

McPherson generally relocated witnesses within a one-hour drive of his house in Los Angeles so he could reach them quickly if they called for help. He settled nearly a hundred witnesses in Orange County alone, and that soon proved to be a mistake. "We were flying witnesses back to New York to testify, and rather than keeping them separated in different hotels, we put them all in one place so it would be easier and cheaper to protect them," McPherson recalled. "We put them all on one floor of a New York hotel, and at night the witnesses would get together and talk." Several discovered they were living near each other in Orange County, so they exchanged telephone numbers and addresses. When they returned home, they got together and decided to muscle in on the local drug business. The police didn't have a clue what was happening in Orange County until October 1977, when an area drug dealer was shot to death as he was leaving a restaurant. All three shooters turned out to be relocated mob witnesses.

An outraged Orange County sheriff demanded that McPherson tell him the name of every WITSEC witness he had relocated in the county, but the deputy refused: "That would have been a breach of security." The sheriff complained to the Marshals Service headquarters, then to the Justice Department, and finally to the White House. But each time, his complaints were sent back down the line to McPherson to answer.

"The sheriff got his revenge, though," McPherson said. "He spotted me at a convention of California police officers and announced from the speaker's podium: 'There's Bud McPherson. He's the guy who relocated the Mafia to Orange County.' "

Under pressure from a local congressman, the Justice Department told McPherson not to relocate any more witnesses in Orange County for one year. But Hollywood took a lighter view of the escapade. It used it as the basis of the movie *My Blue Heaven,* starring comedian Steve Martin as Vinnie Antonelli, a New York wiseguy who is relocated in a San Diego suburb and soon finds the community crawling with other mob witnesses. "The movie was a comedy," McPherson said, "but it was more accurate than other movies and shows I've seen about relocated witnesses. Steve Martin was just like dozens of mob guys I knew. There's a scene where Martin, who has never mowed grass in his life, learns how. So he is out mowing the lawn one day in his silk suit and he calls to his neighbor, 'Hey, good day for a mow.' That's how these guys were. They didn't fit in."

Although McPherson was friendly with witnesses, he knew most would turn against him in an instant. "They were testifying against criminals who used to be their very best friends. If they'd turn on those guys, they'd damn well turn on you, especially if they had something to gain by doing it. I used to warn younger deputies to be careful when it came time to terminate a witness and stop giving him monthly subsistence checks. The really smart witnesses would call up your boss and say, 'Hey, you got to relocate me because the inspector guarding me is dirty.' Then they would bring up how you'd cut a corner or broken some law to help them. Your boss would have to relocate them, which meant they would get at least ninety more days of subsistence checks, which is what they wanted. Meanwhile, you'd be in trouble."

Sometimes deputies in the field would find themselves being drawn into a scam and wouldn't be able to do anything to stop it. "In the early 1970s, it wasn't uncommon for relocated witnesses to run up debts and then claim their lives were in danger and demand that we move them," McPherson said. "When the creditors came looking, you had to lie. You knew where the witness was, but you couldn't tell anyone. I had a witness order a freezer full of steaks the day before we were going to relocate him to Phoenix. He packed all the meat in ice chests and took it with him, leaving me to deal with an angry butcher."

Another example of the sort of sticky situations that

deputies faced was a 1977 incident when two relocated mobsters called McPherson in a panic from a Dallas, Texas, jail. "Believe me, as soon as a witness has any type of problem, you become his best friend," said McPherson. Eddie Greene and Salvatore Cardinelli had just been convicted of defrauding a bank out of a $9,000 loan and were about to be sentenced. They begged McPherson to intervene.

Greene, whose real name was Edmund Graifer, had been nabbed by the FBI in 1972 trying to fence $3.5 million in stolen Wall Street securities. He had entered WITSEC after testifying against a bigger fish involved in stock fraud—John "Johnny Dio" Dioguardi, the Mafia's so-called New York labor expert and the gangster behind the 1956 acid blinding of newspaper columnist Victor Riesel. Prosecutors had used Graifer's sidekick, Cardinelli, to corroborate his testimony, and Dioguardi had been given a fifteen-year prison sentence.

McPherson flew to Dallas, but Judge Sarah T. Hughes had already decided that Graifer and Cardinelli were bums living off monthly WITSEC checks. "Inspector McPherson," she declared, "I don't care what Graifer and Cardinelli did for the U.S. government. I wish I could give them twenty years." The maximum sentence was three years each, but Hughes added her own special twist. "I am specifically ordering you to take these men directly to the federal maximum-security penitentiary in Leavenworth, Kansas, not one of your cushy country-club prisons," she announced. "I want them delivered directly to Leavenworth today, where I can be sure they will do hard time."

McPherson began to protest, but the judge refused to listen to him. "We had put several New York wiseguys in Leavenworth," McPherson said later. "Graifer and Cardinelli weren't going to last twenty-four hours there without being stabbed. I had to do something." McPherson ducked outside the courthouse to a pay phone and called his boss, who in turn connected him to the federal Bureau of Prisons. Its director explained that federal judges could only recommend where they wanted a prisoner sent; they couldn't mandate it. The director gave McPherson verbal authorization to take Graifer and Cardinelli to a San Diego prison, where they would be safe. McPherson dashed back inside the courthouse to collect them. The three were then unceremoniously escorted by local deputies to the Dallas airport. "The U.S. marshal in Dallas was angry at me because I had put two criminals in his jurisdiction, so he told his deputies to make sure all of us got on the flight going directly to Kansas City, just as the judge had ordered." While the local deputies watched, McPherson bought three tickets and boarded the airplane with his two prisoners. But just before the jet pulled away from the terminal, he hustled Graifer and Cardinelli off the plane. Just as he had expected, the local deputies had left, so McPherson raced to a nearby ticket counter and bought three new tickets for a flight going to California. It already had started boarding, so he and his prisoners ran to the gate. Just then McPherson realized there was a hitch in his plan. He hadn't told the airline that he was transporting two prisoners, and the only way he could get them on the flight without a delay was by removing their handcuffs. "I am saving your fucking necks," he told both men, "so before I take off the cuffs, I want your word you won't try to escape." Both gave it and walked onto the plane. He delivered them to the San Diego prison without a problem. But when news reached Dallas, an enraged Judge Hughes cited him for contempt of court and issued an arrest warrant. "If you ever enter Texas, your ass is mine," the Dallas marshal told him. The judge didn't cool off for several months.

"Graifer turned out to be one of our success stories," McPherson said. After he was paroled, he got a job selling cars in the San Francisco Bay area, and when he died in 1999, he owned a dealership worth more than a million dollars. Cardinelli was relocated and is still alive.

The problems McPherson faced with other witnesses during his career were minor compared to the demands that Jimmy the Weasel made. After Fratianno was paroled in 1979 and given the alias Jimmy Marino, McPherson stashed him in Boise, Idaho, for safekeeping. "We still needed him to testify in dozens of cases," McPherson recalled. "I had to keep him safe and happy. Neither was easy." Fratianno was on the telephone complaining to McPherson less than twenty-four hours after he was relocated. "Someone in your program has sold me out!" he shouted. "I saw a hitter I knew outside this motel."

McPherson didn't believe him. "Why didn't he kill you?" he asked.

"It don't work that way," Fratianno replied. "We don't carry guns when we're looking for someone. You don't want to get caught with a gun. What they do is they go to a town with three, maybe four guys, and look for you. And when they know where you are at, they set it up with a getaway car. You don't just kill a guy when you see him. Now you get me out of here or I'm not testifying."

McPherson moved Fratianno and his wife, Jean, who by this point had asked to be reunited with him, into a house in Charlotte, North Carolina. "I don't want nobody to know where I am except you and Safir," Fratianno declared. Two months later, he got up one morning and told Jean that he was taking off on his own. "I'll arrange to see you every so often," he said.

"I think Jimmy just wanted to get away from Jean," McPherson recalled. "He always kept a girl or two on the side, and having the mob chasing him was a good excuse to leave home." McPherson found him in California and arranged to relocate him again, this time without Jean.

During the next five years, Fratianno testified in a series of sensational Mafia trials. In Kansas City, he was the key witness in what then was the largest mob case ever undertaken. Fifteen defendants, a virtual who's who of the midwestern mob, were convicted of paying kickbacks in return for $67 million in Teamsters union pension fund loans used to build Las Vegas casinos. In New York City, newly appointed U.S. attorney Rudolph Giuliani used Fratianno in five major Mafia cases that were going on simultaneously. Overall, Fratianno helped convict six crime bosses during the early 1980s and sent scores of lesser-known mobsters to prison. In the process, he became a nationally recognized celebrity. His photograph appeared on the cover of a half-dozen national newsmagazines. He was interviewed by every major television network news show, and his exploits were recounted in two best-selling memoir-confessionals: *The Last Mafioso*, by Ovid Demaris, and *Vengeance Is Mine*, by Michael J. Zuckerman. With typical Fratianno bravado, he would later claim that he had never bothered to read either book, but that didn't stop him from suing the first author for allegedly misquoting him, and later quarreling with his second biographer.

McPherson's career rose along with Fratianno's notoriety. Other WITSEC inspectors began modeling themselves after him, adopting his quiet, self-confident style and copying what became known as the "McPherson look." Unlike other deputy marshals, who wore off-the-rack suits and favored cowboy boots, McPherson dressed in tailored clothes as expensive as those worn by wiseguys. But it was his sunglasses that became his trademark. Regardless of the hour, season, or whether he was inside or outside a courtroom, McPherson hid his eyes behind sunglasses. "You never could tell what the guy was thinking," one mobster later commented, "because of those damn sunglasses." They became an inside joke: How can you tell which deputies are WITSEC inspectors? Answer: They're the ones who wear sunglasses when they fuck their wives.

One reason Jimmy the Weasel was in high demand was because the Justice Department had begun using the RICO Act to go after mobsters. Although it had become law in 1970, juries had failed initially to convict mobsters under it and federal appeals courts had disagreed in their interpretations of it. But in 1981 the Supreme Court gave prosecutors wide authority under RICO, and overnight it became the most popular charge filed in LCN cases. There was good reason for its use. The Mafia operated much like a hydra, the mythical marsh serpent with nine heads. If one of its heads was cut off, two grew back in its place. A Mafia soldier and capo might be successfully prosecuted now and then, and sent to prison, but the beast survived and other soldiers and capos quickly filled the void. Because crime bosses hid behind legions of wiseguys, it was nearly impossible to kill the brain and heart of the monster. RICO gave prosecutors the weapon they needed. For the first time, being a leader or a participant in a criminal syndicate was itself a crime, a serious one with a serious punishment. If a U.S. attorney could prove a criminal "enterprise" existed, then every known member from the crime boss on down to the soldier could be convicted, regardless of whether or not they had dirtied their hands by breaking a kneecap or committing a murder. Under RICO, the government could also seize illicitly obtained wealth, which meant it could confiscate mob-run businesses. "Sometimes," said McPherson, "Fratianno would be only asked one question by a prosecutor at a RICO trial: 'Was the defendant a made member in the mob?' That's all the government put him on the witness stand to say."

As expected, defense attorneys accused Fratianno of being a "mouth for hire," willing to smear any defendant so he could continue hiding in WITSEC and pocketing rewards. "The truth is, we were buying his testimony to some degree," said McPherson. "I know the Justice Department will deny it, but it was what we did. But how else would we ever get inside the LCN?"

Despite the strict guidelines and policies that Safir implemented after he became WITSEC chief in 1978, Fratianno proved that all witnesses may be equal, but some were more equal than others. To this day, he remains the one who wrung more special favors out of the Marshals Service than any other known WITSEC witness. It paid all of his telephone bills for several years, sent monthly subsistence checks to his mother-in-law, and paid for a facelift, capped teeth, and even breast implants for Jean. "He was an expert at manipulating the system," said McPherson. "I saw Fratianno turn U.S. marshals against one another, turn the Marshals Service against the Justice Department, turn the Justice Department against U.S. attorneys, turn FBI agents against prosecutors. He nearly always got what he wanted, and he made more money milking WITSEC than he ever did committing crimes."

Over the years, Shur received dozens of calls from Fratianno asking for money. "He'd ask for things I often felt were unreasonable," he recalled. "You've got to keep in mind, he had been a crime boss, and now he was dependent on the government for assistance," said Shur. "I believe that in his own mind, he felt he was no longer a free man and wanted to be compensated for his loss of freedom. It also was a game to him. He needed to believe that he was getting away with a scam, forcing us to cross a line."

Fratianno was so prickly to deal with that Safir assigned Marilyn Mode, his special assistant at the Marshals Service's WITSEC operations headquarters, to personally handle Fratianno's demands. She and McPherson, who continued to deal with Fratianno in the field, worked as a tag team. "I used to refer to Fratianno's calls as 'Jimmy's daily screams,' " Mode recalled. The fact that Safir had put a "broad" in charge of him irked the mobster, but the choice proved to be a smart move. Because of Fratianno's macho attitude, he hated looking weak or dependent in front of Mode, and she was able to rein in his hysterics.

McPherson saw Fratianno break down emotionally only once. The gangster's first wife, Jewel Switzer, was dying of cancer in 1980, and Fratianno begged McPherson to let him visit her. Fratianno had first met Jewel when she was eighteen years old and working in Las Vegas as a hat check girl. They married a few weeks later, but he had been put in prison shortly after the ceremony, and her parents had forced her to divorce him even though she was pregnant with their baby. Seven years later, when Fratianno was released, he and Jewel were remarried. They had stayed together for sixteen years, until she wearied of his womanizing and divorced him. McPherson was convinced that Jewel was the only woman Fratianno had ever truly loved. But the timing of her illness couldn't have been worse. He was about to testify in another big case. NBC News, *60 Minutes,* and *20/20* had all scheduled posttrial interviews with him. *Newsweek* had paid him $2,500 for an exclusive interview, and his first book was about to be published. "The mob really wanted him dead," McPherson said. "We knew of several hit men trying to find him, and when I asked Safir about letting Fratianno see her, he said, 'No way!' We couldn't afford to have any slipups and end up with him being killed."

"You can't go see Jewel," McPherson told Fratianno. "Safir refuses to approve it."

"Fuck Safir," Fratianno erupted. "Fuck this program. Fuck

this whole deal. Bud, my wife is dying. She's not going to make it. My daughter is hysterical. I haven't seen my grandkids in years." Fratianno became teary-eyed. "I really have to go. You got to let me go!"

McPherson noticed that Fratianno had referred to Jewel as his "wife" even though they were divorced and he was now married to Jean. The next morning, McPherson arranged for an armored car to drive Fratianno to a private airfield, where an airplane took Fratianno to the city where Jewel was hospitalized. Another armored car drove him there. They were together about an hour, during which McPherson nervously paced the hallways. Four days later, she died. McPherson had risked his job to help Fratianno. He had not told Safir about the secret visit, but Fratianno never said a word of thanks.

"When Fratianno's role as a witness began to come to an end," Shur recalled, "I let it be known that I expected him to be terminated from subsistence. He didn't take the news well." McPherson had tried to prepare him, but the mobster didn't believe the government would ever stop giving him money for his rent and food. "None of the really major witnesses ever believed we'd let them go," said McPherson. "They thought they were so important they'd get checks forever. I'd seen the same thing happen with Vinnie Teresa. I used to whisper in his ear all the time: 'Vinnie, when you get off that witness stand and the government doesn't need you anymore, you aren't going to have as many friends as you do now.' I told him we had to begin thinking about his future, but he was just like Jimmy. They all think they are indispensable."

Fratianno had been in WITSEC for five years when Shur and Safir first tried to ease him out. Fratianno reacted by flying with his attorney to Washington, D.C., and going over both men's heads by appealing directly to Stephen Trott, an assistant attorney general.

"We're not treating you any differently from any other witness," Shur told Fratianno during a hastily called meeting.

"Well, you should treat me different," he replied, "because I am not like ninety-eight percent of the bums in your program. I'm too old to get a job, and I don't want to go on welfare."

Shur tried to point out that WITSEC subsistence was akin to a welfare program, but the gangster didn't buy it. "I have given you plenty for my help," he declared. "You owe me!" By the time the meeting ended, Trott decided that Fratianno would be kept on subsistence for two more years. In effect, Fratianno had negotiated himself a yearly salary of $33,477 tax-free, plus a lump-sum payment of $11,300 to help pay a wide range of his personal expenses, including his auto insurance, real estate taxes, and the cost of gasoline for his car. The Justice Department also agreed to resettle him anywhere inside the United States as long as the Marshals Service and Shur felt it safe. Fratianno chose a hillside outside the tiny Montana town of Bellingham. He built a $190,000 house there, with a 55-by-20-foot grand hall. Every room had a color TV hooked to a satellite dish because Fratianno loved to watch professional football games. There was a huge crystal chandelier in the grand hall and original artwork. He got the government to pay the $400 sewer connection. Fratianno asked McPherson to move Jean to Montana from Brunswick, Georgia, where she had been in hiding. Fratianno was now seventy-three and beginning to show early signs of Alzheimer's disease. It finally looked as if he was settling down. But McPherson knew better. "Jimmy was going to be hustling until the day he dropped dead."

Sure enough, Fratianno was back in the news in a matter of weeks. Without telling WITSEC, he had given an exclusive interview to Thames Television in Britain in exchange for a hefty cash payment and a promise that the show would never be broadcast in the United States. He didn't think anyone would find out, but the Thames network sold the show to a Canadian network, and on Thanksgiving Day in 1985 Fratianno got top billing on a segment called "Murder Inc." Many of Fratianno's Montana neighbors watched Canadian channels because they lived close to the border, and his alias was blown. A furious Safir sent McPherson to haul Fratianno into Washington for a dressing-down.

"We're going to have to move you again, Jimmy," Safir

snapped. "Only this time, we're cutting back your subsistence be-cause you violated the rules."

"You can't do that!" Fratianno yelled. "I won't be able to make my house payments." Fratianno demanded to see Trott again, but his secretary told the gangster that Safir was now call-ing the shots. For two weeks, Fratianno holed up in a hotel, calling FBI agents and federal prosecutors for support, but it didn't do any good. He returned to Montana depressed, and on December 31, 1985, Safir sent McPherson to tell him that the checks were fi-nally coming to an end. McPherson assured him that he would be okay financially. He was being paid book royalties and had in-vested wisely.

Jean left him a week later. She had quietly contacted Safir and arranged to be relocated. Fratianno had no clue she was leav-ing nor where she had gone. Now alone, he called McPherson. "This ain't over, Bud. Trust me, I'm just starting to fight." During the next few weeks, he waged a one-man telephone campaign to get back onto WITSEC's subsistence rolls, and he finally won. Shur and Safir were told to take him back for two more years after Fratianno persuaded an assistant U.S. attorney in New York to add his name to the list of witnesses scheduled to testify against Carmine "the Snake" Persico, who by then had become the boss of the Colombo crime family.

Safir ordered McPherson to relocate Fratianno in a place where no one would know him, so McPherson chose the U.S. Vir-gin Islands. Fratianno lasted there only one month. He com-plained there was nothing to watch on television because the island had only one channel. McPherson resettled him in Corpus Christi, Texas. As before, when Fratianno's two-year extension was near an end, McPherson was sent to cut him loose.

"Jimmy, you've had ten years in the program, more than any-one else," McPherson said. "It's been a good long ride, but it is over." Fratianno called a reporter at the *Los Angeles Times* to complain. "The government threw me out on the street," he said. "I put thirty guys away, six of them bosses, and now the whole world's looking for me. They just get finished using you and they throw you out on the street." A Justice Department spokesman re-sponded that Fratianno had received nearly a million dollars in support payments during his ten years as a witness.

"It was sad, but it was over for him," McPherson said. Three years later, McPherson retired, and two years after that, in 1993, Fratianno died alone in his sleep inside his Montana house. The government had told reporters Fratianno had sold the house, but he hadn't. He had been living there almost as a hermit.

"When Fratianno's first book, *The Last Mafioso*, came out, he sent me a copy as a gift," Shur recalled. "To make sure he knew where I stood, I sent him a money order for the fifteen-dollar price of the book. It may seem like a small thing, but I didn't want to be indebted to him, even for fifteen bucks. You had to understand that when you dealt with someone like Jimmy, there were no idle conversations, no real gifts, no free favors, and that was true up to the moment he died. A racketeer said to me once, 'Shur, I don't al-ways like what you say, but I know what you say is so.' When you dealt with a witness like Jimmy, you had to understand that it was your reputation for integrity that made him respect you, even though he was trying to corrupt you every step of the way."

CHAPTER
FOURTEEN

ROUND THE SAME TIME that Jimmy the Weasel first began to cooperate with FBI agents, a vicious murder inside a federal penitentiary prompted Shur to expand the WITSEC program in a new direction. The change was set into motion one afternoon in 1978, when a bus carrying William Zambito and twenty-one other prisoners arrived at the maximum-security penitentiary in Atlanta, Georgia. Zambito was a state prisoner who had provided information to Miami prosecutors about Florida drug dealers. In exchange, his own prison sentence for drug peddling had been shortened. Although he was not a federal prisoner, the federal Bureau of Prisons (BOP) had agreed to hide him in one of its facilities because inmates in state prisons in Florida were threatening to kill him. He was en route to a federal facility in the southwest when the bus stopped for the night.

As he was being led into the prison wearing leg irons and handcuffs attached to a belly chain, Zambito briefly considered asking to be put in the "hole," the nickname inmates used for isolation cells. He would be safe there overnight and sent on his way in the morning. But he was worried that other prisoners riding on the bus with him would notice he had been afraid to stay in a regular cell block and correctly surmise that he was a snitch. That wasn't a label Zambito wanted following him to his final destination, so he kept quiet and trudged along with the others into an area called A&O, shorthand for Admissions and Orientation, where prisoners in transit were housed with other newly arrived inmates not yet assigned permanent cells. Zambito had reason to be worried. Allen "Big Al" Benton, one of the drug dealers whom he had helped convict, was also in the Atlanta prison.

Zambito was taken to a six-man cell, which was kept unlocked so inmates inside it could move freely around the tier. He had two cellmates: a Hispanic inmate, who didn't speak much English, and Marion Albert Pruett, a bank robber who had arrived a few days earlier, having been sent to Atlanta because he needed surgery on his left leg that could only be done there. Pruett would later tell investigators that Zambito had been jittery from the moment he entered the cell. "He said to me, 'Hey, what's the hole like?' which I thought was an odd question," Pruett recalled. "And I said, 'What's the problem?' and he says, 'I just don't like it here on this compound.' That's when I knew something was going on."

Pruett would later testify that he had been sleeping in his bunk when he was awakened by a noise shortly after 4 A.M. "I had my eyes closed," he said, "but I could see what was coming down." What he saw, he said, was Big Al Benton slashing a knife across Zambito's throat and repeatedly stabbing him. Afraid Benton might kill him, too, Pruett said, he pretended to be asleep.

When Miami prosecutors heard that Zambito had been murdered, they accused prison officials of being both incompetent and stupid. But an internal investigation by BOP director Norman Carlson showed his officers were not to blame. "The warden in Atlanta had not been told anything about Zambito, and there was nothing on his case jacket that identified him as a government informer or witness," Carlson said. "The prosecutors had simply assumed we would know who Zambito was and would take precautions to protect him. It was a total lack of communication." A jury convicted Benton, and Pruett, who was the star witness against him, was hustled off to a different prison under an alias.

The Zambito killing was not the first time the BOP had run into problems because of prison inmates who needed special handling because they were government informants and witnesses. "For years," BOP director Carlson later explained, "I had been getting calls, mostly from FBI special agents but sometimes from FBI headquarters or from U.S. attorneys all across the country, asking me to do favors for their witnesses. They felt these witnesses had really helped them and deserved special privileges. Unfortunately, they would often make unrealistic promises to them and then expect us to carry them out. One prosecutor told me, 'By the way, I told this witness he could have a conjugal visit with his wife now and then. You don't mind, do you?' Conjugal visits were totally against our policy, and I was stuck being the bad guy because I'd be the one who had to tell these witnesses we were not going to follow through." Carlson decided something had to be done, so he contacted Shur.

Looking back later, Shur would note that a natural evolution had occurred. Before WITSEC, there weren't many government witnesses, and when the program began in 1970, federal prosecutors had been so eager to recruit mobsters that many of them were granted full immunity and didn't have to spend a day in prison. But as more and more LCN members agreed to testify, prosecutors and judges became more selective about who was let off without being punished, and by 1974, almost every criminal who entered WITSEC had to serve some time in prison before he was paroled and relocated. This created a new problem: where to house them. The Marshals Service initially let LCN witnesses do their time in safe houses. It also tried military brigs and county jails. But none of these facilities proved to be suitable. Safe houses weren't designed to hold prisoners for long periods, mobsters objected to the rigid regimen of military prisons, and witnesses didn't feel secure in county jails.

Working together, Shur and BOP director Carlson came up with a solution. They decided to build a special prison exclusively for government witnesses. Carlson already had a location in mind. He had his architects reconfigure the third floor of the high-rise Metropolitan Corrections Center the BOP was constructing in New York City, and when the prison opened in mid-1978, Shur moved twenty-one government witnesses into the new WITSEC prison unit.

Not everyone liked Shur and Carlson's "prison within a prison."

Prosecutors in New Jersey and New York were afraid that putting witnesses in the same prison as the mobsters who wanted to kill them was foolhardy. But Shur felt confident. "I considered Norman Carlson one of the best administrators in the federal government. He was not going to let a witness be poisoned, stabbed, or harmed."

Carlson used strict security guidelines to keep the third-floor unit separate from the rest of the prison. It had its own secure entrance, and every witness in the unit was given an alias to prevent other inmates in the prison from knowing who was being housed there. The only prison official who was told the inmate's actual name was the warden. Each witness was assigned a one-man cell, and if he wished, he could ask for his cell door to be locked when other witnesses were free to watch television or play pool in the unit's common area. Before any visitors were permitted to enter the unit, they were required to stand in front of a two-way mirror so the WITSEC witness they were coming to see could verify that the visitor was actually who he said he was. To prevent witnesses from being poisoned, a BOP lieutenant selected trays of food at random from the prison's mess hall and locked them inside a cart that was then taken into the WITSEC unit.

Carlson required every witness to pass an FBI-administered lie detector test before he was allowed to be housed in the WITSEC unit. Carlson wasn't trying to discover whether or not he had testified truthfully in court. He wanted to be certain no one was trying to sneak himself into the unit to kill another witness. And even after a witness passed the test, he wasn't automatically admitted into the unit. First, a photograph of him was distributed to everyone already housed there so they could tell correctional officers if they were afraid of the prospective new arrival. "In some Mafia cases," Shur explained, "we would get a low-ranking guy to testify against his gangster boss. Then that gangster would testify against someone higher up in the organization, and up the chain we would go. This meant there were a lot of WITSEC witnesses who had grudges against each other and couldn't be housed together."

In most of the BOP prisons, Carlson tried to keep rival prison gangs and various hate groups separated from each other to prevent trouble, but that wasn't possible inside the tiny WITSEC unit. "We had Ku Klux Klan members living in cells next to Black Panthers, the Aryan Brotherhood—with swastikas on their arms—sitting with Jews at the dinner table. All these groups who normally would not associate with each other were housed together in our unit," Shur explained. "It worked because there was a common threat that kept them in line. They knew they'd be kicked out of the unit if they caused problems, and no one wanted to be sent into the main prison population because he'd have to check himself into an isolation cell to keep from being murdered."

When it first opened, the WITSEC unit was a spartan affair. It had one communal television set, a pool table, table tennis equipment, some exercise equipment, and a small visiting room. At night, prisoners were taken up to the roof for fresh air and to exercise. Carlson assigned his most senior correctional officers to work there. "I needed strong, experienced officers because these inmates were sophisticated and conniving," he recalled. He also wanted his staff to know that the WITSEC unit was a top priority.

The Manhattan unit was so successful that within months Shur and Carlson had opened two more in federal prisons in San Diego and Chicago. Two years later, a fourth unit opened in Otisville, New York. Together, these four housed a total of four hundred WITSEC witnesses, some serving sentences as long as life. "I felt bad for many of our WITSEC prisoners because they had helped the government," said Shur, "and we were imprisoning them under harsher conditions than the criminals whom they had testified against. We didn't have jobs in the WITSEC units that our witnesses could do to earn money. There was no vocational training, no recreation areas. Boredom was a real problem, and that concerned me because I knew that a bored, idle prisoner could be a dangerous person."

Carlson tried to make life easier by having small color television sets installed in each cell, but, he recalled, "that was about all I could do." Because there were only four units nationwide, relatives often had to travel across the country to visit, and when they arrived, correctional officers had to sneak them inside at odd hours to prevent other prison visitors and inmates in the main prison from seeing them. "We didn't want anyone to discover who we had hidden in the unit based on the visitors coming to see them," Shur explained. Arranging visits was such a nightmare that Shur arranged for witnesses to call home on government lines without charge once each week so they could keep in touch with their families.

Not every WITSEC witness was sent to one of the units. "If we thought it was safe," Shur said, "we would hide witnesses in state prisons under an alias. It gave them a chance to take advantage of educational and vocational classes and live a more normal prison life." But some witnesses were afraid to be housed anywhere except inside the units.

Shur now had to deal with two separate agencies: the BOP and Howard Safir's WITSEC operations office at the Marshals Service. The BOP was responsible for keeping the witnesses safe while they did their time. As soon as they were paroled, the Marshals Service took over protecting them.

While the BOP ran the WITSEC units, Shur had the final say over who was housed in them. He visited each unit at least twice a year to hold "town meetings." He always began by asking: "How are things going?" After listening to the witnesses' complaints as a group, he met individually with anyone who wanted to speak to him in private. "A few inmates in the WITSEC unit tried to run cons on me," said Shur, "and they were the most interesting to deal with because they'd lie, scheme, and try to manipulate me."

At one town meeting, WITSEC inmates demanded that Shur complain to the BOP's Carlson and get a correctional officer transferred out of the WITSEC unit because no one there liked him. But when Shur met separately with several inmates, they admitted the group meeting had been staged. One of the witnesses in the unit had a grudge against the officer and was trying to get him transferred. Everyone else had simply been going along. In a unit that housed only informants, Shur found it easy to keep track of what was happening. For instance, one afternoon a witness called

Shur with a disturbing tip. He said a female BOP caseworker was periodically engaging in sex with a witness in the unit. Shur was skeptical, even when he went into the unit and confronted the witness who reportedly had seduced the woman.

"Yes, I've had sex with her," he admitted. "Who told you?"

Shur, who knew the woman personally, decided to see if he could catch the witness in a lie.

"If you had sex with her, I assume you have seen her nude," Shur said.

"Yep," the witness replied, grinning.

"Then you must have noticed the scar she has on her left leg?" he continued.

"Ah, no," the witness said after a few awkward moments. "I don't remember a scar."

"Well, you had to have noticed that she had a breast removed because of cancer?"

"She did?" the witness asked, seeming genuinely confused. "No, I guess it's possible I missed that. We did it real quick and I didn't always look at her breasts, but I thought for sure she had both of them."

Shur had made up the scar and cancer stories, hoping to trick the witness into confirming them.

"When was the last time you had sex with her?" he asked.

"The twenty-fifth of the month."

At that moment, Shur was called away to answer an emergency phone call. He took it in a tiny office. As he was talking on the phone, he glanced down and noticed that someone had drawn a heart in red ink on the desk calendar. It was on the twenty-fifth. "Whose office is this?" Shur asked a correctional officer. "It's our caseworker's," he replied.

"I had been absolutely convinced the witness had been lying to me," Shur said later, "but seeing that heart had made me suspicious enough to confront the woman, and she admitted having sex with him. She had to resign." The incident reminded Shur of how treacherous witnesses could be. "I warned my staff constantly never to meet alone with a witness in a WITSEC unit, no matter how much they liked them or thought they were a friend," said Shur. "You didn't want to put yourself in a position where it was your word against theirs."

Whenever Shur found himself wondering if a witness was lying, he'd look for corroborating evidence and motive. "That was what prosecutors were supposed to do when they dealt with these guys, too. I'd ask myself, 'Okay, what's this guy's motivation? What's he trying to get out of me?' Then I'd look for other evidence. If everything else failed, I'd go with my gut, but that was extremely risky."

As the years passed, Shur watched some witnesses grow old. "Time was frozen for them. They were stuck in the same WITSEC unit year after year, and a lot of them, especially witnesses in the Mafia, were filled with self-loathing because they had testified against their former friends. I had one witness who tried to kill himself by eating a hundred paper clips."

Shur met with another witness after he had tried to commit suicide because he had tested positive for HIV, the virus that causes AIDS. "I violated my own rule and saw him alone," Shur recalled. "He was angry and upset and desperate. He was not only afraid of dying from AIDS, he was terrified other inmates in the unit would think he was homosexual." Shur tried to reassure him, but he got nowhere.

"What the hell do you know?" the inmate snapped. "I could die tomorrow! You don't know what it feels like—not knowing if you are going to wake up in the morning!"

"Can you read?" Shur asked.

As the inmate glared, Shur lifted his wrist, revealing the Medic Alert bracelet that identified him as suffering from multiple sclerosis. "I know what it's like to live with that same uncertainty," Shur explained, "so if you want to talk about it, we'll talk. If you want to pray about it, we'll pray. But if you want to feel sorry for yourself and feel pity for yourself, we are both wasting what time we have left here."

Shur made certain word spread through the unit that the witness had contracted AIDS from a contaminated needle. Later, Shur had mixed feelings about their confrontation. "Here was a man responsible for killing innocent people. Society considered him to be evil, but I was there trying to keep him from killing himself, telling him that his life was worth saving. I discovered my feelings about these witnesses were complicated. As I got to know many of them, things were less black and white. I remember an arsonist whom I got to know well. This man always made certain the buildings he was going to torch were uninhabited, but he made a mistake one day and a pregnant woman was burned to death. He couldn't talk about his crime without breaking down in tears— not tears to arouse pity, but tears of real remorse. He was truly haunted by what he had done. I saw that as a sign that there was a spark of redemption in him."

Other witnesses were not as easy to stomach. When a warden told Shur that a WITSEC inmate had been caught using a pay phone to make sexually explicit calls to children while he masturbated, Shur told the warden to immediately kick him out of the unit.

"I can't do that," the warden replied. BOP rules required that he hold a disciplinary hearing first before punishing an inmate, he explained.

"Maybe the BOP has to hold a disciplinary hearing," Shur replied, "but I don't have to hold a hearing to remove someone from the WITSEC program. If I say he's out of WITSEC, he's out. And if he's out of WITSEC, then he can't live in the WITSEC unit." Within the hour, the witness had been put into solitary confinement and transferred. "I wanted him out of the unit so other witnesses there would know that conduct like his was totally unacceptable," said Shur.

Shur eventually developed his own philosophy about witnesses in the units. "I decided the world is not made up of good people and bad people. Rather, I chose to believe it is made up of people who are not by definition either good or bad, but simply people, some of whom do good things and some of whom do bad things, and most of whom do some of each. I encountered men who had done horrible and unspeakable crimes, yet I saw them

Gerald Shur, now retired, sitting on the patio rail facing his backyard.
(Photograph by Dudley Reed)

A SHUR FAMILY ALBUM

A beaming young Gerry Shur in a policeman's outfit—his first appearance in law enforcement.

1949

Ready to audition for the Ted Mack Amateur Hour in 1949: drummer Shur with his boyhood friends, Edward Schwarzer (left) and Bernard Breslin (right). They didn't make it.

Miriam and Gerald Shur a few weeks before their secret elopement in 1952. Both were underage, but four months later their parents consented to their marriage.

The Marshals Service was ordered by President Kennedy to protect black students in the South enrolling in previously all-white schools.
(U.S. Marshals Service photo)

WITSEC inspectors protecting a hooded witness. This is a training exercise, so the witness is also a deputy marshal.
(U.S. Marshals Service photo)

A witness testifies before Congress behind a screen while WITSEC inspectors stand watch.
(U.S. Marshals Service photo)

Former mob hitman Joseph "The Animal" Barboza testifying against the New England mob at a congressional committee hearing. A marshal sits on each side, and two more are facing the audience. *(U.S. Marshals Service photo)*

Marshal John Partington takes New England crime boss Raymond Patriarca to jail after Barboza's testimony led to his conviction. *(Courtesy of John Partington)*

An armed John Partington (right) and another marshal dashing off a helicopter with an unidentified witness hiding his face. *(U.S. Marshals Service photo)*

Reis R. Kash, a deputy U.S. Marshal who became the first chief of WITSEC.
(Courtesy of Reis Kash)

Former FBI agent William Hall, who inherited a troubled WITSEC program when he became director of the U.S. Marshals Service and brought in Howard Safir from the DEA to turn it around.

(Courtesy of Gerald Shur)

Howard Safir, who as chief of WITSEC shaped it into the best witness protection operation in the world.   (Courtesy of Eugene Coon)

WITSEC chief Eugene Coon, who built on Safir's changes to further improve its operation.
(U.S. Marshals Service photo)

A hooded witness testifying before a Senate Foreign Relations subcommittee investigating Panamanian ruler Manuel Noriega.
(AP Worldwide Photos)

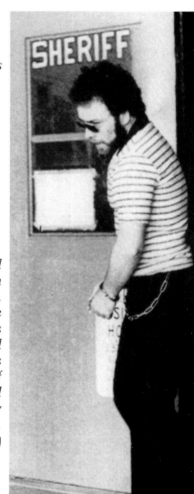

James Cardinali, who testified against John Gotti, charged that he was an easy target for organized crime after getting dumped by WITSEC. He was relocated soon after he appeared wearing this placard in public.
(AP Worldwide Photos)

Former protected witness Marion "Mad Dog" Pruett, who killed his wife and four others during a lethal rampage, and was convicted of murder and eventually executed.
(AP Worldwide Photos)

Joseph Valachi, the first Mafia member to break the code of omertà, testifying before Senator McClellan's Permanent Investigations Subcommittee in 1963.
(AP Worldwide Photos)

Vincent "Fat Vinnie" Teresa, one of WITSEC's first bigtime mobster witnesses, was given numerous chances to reform but couldn't stay straight.
(AP/Worldwide Photos)

Protected witness Sammy "The Bull" Gravano, whose testimony put crime boss John Gotti in jail, didn't stay out of trouble for long. In May 2001 he pleaded guilty to running a drug ring.
(AP Worldwide Photos)

Attorney General Janet Reno and Assistant Attorney General Jo Ann Harris present Gerald Shur with the Attorney General's Mary C. Lawton Lifetime Achievement Award for his 33-year career with the Criminal Division of the Justice Department.
(Courtesy of Gerald Shur)

perform extraordinarily decent acts in prison. I used to give speeches to various groups and I would say, 'To concede that there is a group of "bad" people by definition would be an admission that there is no hope for any of them. That means any effort I put forth to help them is going to be futile, and I refuse to believe that.' " The BOP's Carlson began referring to Shur as the Criminal Division's "social worker."

In 1979, the Justice Department reorganized its Criminal Division, and Shur was named senior associate director of a new section, called the Office of Enforcement Operations (OEO). It was being formed to oversee the department's use of "sophisticated investigative tools," a bureaucratic catchall term that covered such things as the WITSEC program, requests for federal wiretaps, and secret operations that the FBI, DEA, and other agencies occasionally ran. Philip Wilens, another former Organized Crime and Racketeering Section attorney and close friend of Shur's—they had eaten lunch together at work almost daily since 1961—took over supervision of federal wiretaps, leaving WITSEC and whatever other matters arose for Shur to oversee. One afternoon the BOP's Carlson called Shur with a request that seemed to fit his new responsibilities. Carlson explained that federal statutes gave him the authority as BOP director to grant prisoners a furlough from prison for up to thirty days. Historically, furloughs had been given to prisoners so they could attend family funerals. The prisoners weren't turned loose. They were escorted to the memorial service by armed guards. Carlson was calling because federal prosecutors and various FBI and DEA agents had begun asking him to grant furloughs to inmates so they could be used in undercover sting operations. Carlson didn't know the U.S. attorneys or the federal agents as well as Shur did, so he asked if he would review their requests and decide which ones were worth pursuing. "Here's how it worked," Shur recalled. "A DEA agent would ask the BOP to furlough an inmate because he knew a drug dealer in Miami. Obviously, the dealer didn't know the inmate had been put in prison. If I agreed with the plan, Carlson would grant the inmate a furlough and the DEA would set up a meeting between the inmate and the drug dealer. These usually took place in a motel room that had been rigged with video cameras. As soon as the inmate bought drugs from the dealer, the DEA would move in and make the arrest. The inmate would then be brought back to prison." In return for his help, the inmate hoped time would be taken off his sentence.

Shur agreed to begin screening requests, and soon he was reviewing an average of 150 furlough requests each year. He recommended that Carlson release prisoners in about half of those cases. Today, prison furloughs are still being used, although they are rarely discussed by the government.

"I had to weigh three factors when I reviewed a furlough request," said Shur. "Was this inmate an escape risk, was there a chance the inmate might be murdered or murder someone else, and what would be gained by furloughing him?" Because the agents who had asked for the furlough were responsible for making certain the inmate was returned to prison, an inmate was rarely left unguarded when he was on the streets. A common trick that the agents used to foil escapes was to lie to the inmates about when they would be sent back to prison. The prisoner would be told a specific date, but actually be hustled back behind bars several days earlier. Only two prisoners escaped during the two decades that Shur oversaw the program, and both were recaptured before they had a chance to commit new crimes.

"Getting prisoners out of prison wasn't as easy as you might think," said Shur. "We had to make certain that other inmates didn't know what was actually going on because they would have killed inmates who helped us." Sometimes inmates were taken out of prison in ambulances under the guise of needing special medical care. Others would "disappear" while they were being moved from one prison to another.

"I was once asked to recommend a furlough for an inmate who knew the ringleaders of a gang that had stolen military weapons," said Shur. "Agents were going to send him to make a buy and then follow him to where the guns were being stashed. The catch was that we were going to have to put this inmate in a car by himself, because he was supposed to meet the gun traffickers by himself at a fast-food restaurant and then follow them to where the weapons were hidden. The agents were going to follow him and the traffickers, and move in as soon as the deal went down. I talked it over with my staff, and one of them suggested we give him a car with just enough gas in the tank to drive about five miles, so he couldn't run too far if he tried to escape. But the more I thought about it, the more I decided it was just too dangerous. We knew he was going to have access to a car and also weapons. What if he grabbed one of the guns and opened fire on the agents? Or double-crossed them in some way? I was getting a lot of pressure to approve the request because it was a major operation, but I said no. The problem with furloughs was that the agents' priority was making an arrest, so they were more willing to take risks than I was. Not only did I have to balance the risks, I had my firm belief that a prisoner ought to serve his time in prison, not on the streets. Sometimes agents would ask me to get Carlson to extend a furlough for another thirty days. I knew these agents were simply keeping a prisoner they liked from going back to prison. The stupidest reasoning for a request I ever got was from a U.S. attorney who wanted me to recommend a furlough for a prisoner with a very long sentence. He told me he could tell by looking into the inmate's eyes that he wasn't going to run away. I rejected that request."

Shur soon began getting other tasks in his new job. He became the Criminal Division's liaison with the federal parole board, an assignment that gave him even more clout when it came to the board's deciding which federal prisoners would be paroled and which would stay behind bars. Shur also advised it about organized crime figures who were being considered for parole, and about relocated WITSEC witnesses who had committed new crimes and been sent back to prison. By 1980 he had become an even more powerful figure when it came to determining the fate of federal witnesses. Not only did he decide who got into the WITSEC program, but also whether they would be protected in a WITSEC prison unit or sent to a state prison to be hidden under an alias. He could single-handedly remove a witness from the safety of a WITSEC unit, forcing him to be sent back into the regular prison population, where he'd have to hide in the hole to survive. Because of his federal parole board contacts, Shur was in a position to influence whether a WITSEC witness was released early or had to serve all of his prison sentence. Finally, he alone decided whether a witness was turned over to the Marshals Service after he was paroled and given a new identity, or simply shown out the front prison gate.

It was not surprising that some WITSEC witnesses began referring to him behind his back, not always kindly, as "the little god."

CHAPTER
FIFTEEN

HOWARD SAFIR was having too good a time as WITSEC chief to return to the DEA, as he had originally planned, after his year "on loan" ended in 1979. Nor did the Marshals Service's director, William Hall, and its deputy director, John Twomey, want him to go. They offered to make him an assistant director for operations if he would join the Marshals Service, a promotion that would give him more pay and power. He accepted.

Twomey already had a new assignment in mind. When he was a prison warden in Illinois, he had noticed the Marshals Service was still responsible for capturing escaped convicts and other federal criminals on the loose, just as it had in the old Wild West days. But over the years, the FBI had taken over the task of tracking down federal criminals. While it had done a great job of catching the notorious felons on its Most Wanted List, it hadn't had the time or funds to go after the smaller fish, or much interest in doing so. By 1979, there were fifteen thousand federal fugitives free on the streets with no one actively pursuing them. Twomey asked Safir if he was interested in helping the Marshals Service reclaim its turf, and he jumped at the chance.

It took some wrangling, but after several meetings the directors of both agencies signed an agreement in October 1979 that divided up the government's manhunting duties. The FBI kept jurisdiction over the cases its agents developed and criminals charged with "unlawful flight to avoid prosecution," including bank robbers, kidnappers, and other high-profile felons who crossed state borders. The Marshals Service got the leftovers—escaped federal convicts, bond jumpers, and parole and probation violators. At first it appeared the FBI had gotten the better end of the deal by shedding the warrants that it didn't want to pursue anyway. But Safir jumped in with both feet. In 1980 his deputies nabbed ninety-five hundred of the long-overlooked fifteen thousand wanted fugitives. Showing the same creativity that he had used in revitalizing the service's WITSEC operations, Safir created an elite Fugitive Investigation Strike Team (FIST) and dispatched it to Miami. There it joined state and local police officers in a concentrated effort to track down fugitives, and in a five-week period, seventy-six felons were arrested. In Washington, D.C., Safir's deputies used an ingenious ruse to arrest more than a hundred felons. Rather than staking out the wanted men's last known addresses and hoping they would show up, FIST mailed letters to them announcing they had won free tickets to a Washington Redskins football game. Their relatives made certain the letters were forwarded, and when the fugitives arrived on game day to board a bus to the stadium, they were handcuffed and instead driven to the D.C. jail.

The real test for Safir, however, came after Christopher Boyce escaped in January 1980 from a federal penitentiary in California where he had been serving forty years for espionage. Along with a childhood friend, Boyce had sold military secrets to Russia's KGB in the early 1970s that he had stolen from a U.S. defense contractor. Known as "the Falcon" because of his love for the birds, Boyce had been profiled in a best-selling book called *The Falcon and the Snowman*. A motion picture by the same name was being filmed about the case, and Boyce was so daring that he called the Hollywood set to ask about the movie's progress while he was on the run. Safir turned the hunt for Boyce into one of the most extensive and expensive in American history. His deputies investigated tips in South America, the Middle East, Europe, and Australia. He began every day's staff meetings with the same question: "Where is Christopher Boyce?" and as the months began to roll by, he started to worry that Boyce would surface in Moscow and thumb his nose at the Marshals Service, causing it to once again become the butt of jokes by other federal law enforcement agencies.

It was in the midst of the hunt for Boyce in the late summer of 1980 that a security guard at the Marshals Service's operations center called Safir from the front desk and told him that ABC newsman Geraldo Rivera and a film crew were in the lobby demanding to see him. Safir assumed Rivera wanted to interview him about the Boyce manhunt, but he was wrong. Rivera, who had launched his career by exposing government neglect of the mentally handicapped, felt confident that he'd found another exposé: federal ineptness in the running of WITSEC. Safir suddenly found himself being forced to defend WITSEC and push the hunt for Christopher Boyce to the side. This is how Safir would later recall what happened next.

"I told the guard: 'Tell Geraldo to call our public information office and make an appointment,' and Geraldo grabs the phone out of the security guy's hand and says, 'Safir, come on out!' I said: 'I don't think so. Call our public information people, make an appointment, and then maybe I will talk to you.' Geraldo says, 'You're a liar and I know you're a liar and we are going to prove it.' After he said that, I hung up on him."

For several days, Rivera and his film crew staked out the lobby. Each time a male employee passed by them, Rivera dashed up with his crew's cameras running. "Are you Howard Safir?" he'd ask, since he didn't know what Safir looked like.

"I finally told the guards," Safir recalled, "to kick his ass out!" A few days later Safir got a call from a top Justice Department official who was a friend of an ABC News executive. "I was told, 'You ought to do this interview.' " Bowing to pressure, Safir agreed, but he didn't trust Rivera. "I hired my own audio-recording company," Safir recalled, "and when Geraldo walked in my office for the interview, there was a guy with a reel-to-reel recorder and microphone sitting there. Geraldo says, 'What's this?' and I say, 'You are going to record, I am going to record.' He says, 'Well, we are not doing this if you are going to record,' and I say,

'Okay, see ya, have a nice day.' So then Geraldo says, 'Okay, we are doing this under duress.' "

An ABC producer later remembered the encounter differently. He claimed Safir had hidden a microphone beneath a tabletop, putting Rivera under electronic surveillance. Regardless, both sides would later describe the interview as confrontational. "There was hostility," Rivera recalled, "no question about it." An ABC producer added: "You could cut the tension with a knife."

Rivera called his report "Hostages of Fear" when it was broadcast on the prime-time news show *20/20* in October 1980, and just as Safir had feared, it lambasted the Marshals Service. An indignant Rivera told viewers that Safir's deputies had done such a horrible job relocating and protecting federal witnesses that scores of them were living in fear. Some had become so distraught that they had committed suicide. Others had been murdered by the mob.

Much of the program centered on the tragic case of Frank Calimano, who had entered WITSEC in 1978 along with his wife, Vivian, and their two teenage sons. Calimano was not the usual WITSEC witness because he was not a criminal. In fact, he had never been in any sort of trouble with the police. In 1976, he had agreed to let the FBI run an undercover operation inside the air-conditioning and heating company that he owned on Long Island, New York, and during the following year the FBI secretly videotaped members of the Gambino crime family in Calimano's office bribing and threatening union officials and construction company owners. When the FBI was ready to begin making arrests, federal prosecutors asked Calimano to testify in front of a grand jury. His wife urged him not to do it, saying: "You've done enough." But Calimano, a Korean combat veteran, told her that every American had a civic duty to step forward if he had information about a crime. As soon as he testified, he became a marked man, and prosecutors urged him to enter WITSEC and disappear.

WITSEC relocated Calimano and his family in Houston, Texas, and everything went smoothly at first. He opened another air-conditioning and heating business, which he financed completely on his own by taking out a bank loan. "I don't want any government handouts," he told deputies. But there was a hitch. Because he had lost his good credit standing when he was given a new identity, the only way he could qualify for the loan was by putting up as collateral several expensive pieces of business equipment that he owned.

Two years later, Vivian was buying groceries when someone called out her old name. It was a former friend from Long Island, and it turned out that she and her husband had bought a house only a few blocks from where the Calimanos now lived. The local WITSEC inspector told Calimano that he and his family needed to leave Houston immediately because their cover had been blown. But Calimano said he needed time to close down his business. Besides, he didn't have enough cash to pay off his bank debt.

By this time, Safir and Shur had implemented a number of regulations that made it more difficult for witnesses to flee town without paying their debts. Those who tried could be sued in civil court or even prosecuted for fraud. Rivera told viewers that Calimano felt trapped. If he didn't flee immediately, he would be booted out of WITSEC for not following its orders, but if he left Houston, he wouldn't be able to pay off the bank loan. At the least, he would lose his collateral, and he might possibly be sued.

Calimano turned to Safir for help. In an emotional letter, he asked if the Marshals Service would pay the interest on his bank debt for six months, giving him time to relocate and get a new business off the ground. To Calimano, it seemed a reasonable request, especially since he had made significant sacrifices for the government and had never demanded anything in return. "Frank believed our government would always do the right thing," a tearful Vivian told Rivera.

But Safir flatly rejected Calimano's request. In a stern letter, he explained that the Justice Department had decided it was illegal for the Marshals Service to get involved financially in business deals with witnesses. This included paying their debts. Continuing, he warned Calimano that if he didn't leave Houston at once, the Marshals Service could not guarantee his safety and he would be terminated from the WITSEC program for failing to follow its rules.

Calimano became so severely depressed that on June 1, 1980, his family arranged for him to enter a Veterans Administration hospital for psychiatric help. The night before Calimano checked in, he recorded his thoughts on tape. "I feel betrayed," he said. He and his family were "hostages of fear"—afraid of mob retribution yet trapped by WITSEC's rules. "I have a funny feeling about walking into that hospital," he added. "I am not going to survive this."

Six days later Calimano hanged himself.

"We didn't know what to do," Vivian Calimano told Rivera. "There was no way for us to leave, because of the business."

After reminding *20/20* viewers that Calimano had been an honest citizen who had responded heroically when the FBI asked for his help, Rivera assessed blame. "According to the people closest to Frank Calimano," he announced, "it was the inflexibility of Mr. Safir and the Marshals Service that eventually drove Calimano over the brink."

Rivera's cameras then cut to a stiff Howard Safir sitting at his desk at the Marshals Service operations center with an American flag perched behind him. When Rivera asked him about the suicide, Safir said he was prohibited by WITSEC rules from discussing individual cases. "There are privacy issues here," he declared.

"Why?" Rivera retorted. "Calimano is dead." He then switched subjects. "Have you ever lost a witness to an assassin's bullet or a knife or poison?" he asked.

"In the ten years that the program has been in operation, we know that no witness under the active protection of the Marshals Service has ever been killed," Safir replied.

The cameras immediately cut to Rivera, now standing outdoors.

"But Mr. Safir was either badly misinformed or intentionally lying about the unblemished record of the Federal Witness Protection Program," Rivera declared. "On July twenty-sixth—that was less than two weeks before our interview with Mr. Safir—the badly decomposed body of a woman was found in this rock quarry near Little Rock, Arkansas. The woman was identified as Sheila Anne Bishop. A federally protected witness, she had been murdered."

The camera then cut to Pulaski County sheriff's investigator Larry Dill, standing with Rivera at the spot where Bishop had been shot in the back of the head.

> RIVERA: Did the marshals cooperate in your investigation?
> DILL: No, they didn't.
> RIVERA: Let me ask it another way: Did the marshals, in effect, obstruct your investigation?
> DILL: Yes sir, they did.

> The cameras immediately cut back to Safir.

> SAFIR: Our policy is that we assist all law enforcement—federal, state, and local—in all investigations.

> Cut back to Dill.

> DILL: I never ran into another agency that not only would obstruct an investigation into a homicide, but on numerous times . . . the marshals gave me information that turned out to be completely false.
> RIVERA: They lied?
> DILL: They lied.

Rivera's cutting back and forth left a vivid image in the minds of viewers: Howard Safir was a liar. And WITSEC was a program run dangerously amok.

Safir was furious. "My kids were watching it," he recalled. "My mother was watching it. I'm getting calls from all my friends saying, 'What the hell is going on here?' "

Safir was so incensed that after several weeks of stewing, he filed a $10 million defamation suit against Rivera and ABC. The thrust of his suit was that one of his answers to a pivotal question had been intentionally distorted to make it appear as if he were lying. Midway in the broadcast Rivera had asked whether any witnesses had ever been murdered. Safir had replied that none had, and at that moment the cameras had cut to the Arkansas rock quarry where Rivera was standing. Rivera had then said: "Mr. Safir was either badly misinformed or intentionally lying."

In his lawsuit, Safir revealed that the second half of his answer to that question had been edited out by Rivera. Because Safir had taped the entire interview, he was able to reconstruct exactly what he had said. Television viewers heard Safir say: "In the ten years that the program's been in operation, we know that no witness under the active protection of the Marshals Service has ever been killed." Rivera had cut away from Safir at that point. On Safir's tape, however, he could then be heard saying: "There have been thirteen witnesses, who were in the program at one time, killed, and in all of those cases, it was as a result of a breach of their own security."

Safir thought he had caught Rivera and ABC red-handed, but the network's attorneys claimed that Rivera had actually been practicing "responsible journalism" when he edited out the second half of Safir's comment.

"We knew at the time that the number Safir used [thirteen] was not true," Rivera explained later. His producers had discovered that at least seventeen WITSEC witnesses either had been murdered or had committed suicide since 1970. "We have no obligation to broadcast a person's statement if the statement isn't true," Rivera declared.

Safir and his lawyers argued that Rivera and ABC's response was a red herring raised by the network's lawyers to deflect attention away from the basis of the suit, which they said was Rivera's biased editing. Whether thirteen or seventeen witnesses had been killed really wasn't the issue, they said; the fact remained that Safir had acknowledged on camera to Rivera during the interview that WITSEC witnesses had been murdered. But Rivera had edited his answer to make it appear as if Safir had said that no witness had ever been killed. Since the next *20/20* scene showed Rivera standing at the spot where a witness had been found dead, viewers were led to believe Safir had lied, especially when Rivera himself suggested that "Mr. Safir was . . . intentionally lying."

As is customary in such cases, legal costs skyrocketed. Safir contacted a media watchdog group in Washington called Accuracy in Media, and it agreed to help pay his legal bills.

Safir was not the only WITSEC official angry about Rivera's story. "During my career," Gerald Shur said later, "I'd dealt with dozens of reporters, and I'd always felt comfortable around them even when they disagreed with me. But I felt Geraldo had taken a single suicide and statements by a few angry witnesses and contrived to turn them into a sensational and misleading story just in order to get a shocking story on the air. I was furious when I learned he had edited Howard's words to make him look like a liar. It was lousy journalism."

Although WITSEC had been criticized in newspaper and television reports periodically in the past, nearly all of those stories had focused on gripes by individual witnesses about problems they had encountered after they were relocated. Rivera's was the first report that suggested the Marshals Service was not adequately protecting witnesses from the mob. "I knew witnesses were not being killed by the people they testified against," Shur recalled, "and I was afraid the *20/20* program was going to have a negative impact on the number of witnesses coming forward to testify."

Shur had asked an independent panel in the Justice Department in 1977 to determine if WITSEC witnesses were being adequately protected by the Marshals Service. It had investigated every death that had occurred in the program from its start in 1970 through early 1978, including murders, suicides, and any deaths under unusual circumstances. Its findings:

• Daniel LaPolla was identified as the first WITSEC witness murdered by the mob. He had come out of hiding in 1972 to attend a funeral in his hometown and had stopped after the ceremony to check on his house. When he opened the front door, a booby trap exploded, blowing him to pieces. The panel told Shur that LaPolla's death could not be blamed on the Marshals Service because he was being protected by agents from the Bureau of Alcohol, Tobacco, and Firearms at the time, and they had told him to stay away from the funeral and his house.

- In 1974, protected witness James E. Berry's body was found in a field outside Mansfield, Texas, but once again, the panel ruled his death had not been caused by the Marshals Service. An investigation by the Fort Worth Police Department showed that Berry had been tortured and killed by local drug dealers after he tried to cheat them out of money. Berry, a known drug addict, had violated WITSEC rules when he contacted the dealers, the panel said. In addition, his murder had nothing to do with the testimony he had given against the mob.

- In 1975, Louis Bombacino was murdered when he turned the ignition key in his car and set off a bomb. The panel said there was no doubt that the former Chicago mobster was the victim of a mob hit. But its investigation showed Bombacino had been relocated in Tempe, Arizona, by the FBI in 1967, some three years before WITSEC was formed. The Marshals Service had nothing to do with him.

And the list went on and on: George Marshal, a known drug addict, died in 1974 from an accidental overdose of morphine; witness Reinaldo M. Morales drowned in 1976 after getting drunk at a party and trying to hold his breath under water for several minutes to impress his friends; witness James P. Coffee was killed in 1976 when he lost control of the car he was driving, but there was no evidence it had been tampered with. Of the fifty-five instances where protected witnesses had died, only two could not be fully explained.

- Ernest Pacaro died on April 12, 1975, in the garage of his Las Vegas house after inhaling his car's exhaust fumes, the panel said. The Clark County coroner's office decided his death was a suicide, but the Las Vegas Police Department listed it as a "possible murder." The police were leery because Pacaro's body had been found next to the open door of his car and his head was resting on the driver's seat. Police theorized that Pacaro had been locked in the garage by his killers, and when he couldn't open the overhead door, he had crawled to the car, opened its door, switched off the engine, and passed out. However, there was no evidence to support this theory.

- Armando Zatarin's death also had been identified as a "suspicious suicide." He was believed to have shot himself in the head in 1977 while he was talking on the telephone with a DEA agent. The coroner's report said the wound was consistent with a "close-range, self-inflicted gunshot," and the DEA agent said Zatarin had been threatening to shoot himself during their conversation. But police believed someone had been with Zatarin at the time of the shooting, and they refused to rule out the possibility that this unknown person might have pulled the trigger.

In its final report to Shur, the panel concluded that there was absolutely no evidence that witnesses in WITSEC were not being adequately protected by the Marshals Service. The panel wrote:

> Even if the two suspicious cases [Pacaro and Zatarin] are accepted as security failures, the WITSEC program failure rate is still two in 2,225 witnesses over a period of almost eight years, against organized criminal elements with extensive resources and presumably strong motivation to locate and destroy witnesses—both as matters of personal vengeance and organizational discipline.

Even though the panel's study had been conducted before Safir had become WITSEC chief and no one had reviewed deaths in WITSEC that had occurred within the past two years, Shur was confident that witnesses were being well protected by Safir and his inspectors. "If anything, security had improved after Howard Safir arrived in 1978," Shur said later. "Complaints from witnesses had dropped ninety percent since he had taken charge, and I knew of no instances where any witnesses who had been following the rules had been murdered. Absolutely none! The Calimano case was tragic, and yes, there had been other suicides in the program. Every suicide concerned me, but I had my analysts compare the number of suicides in WITSEC to the number of suicides in the general population, and WITSEC was not out of line."

Nonetheless, Rivera's *20/20* broadcast prompted Senator Sam Nunn to call Shur and Safir before another investigative congressional subcommittee in December 1980 to defend WITSEC.

Following Rivera's example, the Georgia Democrat opened the three days of televised hearings by calling Vivian Calimano as the subcommittee's first witness.

"I do not want anyone to go in this program the way it is now," she testified. "I do not want anybody to have to suffer this."

Despite that emotional start, Nunn's investigation turned up few surprises and uncovered no evidence that supported Rivera's claim that witnesses were being slaughtered. What Nunn did discover was that witnesses were still having trouble getting new documents from the Marshals Service despite Safir's reforms. Some nine hundred witnesses were waiting, some as long as two years, for their paperwork. Despite this, a survey by the subcommittee of fifty-seven witnesses and eighty-nine of their family members found that three-fourths of them were satisfied with how they had been treated. They credited WITSEC with having saved their lives.

After Nunn's hearing, WITSEC fell from the front pages and Safir went back to focusing his full-time attention on trying to capture missing spy Christopher Boyce. "It was a very difficult time for Howard," said a close friend and WITSEC inspector. "He believed he had done a fantastic job in rebuilding WITSEC, and he was proud of what he was accomplishing in arresting fugitives. And then Geraldo goes on television and busts his chops, and others in the media begin criticizing him because Christopher Boyce was still running around loose a year after his escape. I remember running into Howard in the hallways and saying something about how I felt bad about the pressure he was under. Safir seemed offended. 'If you can't stand the heat, then you get out of the kitchen,' he said. Then he added, 'I'm not even feeling warm yet.' "

It was about to get hotter.

CHAPTER
SIXTEEN

C HARLES SONNY PEARSON sauntered into the Sandoval County sheriff's office in Albuquerque, New Mexico, in April 1981 and said he thought an unidentified, badly burned corpse that had been found in the desert a few days earlier might be his wife, Michelle. He had reported her missing six weeks earlier. Then, as if it were an afterthought, he added: "I'm a protected government witness and so was she. Maybe someone got to her."

Sheriff Gennaro Ferrara was immediately suspicious. Pearson showed no emotion even when he identified the horribly battered corpse as Michelle. Nor did he ask any questions about how she had been killed. An autopsy showed she had been beaten with a blunt object, strangled, dumped in the desert, doused with gasoline, and set on fire. Her remains had been found by two gas company workers who had stumbled upon them while doing a land survey.

Pearson's story about the last time that he had seen Michelle also struck Ferrara as odd. He said they had argued and that she had bolted from the trailer they rented in a rural area north of the city at around 2 A.M. on March 2. The last he saw of her, she had started walking down the railroad tracks toward town.

Why had Michelle walked along the railroad tracks rather than speeding away in their car? Ferrara asked. Pearson didn't know. He was even more evasive when asked about his past. He wouldn't divulge his former name or tell Ferrara who might be hunting him. All he would reveal was that he had once served time in the Atlanta federal penitentiary on a bank robbery conviction.

The Marshals Service's office in Albuquerque sent WITSEC inspector Ruben Chavez to confer with Ferrara, and Chavez confirmed that Charles and Michelle had been secretly relocated in New Mexico by WITSEC nearly three years earlier. But Chavez said federal regulations prohibited him from telling the sheriff anything more about the couple.

"This is a homicide investigation!" Ferrara protested. "You've got to tell me *something*." He needed basics: Where was Michelle from? How extensive was Pearson's criminal background? Why had the couple been forced into hiding? And, most important of all, who was trying to kill them?

But Chavez refused to give him any details. The fact that Michelle was dead didn't change the constraints under WITSEC because the Marshals Service was still obligated to protect her husband. He could not breach Pearson's security by revealing personal information about his wife. And then Chavez dropped a bombshell. He said Michelle had called him late on the night of March 1 and told him she was afraid of her husband. A friend had warned her that Pearson was planning on murdering her. Chavez said he urged Michelle to call the police, but she said she didn't trust them. They agreed to meet the next morning, but just before their scheduled rendezvous, Pearson had called him and said that Michelle had run off at 2 A.M. and disappeared.

Based on this scanty information, Ferrara had Pearson jailed as a material witness and sent his photograph and fingerprints to the FBI for identification. Under New Mexico law, he could keep Pearson locked up for three days; then he either had to charge him with a crime or release him. The sheriff hurried to find evidence.

A customer at the Big Chief Truck Stop and Cafe, where the Pearsons frequently drank coffee, said he had overheard Pearson threatening to kill Michelle. But that was the only incriminating evidence Ferrara could find within the three-day deadline. A local judge ruled it wasn't sufficient, and Pearson was released. When Ferrara checked a few days later, he discovered that Pearson had fled.

A month later a friend of Pearson's was arrested in an unrelated case, and he offered to tell Sheriff Ferrara what had really happened to Michelle in return for a plea bargain. He had been visiting the Pearsons in their trailer on March 1 when they had started arguing. But Michelle had not run outside. She had gone to bed, and Pearson had waited until she was asleep and then attacked her with a claw hammer. When he discovered she was still breathing, he strangled her with his belt. And there was more: Charles Pearson's former name was Marion Albert Pruett.

Ferrara was furious when he ran a background check on Pruett and discovered he had a long criminal record. He had been admitted into WITSEC after he testified in a murder trial against Allen "Big Al" Benton, who had been accused of slashing the throat of snitch William Zambito in the Atlanta penitentiary in 1978. Sheriff Ferrara felt betrayed. The FBI had told him that a check of Charles Pearson's fingerprints had found "no known criminal record." Ferrara suspected the Marshals Service had tampered with the files to hide Pearson's true identity. "Had I known what sort of criminal I was dealing with," Ferrara said later, "I am certain I could have persuaded a local judge to keep him locked in my jail."

Ferrara swore out a murder warrant for Pruett, but when he notified the FBI, he discovered he would have to get in line. Marion Pruett, a.k.a. Charles Pearson, had gone on an interstate crime spree.

He had fled New Mexico in May, headed north, and robbed a bank in Seattle, Washington, less than two weeks later. In July, he robbed another bank, this time in Corpus Christi, Texas. In August, he hit a third bank, in Tallahassee, Florida. In September, he upped the ante. While robbing a bank in Jackson, Mississippi, Pruett took loan officer Peggy Lowe hostage. When they reached the Alabama state line, he shot the forty-two-year-old mother of two in the head and dumped her body beside a deserted road. She bled to death before anyone found her. Two weeks later, he robbed a bank in Bridgeville, Pennsylvania, and then turned southwest, driving to Fort Smith, Arkansas, where he robbed a convenience store and took its clerk, Bobbie Robertson, hostage. He shot her and tossed her dead body out of his car as he left town. Thus far, he had killed two women and robbed six banks in a five-month period. And he wasn't done. Pruett headed next to Colorado and on October 16 robbed two different 7-Eleven stores, one in Loveland, the other in Fort Collins, executing clerks in both. James Balderson and Anthony Taitt, both college students who had been working night shifts at the stores to earn money for tuition, were forced onto their knees by Pruett and executed. His combined take from the two robberies was $58. Seventeen hours later, Pruett's crime spree came to an end when a Texas highway trooper stopped him for speeding. When he was interrogated later in jail, Pruett bragged that he had also killed a man outside a bar in New Orleans, then kidnapped the man's girlfriend and killed her, too. That brought the total number of his victims to eight, but the New Orleans police were unable to find their bodies. Incredibly, Pruett insisted that he was not to blame for any of the robberies or killings. "I've become a mad dog killer," he declared, "because I've done so much cocaine." He said he had been robbing banks to feed his $2,000-per-week habit.

Shur was appalled when he learned all this. "I knew when I first created the witness program that someday a protected witness might commit a crime, but I never, ever conceived that anyone would do what Pruett had done. I had gone into the Justice Department because I cared about helping people. My heart went out to his victims—to this day, I still think about them and grieve for them. But, as I usually did during crises, I moved into my clinical mode and immediately began examining our records to see what we could do to help the prosecutors. I wanted Pruett punished."

Shur's records showed that the U.S. attorney's office in Atlanta had asked him to admit Pruett into WITSEC after he agreed to testify against Benton. The Zambito murder case was the ninth killing at the penitentiary in eighteen months, so prosecutors had made the case a top priority. Benton had originally been charged with murder, but the jury refused to convict him of killing Zambito after a prison priest testified that at the time of the murder, he had seen Benton helping other inmates in the prison kitchen prepare the morning's breakfast. Instead, the jury had found Benton guilty of conspiracy to commit murder, which carried an automatic life sentence.

Fearing Pruett would be murdered in Atlanta, Shur had admitted him into WITSEC on May 3, 1978, and immediately had him moved to a different prison, where he was hidden under an alias. Pruett served another eighteen months of his bank robbery sentence, and during that time called Shur's office and asked that his wife, Pamela Sue Canuteson, a.k.a. Michelle, also be protected because she was receiving death threats. The parole board voted to release Pruett eleven months early, after Pruett appealed to a congressman for help. A member of his staff had asked the board to release Pruett early because of his testimony against Benton. According to Shur's file, one of Safir's WITSEC inspectors had recommended against giving Pruett a new identity and relocating him. But Shur had disagreed. "I was focused on the number of murders that had happened in the Atlanta penitentiary, and I believed that if we successfully relocated Pruett, other inmates might come forward," said Shur. "Yes, his record was of concern to me, but witnesses with even lengthier criminal records than his had successfully begun law-abiding lives after entering WITSEC, and the Marshals Service had objected to many of them, too."

The "Pearsons" had arrived in New Mexico on November 15, 1979, and were paid a monthly allowance for nine months, until Pruett had landed a job as a dump truck driver. At that point, they were terminated from the program. No one in WITSEC had heard from them again until Michelle's panicky call to Deputy Chavez on March 1, 1981.

The fact that a relocated WITSEC witness had gone on a multi-state murder spree brought an immediate public outcry. Pruett fanned the flames when he bragged to reporters from the *Denver Post* that he had lied to get into the protection program.

"I actually killed William Zambito," he declared. "I framed an innocent man and I got rewarded for doing it."

Pruett now described the murder this way: "Big Al [Benton] said he'd pay me to kill Zambito when he found out they'd put the snitch in my cell. I took my shank [homemade knife] and started stabbing him in the morning while he was sleeping. He stuck his hand up to block the blows. I cut his hand real bad. Then I stabbed him in the face about three or four times. I hit him in his throat and he suddenly bolted up and was gurgling and I spit on him and said, 'Die, you motherfucker!' Then he fell back and stopped gurgling."

Pruett said he had turned against Benton after the murder when he reneged on paying him, and instead hired another inmate to kill him. In a written statement, the U.S. attorney's office in Atlanta said it did not believe Pruett's newest version of the killing. But even if it were true, Benton still was guilty of conspiring to kill Zambito, and that made reopening the Zambito case pointless.

"People were really furious at WITSEC," recalled Shur.

They got even angrier when Sheriff Ferrara accused WITSEC of tampering with Pruett's fingerprint records to help hide his true identity. "When I read the sheriff's accusation, I immediately called up the FBI and asked it to check on what had happened," said Shur, "because I knew it wasn't going to lie to protect a WITSEC witness and neither was I."

Shur and the FBI had worked out a simple procedure for keeping track of WITSEC witnesses' fingerprints. Shur's staff gave the FBI the name of every criminal enrolled in WITSEC, and their fingerprint records were flagged. If fingerprints were sent to the FBI for review and they matched the prints of a WITSEC witness, the FBI examiners would spot the flag and immediately notify Shur's office and the Marshals Service. At least, that was how the system was supposed to work. "I was worried that maybe someone had made a mistake," said Shur, "and someone had—but it wasn't my staff or the FBI." The FBI told Shur that Pruett's fingerprints had arrived smudged, which caused an FBI examiner to misread them. They had been smudged, the FBI added, at Ferrara's jail. "There was nothing devious about any of this," said Shur. "There was no WITSEC cover-up, no conspiracy or secret scandal." However, there was another ironic bit to the story. The FBI said Ferrara had mailed Pruett's fingerprints to Washington by regular mail. "Even if they had not been smudged and an examiner had identified them as matching Pruett's, there still was no way the FBI's report would have gotten back to the sheriff within the three-day time limit; it had taken three days for the prints to reach the FBI in the first place. The crimes were horrible, but I still felt we were being made a scapegoat."

Senator Thad Cochran, whose hometown of Jackson, Mississippi, had been the site of Pruett's first hostage murder, held a special congressional subcommittee hearing to investigate WITSEC's handling of Pruett. "As I had done before," Shur said, "I met in advance with Cochran's staff and told them everything we knew." At the hearing, he explained that the Marshals Service did not routinely notify local law enforcement when it relocated a witness within its borders because that would have been prejudicial to witnesses who were trying to make a fresh start. WITSEC inspectors were also concerned that dishonest cops might tip off the mob. Howard Safir told Cochran that Inspector Chavez had been following WITSEC procedures when he had refused to tell Ferrara about Pruett's past. His decision to tell him about Michelle's call had been correct because it did not reveal anything about her new identity.

Shur reminded Cochran that Pruett was out of WITSEC when he murdered his wife, having been terminated from it eight months earlier. Finally he hammered home what he believed was a critical point. Yes, Pruett had been paroled eleven months early, apparently because he had testified against Benton. But he would have been released from prison in eleven months even if he hadn't been granted an early parole or relocated because he would have finished serving his sentence. Who was to say that he would not have killed Michelle and gone on a rampage then, even if the government had not helped him?

"While I deeply regret what Pruett did," Shur said, "we are not to blame. Pruett is to blame for what he did." Shur assured Cochran that the Pruett case was atypical. A recent study had found that fewer than 21 percent of protected witnesses had been arrested within two years after they were relocated (in later years this figure would fall to 18 percent). That meant 79 percent stayed

out of trouble. "Given the criminal backgrounds of our witnesses," he declared, "these are amazing statistics."

Cochran's hearing was conducted during the July 4 weekend
at a local Ramada Inn in Jackson, and Cochran was the only senator who attended it. Moreover, none of Pruett's victims was called
to testify. While the hearing made front-page news in the local
paper, no one in the national media paid any attention to it, and
the Pruett scandal began to become yesterday's news. It seemed as
though WITSEC had ridden out the worst of the media storm. Better yet, six weeks later Safir and the Marshals Service found themselves being feted in the press and on television for a daring arrest
that seemed to overshadow the bad press the Pruett rampage had
spawned.

Acting on an informant's tip, Safir's fugitive-hunting deputies had finally tracked escaped spy Christopher Boyce to Port
Angeles, Washington, a coastal town in the Pacific Northwest
across the strait from Victoria, British Columbia. He had evaded
them for nineteen months, but the deputies now felt confident
that they were about to capture "the Falcon." However, Boyce did
not show up at the apartment where he had reportedly been living,
and it looked as if they were about to fail once again. And then fate
intervened. On impulse, two deputies pulled into the Pit Stop, a
neighborhood hamburger joint, to show its carhops photographs of
Boyce. As they were waiting for one of the carhops to roller-skate
out to their car, the agents glanced at the driver in the car parked
next to theirs. Sitting behind the steering wheel was Christopher
Boyce. He was reading a book and eating a hamburger. Deputy
Dave Neff slipped next to Boyce's open car window and stuck a
pistol next to the fugitive's left ear. "Drop the hamburger!" he ordered. Minutes later, Safir's phone rang at home. It was after midnight. "The Falcon is back in his cage," a deputy told him. "It's
over."

Geraldo Rivera was not about to let Shur and Safir off the hook
when it came to Marion Pruett. The ABC newsman was con-

vinced the case proved just how out of control and dangerous WIT-SEC was. He decided to interview Pruett and his victims' family members, and in early 1983 ABC broadcast another segment on *20/20*, this time called "A Deal with the Devil."

"Two years ago we told you how a significant number of supposedly protected federal witnesses were turning up dead," Rivera began. "Tonight's report deals with another sometimes fatal defect in the witness program: the apparent lack of screening of potential witnesses."

After describing Pruett's rampage and showing viewers photographs of his murder victims, Rivera turned his camera on the victims' families.

"It is unbelievable that a person like Pruett would be out—them knowing the type of person he is—and turning him lose on society," said Ed Lowe of Jackson, Mississippi. "It's unimaginable."

"I want Pruett in the electric chair, the sooner the better," said another relative.

The parents of the two college students murdered at the 7-Eleven stores in Colorado spoke angrily about WITSEC.

BETTY BALDERSON: The loss of our loved one was the first hurt, and the second hurt was when we found out the government had been involved in it through the witness protection program.
RIVERA: Do you think the federal witness protection program bears at least some responsibility in the murders of your sons?
BETTY BALDERSON: Oh yes.
FRANK BALDERSON: Definitely.
MARY TAITT: They have been co-conspirators.

A belligerent Marion Pruett appeared next on film.

RIVERA: Is it possible that people would be alive today if you were not on the witness protection program?
PRUETT *(laughing loudly)*: I don't think I need to answer that. It speaks for itself.

RIVERA: Do you think the government is a co-conspirator in
  your homicides because they let you out of prison, they let
  you go free?
PRUETT: Yeah, they most definitely did.

Rivera quickly cited three other cases for viewers in which
WITSEC witnesses had committed murders. Roy terHorst, whose
daughter was one of the victims, charged that the government
"gives more to a criminal, if they can get a nickel's worth of testimony out of him, than they do for the citizen walking around the
street."

RIVERA: If you could speak directly to people who administer
  this program, what would you say?
TERHORST: Do away with it. You have done more harm than
  you have ever done any good.

With disgust building in his voice, Rivera told viewers that
no one in the government had ever apologized or offered the injured families any financial compensation. Then he let the mother
of one of the victims have the final word.

FLORENCE BEAULIEU: I pray to God that they change their rules.
  You cannot keep sending those people onto the street and
  saying that they are doing good. Somebody has got to have a
  conscience someday.

Now it was Shur's turn to be angry. Rivera's producer had
asked to interview him for the show, but Shur had said he would
only appear on *20/20* live so Rivera could not edit his remarks.
ABC declined. Rivera then asked associate attorney general
Rudolph Giuliani, who had been appointed by President Reagan in
1981 to be the third in command at the Justice Department, if he
would grant *20/20* an interview, since he had oversight over the
Marshals Service. But he, too, refused unless he could appear live.
Having failed to get either official, Rivera had taken a clip from
the network's archives that had been filmed when Shur testified
before Senator Cochran's hearing in Mississippi. He spliced Shur's
testimony into the *20/20* broadcast.

"To the families of these victims and to the local cops some-times frustrated by the witness program," Rivera had told 20/20's viewers, "Justice Department official Gerald Shur had this to say."

SHUR: The one thing we share with your local law enforcement people is an oath to fight crime and, ah, we do have to strike sometimes difficult balances.

Placed as it was, Shur's comment had come across as flippant when shown after the highly charged scenes of the victims' suffer-ing families. What Rivera never told viewers was that Shur had not been talking about Pruett. He had been answering Cochran's totally unrelated question about witnesses who had refused to pay their debts after they were relocated.

SENATOR COCHRAN: . . . What about the cases that we have cited—the lady from Huntsville, Alabama, who has a judgment against a protected witness for $150,000? Basically, she's out because of a swindle by a relocated witness. What can be done about these incidents?

SHUR: Under previous administrations we were prohibited from doing much more than cajoling and pleading and perhaps pleading some more, and perhaps threatening our relocated witnesses to honor their debts. . . . You would not do that in $400 or $500 cases, and it's one of those things which we regret, because that $400 or $500 may be very meaningful to that individual, but *the one thing we share with your local law enforcement people is an oath to fight crime, and we do have to strike, sometimes, a very difficult balance.*

"In the first 20/20 broadcast, Rivera made Safir look like a liar, and in the second, he made me look callous about the people Pruett had murdered," Shur recalled. "Millions of viewers saw the broadcast, and I couldn't go out and tell every one of them how Geraldo had spliced together my answer. He made it look as if I didn't care that people were harmed. Believe me, I cared. I felt ter-rible about what Pruett had done, and I resented what Rivera had now done to my words. To me, Rivera was the best example of the worst kind of journalist."

Shur had another reason to be upset. The ABC newsman had tried to pressure Giuliani into granting him an interview by using an old reporter's tactic. In a letter, Rivera had told Giuliani that Marion Pruett had accused Shur of knowing that "Big Al" Benton was being framed and that he [Pruett] was the real killer. Rivera then wrote that if Giuliani did not come on television to refute Pruett's charge and defend Shur, 20/20 would have no choice but to broadcast Pruett's accusation unchallenged. Turning up the heat, Rivera had sent a copy of the letter to the U.S. attorney general.

The letter didn't work. Giuliani did not grant him an interview, and Rivera never broadcast the accusation. Still, Shur felt used.

"Rivera was accusing me of sitting quietly by and doing nothing during a frame-up," said Shur. "He was besmirching my reputation in an attempt to twist Rudy Giuliani's arm and force him on camera. It was sleazy."

Not long after Rivera's broadcast, the parents of one of Pruett's murder victims sued Shur, Safir, Chavez, and the Marshals Service, claiming each was responsible for their son's murder because they had helped relocate Pruett. But a federal appeals court rejected the case after ruling that the defendants were not responsible.

Meanwhile, Safir won a key ruling in his still unresolved $10 million slander suit against Rivera and ABC over the first 20/20 show, "Hostages of Fear." A Virginia judge rejected ABC's attempt to remove the case from a state court to a federal court, and set a date for the case to go before a jury.

Safir was convinced that if ABC got the case transferred into a federal court, he'd lose. On the morning the trial was scheduled to start, the network paid Safir an undisclosed cash settlement. The court record was sealed and both parties were barred from discussing how much Safir had received.

"I wanted to be fair in this book," Shur said as these pages were being written, "so I decided to give Rivera a chance to respond to my written account of what happened." This is Rivera's reply exactly as he gave it to us to print:

I have no clear recollection of the gory details of what happened in the Shur controversy, other than to suggest that he sounds from this account like a crybaby who could dish it out but not take it. As to his charge of "sleazy," what was really sleazy was the way promises made to program participants were allegedly not honored. Insofar as Mr. Safir is concerned, what I remember very clearly is how, under his reign as New York's police commissioner, many minority mothers felt they had more to fear from cops than crooks when their kids went out at night. I fiercely opposed settlement of the lawsuit he so cleverly insisted on bringing in his hometown Virginia state court, rather than in the more appropriate, First Amendment–sensitive federal courts. Our strategic legal mistake was countersuing his agency. That made the federal government his co-defendant, and allowed his lawyer to benefit from all the taxpayer-funded discovery that took place. I angrily and publicly objected to the imposed settlement with Mr. Safir precisely because it could allow a one-sided accounting and explanation of the widely publicized problems within WITSEC. The settlement was forced on me by ABC and the insurance company, and didn't cost me a dime; although, as I said at the time I was informed of the settlement, I took a long, hot shower to clean off the stench of it. [Note: Rivera is referring here to Howard Safir's tenure as the police commissioner of New York City, a job he took after he left the Marshals Service.]

"I found Rivera's reply ironic," Shur continued. "What does Howard Safir's later role as New York City police commissioner have to do with the fact that Rivera substituted my answer to a question about debt collection into his report about victims of a horrible crime? When I was in law school, a lecturer told us that if the facts are on your side, yell facts; when the law is on your side, yell law; and when nothing is on your side, just yell like hell. That's Geraldo Rivera."

Pruett was sentenced to four life terms for the murders of his wife, bank clerk Peggy Lowe, and the two 7-Eleven clerks in Colorado. An Arkansas judge sentenced him to death for killing Bobbie Robertson. Seventeen years later, a federal judge set aside Pruett's death sentence, ruling that pretrial publicity had prevented him from receiving a fair trial, but a higher court overturned the judge's ruling. It said Pruett had generated much of the publicity himself when he bragged on camera about his "mad dog" rampage. In April 1999, Pruett was executed by lethal injection in Arkansas.

CHAPTER
SEVENTEEN

A FEW MONTHS AFTER Marion Pruett's rampage, WITSEC came under attack again, and Shur found himself being criticized about the sort of criminals he was letting into the program. Thomas "Big Red" Bryant, a self-admitted murderer, who had once casually cooked himself scrambled eggs while his crime partner beat and terrorized an eighty-six-year-old man during a house burglary, was one reason why.

A former motorcyle gang member, Bryant was one of seventeen government witnesses called to testify by federal prosecutors in San Francisco in 1982 against the Hell's Angels motorcycle club. They had accused thirty members of the notorious biker club of conspiring to manufacture and distribute narcotics. They were charged under the RICO statute in an effort to disband the entire club. Like Bryant, most of the other witnesses were former Hell's Angels themselves, and when the government paraded them through the courtroom, they sickened the jury.

A turning point in the trial came when Bryant admitted during his testimony that a DEA agent had visited him the night before to give him a briefcase stuffed with $30,000 in small bills. The cash, Bryant said, was a reward paid to him in return for his testimony. That admission stunned defense attorneys, who quickly accused the DEA of buying testimony. When the defense grilled each of the other prosecution witnesses, it discovered that every one of them had been paid, too. The DEA had shelled out a total of

$280,000 in "rewards." The witnesses were also receiving other "inducements." Several said federal prosecutors had agreed to reduce or dismiss criminal charges pending against them. Nearly all had been accepted by Shur into WITSEC and were being given new identities and relocated.

The first Hell's Angels trial ended in a hung jury. In a second trial, the jury refused to convict any of the accused. Instead, jurors lashed out at the prosecutors after the trial for depending on such loathsome witnesses to make their case. The jury foreman called Bryant and the others "despicable and beneath contempt." Even the judge said he had been offended by the DEA's cash payments. As expected, defense attorneys were blunt. "This is a case," said one, "where the government simply went out and bought the testimony it wanted to use." A newspaper article described WITSEC as a "carrot" used to recruit witnesses.

Shur had not been told about the rewards in advance and was furious. He wasn't opposed to the government using rewards, but he felt the DEA had been out of line. "Giving rewards before someone testifies is outrageous and wrong," he explained. "Rewards should only be awarded after someone testifies and under strict conditions: A witness should never be told in advance he is definitely going to receive one, and he should never be told before he testifies what amount he will be awarded."

Shur knew jurors were naturally suspicious of criminals who changed sides and were now testifying against their friends. Studies showed most jurors were predisposed to distrust criminal witnesses, especially if they appeared to be profiting from deals made with prosecutors. At the same time, as a Justice Department attorney, he understood that prosecutors sometimes had little choice but to reach down into the gutter to recruit criminal witnesses. Notorious cases such as those of hippie-cult leader Charles Manson and the serial killer known as the Hillside Strangler never would have ended in conviction if prosecutors in California had not cut deals.

"The fact that most WITSEC witnesses weren't Boy Scouts," Shur said later, "did not mean they automatically lied for the government. The same was true about witnesses who were murderers or extremely violent. When I first joined the Justice Department, an old-time narcotics investigator told me the best case he had ever made was based on eyewitness testimony by a schizophrenic. He said, 'Shur, don't ever throw a nut out of your office.' Jimmy the Weasel had been a hit man and he could be violent, but that didn't have anything to do with whether or not he was telling the truth on the witness stand." The question always boiled down in Shur's mind to corroboration, preferably from wiretaps or from other witnesses who weren't criminals.

After the failed Hell's Angels case, Shur decided federal prosecutors and agents had to disclose in advance if a witness seeking WITSEC protection had been promised or paid a reward. He also required them to disclose to his office the details of plea bargains.

Shur moved to tighten WITSEC in other ways. He announced that relocated witnesses could no longer be used in undercover operations or as informants without his specific permission. "We discovered we were moving some witnesses two or three times because they were getting involved in new cases after they were relocated," he said. "We would move a witness from Brooklyn to Minneapolis, and an agent in Brooklyn would call a buddy of his in Minneapolis and tell him that he had just sent him a great guy to use undercover. The next thing you knew, the Minneapolis agent was using this witness to make cases. Here we were, trying to get a witness's kids into school and find him a job, only to have him call us saying he was being threatened again and needed to be moved because of some local case." Not only was it dangerous to keep using WITSEC witnesses, it was expensive. By the early 1980s, it cost WITSEC an average of $40,000 each time it relocated a witness.

"Some witnesses loved the excitement of helping prosecutors," said Shur. "I think it gave them the same exhilaration they felt when they committed crimes. I'd hear a witness talk about 'our case' and say things such as 'we got to get this guy.' One witness told me he had his own desk and his own secretary in a U.S. attorney's office."

Another change in WITSEC had evolved almost on its own. With the opening of WITSEC prison units, WITSEC had become a two-step program. Witnesses could no longer assume they would be automatically given new identities and be relocated after they were released from prison. Shur would decide whether they needed to be relocated or if they could simply be paroled, taking into consideration their conduct in the WITSEC unit and whether he felt they would still be in danger if they were released.

In late 1983, yet another Senate subcommittee held public hearings to investigate WITSEC, the fourth set in five years, and this time, the hearings led to passage of the Witness Security Reform Act of 1984. Written primarily by Senator Thad Cochran, it formalized many of the internal procedures that Shur already had implemented. There was one practice the law toughened. Because of the Pruett murders, the law required Shur and his staff to prepare a formal, written "risk assessment" of every witness, prisoner or nonprisoner, entering WITSEC. As part of this evaluation, each witness was required to undergo a battery of psychological tests administered by a psychologist. The examiner would then try to predict in a report given to Shur whether or not the witness would pose a threat to the community if he was relocated. It was Cochran's way of trying to keep WITSEC from turning another Pruett loose, and it quickly led to a disagreement between Shur and Howard Safir.

Safir said he wanted to use psychologists from the private sector to evaluate potential witnesses. But Shur argued that federal Bureau of Prisons psychologists were better trained to evaluate criminals and were less likely to be fooled. When Safir dug in his heels, Shur sent a detailed memo to attorney general Benjamin Civiletti explaining the benefits of using BOP psychologists. In the end, the two men reached a friendly compromise: Safir retained the right to call in outside psychologists whenever he believed a witness was an obvious risk. Shur agreed to review the outsider's opinion but not be obligated to accept its conclusions.

But the two men were soon butting heads again when Safir announced that he wanted his WITSEC inspectors to decide who got in WITSEC and who was rejected. "My inspectors were the frontline troops," Safir recalled. "They were the experts in the field who were actually dealing with these witnesses day in and day out, yet they had no input whatsoever in deciding whom Shur approved for relocation. That didn't make sense to me. In my opinion, it was pretty easy to tell right out front that some of these witnesses were not going to make it, yet we had to spend our time and resources, and put our people at risk, because some prosecutor wanted to use them as a witness. I told Gerry Shur that we wanted the right to veto any witness who we didn't think was a good candidate for relocation."

Shur was not about to surrender his power over who got into WITSEC. "This wasn't about ego," he explained later, "it was about giving the Marshals Service too much power. I couldn't have inspectors telling a U.S. attorney that he couldn't prosecute a mob case because the Marshals Service had decided it didn't want to protect or relocate a key prosecution witness."

Some inside the Justice Department saw Safir's move as an attempt to seize control of the entire program. "Howard had done a magnificent job revamping the WITSEC branch and getting his inspectors trained in how to handle witnesses," a former top WITSEC inspector who worked in the Marshals Service headquarters said. "He didn't think Shur needed to be calling the shots, and there were others inside the Marshals Service who were, quite frankly, sick and tired of getting the heat for relocating obvious killers like Pruett. The real problem was federal prosecutors. They only cared about racking up convictions. Some didn't care what sort of filth they put on the stand as long as a witness could get them a conviction. Then the Marshals Service was stuck dealing with this riffraff after the prosecutors had closed their briefcases and gone home. It only made sense that the people who actually had to do the job should have power over who got in."

Another Marshals Service manager who worked at its headquarters at the time put it like this: "In the early days, Shur let too many witnesses into the program. He always erred on the side of safety when it came to protecting witnesses. If a U.S. attorney out there said a witness needed protection, it seemed that Shur automatically let him in, and some of these witnesses were dangerous and awful." A WITSEC inspector would later recall how he picked up a witness, as ordered, from a U.S. attorney's office one afternoon and had an ice pick held to his throat without warning minutes later while speeding down an interstate thoroughfare. Luckily, he talked the witness out of killing him.

Shur would later dispute claims that he had been lax about letting witnesses into WITSEC. "Howard's inspectors often assumed that I approved every request I received from a prosecutor and that I never told them no. That was simply not the case. I often rejected a proposed witness for any number of reasons, such as the witness's testimony not being sufficiently significant, or we already had too many witnesses in a case, or in my mind the witness posed too great a threat of future violence. Naturally, I wouldn't notify the Marshals Service of the cases they were not going to be involved in, and since they didn't see the denials, they assumed I was approving everyone."

Regardless, Safir took his suggestion directly to Attorney General Civiletti. Shur, meanwhile, dashed off a long memo explaining why it was a wretched idea. "Giving the Marshals Service the absolute right of rejection of a witness would be abrogating the Criminal Division's responsibilities of determining what prosecutions should go forward," he declared. "To give them such power would allow them to negate years of investigation and grand jury work."

Once again, Shur and Safir compromised. Shur retained the final say over who did and didn't get into WITSEC, but he agreed to first consider written recommendations sent to his office by Safir's inspectors. It was a move that gave WITSEC inspectors more clout, at least in appearance.

"I had to look at factors other than whether this witness was going to be easy or difficult to relocate," Shur said later. Sometimes federal prosecutors needed to utilize criminals, including the likes of Thomas "Big Red" Bryant, for a larger purpose—bringing to justice criminals who were even more dangerous, he pointed out. This always entailed risks: Outcomes were not going to be predictable, compromises were inevitable, and some calls were going to prove wrong. It also meant he had to face the music when bad things happened, as well as become the whipping boy for those who could not acknowledge that complexity or uncertainty, or who had agendas of their own. Shur understood the buck stopped with him whenever WITSEC made a mistake. It was heat he was willing to take.

"Howard and I continued to have a friendly working relationship despite our disagreements," said Shur. "I remember we disagreed about a specific witness whom I had decided to let into the program, and Howard didn't think we should accept him. He felt so strongly, he decided to appeal my decision up the line. I had to leave town, but I trusted him so much that I suggested he present both sides of the argument. When I got back there was a message for me from Howard. It said: 'You won.' The same thing happened a second time when again I had to leave town. Once again Howard presented my side, and this time when I returned I had a message: 'You won again. Next time stay in town and present your own argument.' That says volumes about how much I trusted him."

Although Safir had failed at winning his field inspectors veto power, he had won them the right to make a formal written recommendation to Shur. "I came to value these assessments and rely heavily on them," said Shur. "Oftentimes, they were the first papers I read when my office received a packet from a U.S. attorney asking us to accept a witness into the program. Howard had actually created a new profession inside the Marshals Service, the WITSEC inspector, and I saw these specialists as a strong ally."

Whenever WITSEC inspectors would get together for a beer or in later years at reunions, the war stories would start. Someone would bring up the witness who had demanded that Donald "Bud" McPherson move her Thoroughbred, or the exotic dancer who was furious when three of her five snakes froze to death while they were being transported by deputies through Chicago. There would be mention of James Cardinali, the four-time murderer kicked out of WITSEC because he told his girlfriend his real name, who protested by picketing the federal courthouse in Albuquerque wearing a sign bearing a red bull's-eye and the words "Mob Star Witness." Or someone would mention former New Jersey mobster John Johnson, who was relocated to Austin, Texas, and was earning a good living operating a hot-dog vending business until he decided one day to run for mayor. He announced his candidacy by handing out copies of his seven-page rap sheet and declaring that he had been a thief *before* seeking office, whereas others waited to turn crooked after they were elected. He got 496 votes. Miami businessman Joseph Teitelbaum's name would occasionally surface, too. He was a "nonrelocated" innocent WITSEC witness. The mob tried to kill him after he spent eighteen months helping the FBI secretly collect evidence against the corrupt International Longshoremen's Association. Despite death threats—a crane operator was offered $50,000 to drop a cargo container on him—Teitelbaum adamantly refused to abandon his relatives and his business to enter WITSEC, arguing that he shouldn't have to go into hiding because he had done the right thing. Instead, Teitelbaum forced Safir to send inspectors to protect him at his home. They spent more than two years providing him with around-the-clock protection, at a cost of $3 million.

Of all the war stories, however, few could equal the case of the flaccid penis. A mobster became so depressed after he entered WITSEC that a psychologist warned an inspector that unless the witness's self-esteem was restored, he might not be able to testify. The psychologist suggested a penile implant because the gangster was having trouble getting an erection. The inspector put in the request, Shur approved it, the government paid for it, and afterward the witness's mental health improved dramatically. There was only one problem. One night the WITSEC inspector got a call from the mobster. "They put a button under my skin next to my navel," he explained. "You push it and your dick gets stiff, right? Now, here's the problem. When I lean forward while I'm eating, my gut hits the kitchen table right where this button is located, so boom, the little general shoots to attention. It's uncomfortable and can be very embarrassing."

"Buy a shorter chair or a table," the inspector suggested.

Jerry Lyda, who relocated several hundred WITSEC witnesses before retiring in late 2000, always enjoyed the war stories, but it was a panicked call from an informant in Chicago that he would later remember when asked to describe his thirty-year career as a deputy marshal. Two hit men were on their way to kill a relocated witness, the caller told him. Lyda telephoned a fellow inspector in a nearby city where the witness and his family were hiding. "He got them out less than an hour before the mob showed up to murder them," Lyda said. "It was an extremely close call."

Lyda was one of the first to volunteer to become a WITSEC inspector in 1978, after Safir began revamping the WITSEC operations. "He made the job something you had to volunteer for, a job that you had to want to get into, and he began pulling a different breed of inspectors into the job. Inspectors had a different mentality. You had to get satisfaction out of helping someone rather than arresting them. You had to turn your collar around, because as an inspector, you ended up doing a lot of jobs that were part deputy, part social worker."

Inspectors in the field had two assignments: protecting and producing witnesses in court within their jurisdictions, and successfully relocating them, a task that required finding a witness a new city to live in, making sure he received all of the assistance that was due him and his family, and then helping them become self-sustaining. If the inspector did his job well, no one would notice. Only his failures ever made headlines.

"During my career, I saw two major changes that really improved how we relocated witnesses. The first was the use of MOUs [Memorandums of Understanding], because everything was put down in black and white so there wouldn't be any confusion, or at least not as much as there had been," said Lyda. "The next big change was Howard Safir. He took a job few wanted and gave inspectors more clout, more say, and more respect."

What many witnesses didn't realize, said Lyda, was just how important a WITSEC inspector was going to become in their lives. "Every witness who came into the program would tell you, 'Hey, I'm the most important witness who's ever been in WITSEC.' " They believed that, in part, because federal prosecutors and agents had often fed their egos to get their cooperation. If they had a problem, they simply called the U.S. attorney and said they wouldn't testify unless their demand was met. But after they stepped off the witness stand, the WITSEC inspector was the only official there to help them.

"There were two keys to helping witnesses make the transition from the criminal to the legitimate world: attitude and trust. You couldn't force a witness to go straight, but you could help provide him the tools if he wanted to make the change. That's where the trust came into play. You had to win a witness's trust. Protecting him and his family was the first step to getting close to a witness. Then you helped him relocate. Hopefully by that time you had developed a close enough relationship that he would believe you when you said, 'Okay, when it comes to a job, you'll have to start at the bottom. It's not great, but it's a start. It will help you establish a work history and then we can move on to something better. But you will have to be patient.' A witness had to be able to believe you had his best interests at heart, and that was difficult for many of these guys because they were used to only watching out for themselves. It required a big leap of faith. What made the inspector's job different from other jobs in law enforcement was that it often required you to make a long-term commitment to these people and play a unique role in their lives. You ended up investing a lot of your time, your energy, and much of your personal career in helping them succeed."

The first problem in relocating witnesses was always money. "Few knew how to budget, and many of them were used to making hundreds of thousands of dollars through crime," said Lyda. "Now they had to scale back, and they didn't know how. You had to teach them a lot of basic living skills."

The second problem was secrecy. "I preached to every witness: 'Don't tell anyone where you have been relocated,' and then

I added, 'I mean *anyone*,' because the problem is that everyone trusts someone. A witness would tell me, 'I only told my mother. I can trust my mother,' and then I'd talk to the mother and she would say, 'I only told my sister. I can trust my sister.' Then the sister would say, 'I only told my husband. I can trust my husband.' And on it went. I had a witness who told a U.S. attorney where he had been relocated. Now, that sounds completely safe, but the attorney told a federal agent, and the agent was sitting in a courtroom one day and he told another agent within earshot of some defendants. Suddenly we had an emergency on our hands."

Lyda and other WITSEC inspectors warned relocated witnesses who had been given new identities not to tell anyone they met that they were witnesses, including people they dated or later even married. "Security was the top priority. You had to look down the road: What if there was a divorce and the spouse went running to the mob for revenge? It wasn't uncommon for an angry spouse to be furious at us because we hadn't told them about a witness's past. But we could not risk jeopardizing a witness's security."

The third problem was keeping witnesses from going home. "As time passed, they would begin to lose sight of why they had first entered WITSEC. The desire to go home and get back in touch with one's family and friends would become overwhelming. At the same time, they would convince themselves the risk had passed or there wasn't really that much risk at all. Psychologically, it made them feel safer, too, thinking that no one was really looking for them."

Witnesses would hear stories about other witnesses who had not been harmed when they returned home. One famous tale was about Herbert Itkin, whose testimony had sent Anthony "Tony Ducks" Corallo, a New York mob boss, to prison. After Corallo was paroled, the two men happened to come face-to-face one day outside the Waldorf Astoria Hotel. After several awkward seconds, they both said hello.

"You did a hell of a job on us," Corallo said, and then he walked on.

Lyda warned his witnesses that the risks were too great.

While the mob might not have bothered to send a hit man after a witness hiding in Iowa, it wouldn't hesitate to kill him if he was only a few blocks away. But his warnings were often ignored. One day a witness announced he was voluntarily dropping out of WIT-SEC. He said he had sent out feelers and been assured that the mob boss whom he had turned against was willing to forgive him. Lyda pleaded with him not to return, but the witness ignored him. He was murdered a few days later. "Being cut off from your family was simply intolerable for many of these witnesses," said Lyda. "As the months passed, it became very difficult for many of them not to at least try to sneak back. The inspector, of course, didn't have any way of knowing if a witness was going home, because after we relocated them, we didn't watch them twenty-four/seven." One afternoon Lyda was putting a WITSEC witness on a flight leaving Chicago when he spotted another witness strolling into the terminal from an aircraft that had just landed. He was returning from his "danger area."

"If you are going to survive as a WITSEC inspector, you learn quickly not to completely trust any witness," he recalled, "or you learn to know there are certain things you can trust and others that you can't trust." Another insight: "It seemed to me every one of these guys held something back from prosecutors. They knew if they ever got into trouble later, they could use it as a bargaining chip. They never told you everything they knew." Still another: "No matter how close you got to these guys, you always had to remember they had testified against their very closest friends. I remember getting along great with a witness and then the day came when I told him no. Instantly, he turned completely against me."

The trick was knowing how to walk the fine line that enabled an inspector to get close enough to win a witness's trust but not become a friend. Lyda knew inspectors who went to prison because they had gotten mired in business deals with witnesses. One inspector quit his job to marry a witness. "It was difficult because you put so much time and energy into helping them that you were heavily invested in their lives," said Lyda. Before Safir, deputies gave their home phone numbers to witnesses. Safir issued pagers to his WITSEC inspectors. It was a symbolic but important change.

Despite his years of experience, when he first interviewed a witness, Lyda could not predict whether or not he would make a good candidate for relocation. "No one had a crystal ball and you couldn't always tell from reading about a person's past or the crimes they had committed. There was no way to know when someone was finally ready to change their life. I had a motorcycle gang member who was so cold-blooded that he and another biker murdered this woman, then cut her open and put charcoal inside her to use as a grill. But when I relocated him, he was easy to deal with and really worked hard at going straight. He was a success story, but only for a while. He got a job in a bar and ended up shooting someone during an argument. He was sent back to prison. A lot of them were like that. They could go either way, and you didn't know which way they would choose."

It was that hint of doubt that was on a WITSEC inspector's conscience when he sent a known killer into a community. "You saw this witness as someone who deserved a chance to start over, not as the enemy. The real disappointment, of course, came when you discovered that someone you had helped had gotten into trouble. All your work—finding them a place to live, getting their kids into school, finding them a job—everything you had done to help them succeed suddenly didn't matter. Sometimes you would spend years helping someone, only to have them get into trouble again. I would confront them and tell them exactly how disappointed I was. I'd say, 'We put a lot of effort into helping you become a success, and you failed us.' But then you would have a success. There are dozens and dozens of witnesses out there I relocated who have never gotten into trouble. I know witnesses who had children, and now they're grandparents. I doubt their grandchildren have a clue about their grandparents' past. We helped change three generations of lives because of what we did as inspectors. That's what you focused on and strived for. That's what made all of the frustrations that came with the job worthwhile. At the end of the day, while your colleagues were locking bad guys behind bars, you had the quiet satisfaction of knowing there was a family living in the suburbs who used to be criminals and you helped them turn their life around."

Shur felt WITSEC had reached a turning point in 1984, and so did the Senate subcommittee that drafted the Witness Reform Act. "The Federal Witness Protection Program has become so essential that it is difficult to imagine federal law enforcement without it. That is a high and well-deserved compliment to pay a program that is only fourteen years old—and a program that is replete with the potential for many problems of great magnitude," the subcommittee wrote in its final report.

"We had reached a point where no one, either inside or outside of the government, was arguing anymore about whether or not this was a worthwhile program," said Shur. "They might disagree with who was allowed into the program, but WITSEC was here to stay."

PART THREE

WITNESS X—

A PERSONAL STORY

There is no one for us to talk to. We've become so-cial hermits. We start to make friends, then lose them because we're so inhibited.

Greg Mitchell, witness
As quoted in *The New York Times*, 1980

NO GOODBYES

THIS IS HOW it happens. You're cooking dinner. Your son is playing with Carmine, the kid from next door, and your baby is taking a nap. Your sister has stopped by and you're gossiping about the woman who is having sex with this Jewish guy who owns a corner deli and there's a knock, and when you open the door two men show you badges and your life suddenly ends. I mean, I had tomato sauce simmering. I knew Sal was thinking about cooperating with the cops. The last time I'd seen him in jail, he'd told me he was going to be down a long, long time, like fifteen or twenty. He was worried. I'd never seen him so worried. He tells me there is talk going around about him, you know, and that ain't good. You see, even if you aren't going to rat, if someone thinks you are, then you're going to end up being whacked and you might not ever have said a word to the cops. A guy like Tony, he isn't going to take chances with you, and even if you knew him since you were babies and you had first communion together, it don't matter. "Business is business." That's what Sal used to say all the time. Of course, he also used to say, "No one gets whacked unless they deserve it, because they got greedy or screwed up."

One of the U.S. marshals introduces himself as Larry and he says real polite-like that we got to go, like right now—just toss some clothes for a beach-type resort into a bag and go. He says Sal is in protective custody, which means everybody in jail knows he's a rat, which means Tony may be sending guys over right now to whack us.

This other marshal, he keeps looking outside, like he is making sure it is safe. Anna, she's my only sister, and me send Carmine home and start grabbing swimsuits, T-shirts, baby stuff, and I wake up Marie, my two-year-old. I come out of the bedroom and Anna is arguing with the marshals because they are saying she and our grandfather have to come, too, since Tony might kill them to get to Sal. You see, Sal was close to Tony. He knows a lot and they figure Tony is going to start whacking people just to make sure no one else decides to flip over and start talking. Tony has got to keep control of his crew.

Anna lives with our grandfather a few buildings down and the marshal says there is another marshal down there getting him. Anna and I just looked at each other. We were thinking: "The Captain moving? Oh yeah, like *that* is going to happen." We call our grandfather the Captain, everyone does, because he wears a blue sailor's cap. He has every day since World War I. The Captain spent his entire life in our neighborhood. We all had. But I don't think I had ever seen him outside five blocks from here. Once we asked if he wanted to go into Manhattan. He says, "Why? They got something I can't get here?" His daddy came directly over on the boat. Everyone knows the Captain. He's all the family me and Anna got. Our folks are dead and Sal's mom is dead and his dad married some woman in New Jersey and Sal hasn't talked to him in years.

Anna is telling the marshal she isn't going to go because she is about finished with beauty school, and the phone rings. Everyone looks at each other and I finally answer it. It's a marshal. He speaks to Larry. Then Larry tells me the Captain is refusing to go. By this time, Marie is crying and John, my four-year-old, is getting restless and Anna says, "Okay, I'll go, but I got to be back tomorrow for class," and the marshals are just trying to get us the hell out of there. So we all head downstairs with these marshals looking out into the hallway first and checking out the street. When they give us the all-clear signal, we come dashing down the front steps to a van they got running there and my neighbor, Mrs. Bonavolonta, is sitting on her stoop—she always sits there watching things—and she calls out, "Hey Angela, can you get me some salt if you are going to the market?" It's hard for her to walk because of her arthritis so she's always asking me to run errands. Here I am, running for my life, with Marie crying and John tagging along and Anna carrying suitcases, and Mrs. Bonavolonta is asking me to bring her back some salt!

The marshals drive us down to where Anna and the Captain live and I race upstairs, still carrying Marie, and try to talk to him, but the Captain says he is staying so I signed some stupid paper for the marshals about how they tried but he refused to go and Anna comes and gets in the van with her suitcase and her puppy. He is part German shepherd and part Labrador retriever and John loves him but Marie is scared and starts fussing again. What a sight! We're all crowded in this van with these two marshals and there's another car behind us with another two marshals and we are all afraid Tony's crew is going to come racing up and open fire any second. Meanwhile, all around us, life is going on as normal. People are walking their dogs, talking to neighbors, and us hurrying around. I don't think I really understood what leaving meant until we pulled away. There wasn't time to think and then I looked through the glass and there is the Captain standing on the porch stoop watching us go. For godsakes, how safe is that? The Captain is angry, but he has tears in his eyes and suddenly I am blubbering like a baby and then Anna starts and the kids begin and even the dog starts whimpering and these marshals are trying to get us quiet and the next thing you know, we are pulling out of the neighborhood where I lived my entire life—twenty-seven years—never having gone no further than New Jersey and the shore, and I am thinking, "What the hell is going to happen now?" and I am worried about the Captain being shot and suddenly I remember I had promised to help Mrs. Rizzo at a baby shower she is giving for her daughter-in-law tomorrow and how I had already bought a cute little baby outfit and then I realize I didn't have time to get any of the photographs of my parents from the bedroom. And then I started laughing and Anna says, "What's so funny?" and I am laughing so hard I can't even tell her because, you know, about a week before Sal got pinched by the cops, I had decided to begin putting away money just in case there was an emergency and I had five hundred bucks hidden in a coffee can up on the top shelf in my kitchen. I had thought about spending it a lot of times, but no, I kept saving it, and now it was there and I figured I'd never see it again, and for some reason that struck me as just being really funny, like a good joke on me, you know? I was a wreck.

Angela and her children were taken along with Anna and her dog to a federal building, where they spent six hours. They signed documents, talked to deputies, and waited. Then they left the city and drove for three hours, finally arriving at a small beachfront motel.

We looked at this dump and were in shock. There was some nice rooms there, but they didn't give them to us, and the owners, they treated us like trash. We were the only guests because it was out of season. My room had a pullout couch and a bed and was connected to Anna's room. The bathroom was filthy, the sheets and blankets smelled, the dresser drawers were filled with mildew. But John liked it because it was at the beach, and the dog seemed okay. That night a marshal stayed in a room next door, and me and Anna could hear him talking on the telephone because the walls were so thin and we hear him say, "Hey, I'm all alone out here! What if some heavy-duty shit goes down?" We just looked at each other. I mean, if this guy is scared and he's a big marshal, then what are us two women going to do? Sal had given me a pistol—a little .32 automatic—a long time ago and I had stuck it in my bag without the marshals seeing me and I got it out. Anna says, "Can you shoot?" I said, "Hey, if Tony and his goons come crashing through that door, I'm going to begin blasting and not ask questions. Just hit the floor because I don't aim real well." Anna laughed. We both needed a drink.

I didn't sleep that night. I just sat there with my pistol thinking about Sal and the Captain and the kids and what was going to happen to us. The marshals said we could never go back to Brooklyn. Never. I'd thought they were joking at first. I couldn't believe it. How can you be expected to just pick up like that and leave? I got really angry at Sal for being so goddamn stupid. I was glad my parents were dead. They would have been ashamed. They had never liked Sal. They hated me dating him. They said he was Mafia trash. But I liked how he walked through the neighborhood. He was someone important because he was part of Tony's crew, you know? We'd go out and people treated us with real respect. Sal never paid for a dinner. He always gave big tips. When we spent time with Tony, it was like we were royalty. Tony ran everything. I was lying in bed thinking when suddenly Anna comes into the room and asks if I am sleeping. "I was just thinking," she says. "You think Mrs. Bonavolonta is still waiting for the salt?" We both giggled.

The next morning, Anna and I got into this terrible fight. I was talking about how worried I was and suddenly she says, "Hey, what about me? I'm not even married to Sal but my life is ruined." She had been doing real well in beauty school. Just like me, she'd grown up in the neighborhood. I hadn't thought about her and how this was messing things up. We didn't speak all day. Finally, after dinner I apologized and we had a good cry. We were sitting outside when this car comes down the road directly in front of the motel and dims its lights. There's this young guy in there and he sees us and pulls into the motel and asks us if there is a bar anywhere close. Anyone could see that nothing was open but he sort of hangs around for a few minutes. Anna got his license tag number and we hurried down to the motel office, since we didn't even have a phone in our room, and called this emergency number that the marshals had given us. The marshal who was supposed to be watching us had gone into town to eat dinner. About three hours later, he comes to our rooms steaming mad. He has gotten chewed out for leaving us and he thinks we got him into trouble on purpose because we don't like him. You can tell from his comments he thinks Sal is a piece of garbage who should be locked up forever and you can tell he isn't happy about being stuck out here guarding us. He thinks we are lying about the car, but when he checks, he finds out it belongs to some guy who I guess was trying to pick up a date. The next day, the marshal packed up and left without saying a word. He left us there wondering what was going to happen and not knowing what to do. It was unreal.

Later that same day, a car pulled up and out steps the Captain. He says he started getting threatening telephone calls the same day we left. His friends who he'd played chess with stopped playing with him. Who could blame them? They were afraid. People would leave whenever he went to get a cup of coffee. These were people he'd known all his life and they were scared to talk to him. He told me he would never talk to Sal again. Not another word. We put him in Anna's room. I'd never seen him so sad.

We stayed in that damn motel for a month. It was depressing. We got bored. There was nothing to do. No toys. Nowhere to go. Finally, Sal shows up with four marshals guarding him, like he's some big shot. He said we were going into the witness program. Anna freaked out. She wanted to go back to Brooklyn, but the marshals said we could never go back. We'd be killed. Word on the street was that Tony had a contract out on Sal. Can you imagine what it feels like to know someone is hunting for you and your kids? To know there is someone out there who wants to shoot you? The marshals told us to begin thinking of new names. They said Anna and the Captain were going to be sent somewhere away from us. They told us not to tell each other our new names, but of course I told Anna. Anna was bitter. The marshals told her they'd get her into another beauty school and help her find a job, but she hated Sal for messing up her life. Our last night together, Anna wasn't talking to Sal, the Captain wasn't talking to Sal, and I wasn't talking to Sal. The marshals told us we weren't supposed to contact each other ever again. If someone on Tony's crew found us, they'd make us tell where the others were hiding. They told us we could send letters to each other through them. We were to write our letter, put it inside another envelope, and send it to the marshals so they could open it and forward that letter to the right address. Me and Anna agreed that we would write and tell each other our telephone numbers as soon as we got settled. Of course it was against the rules, but c'mon, did anyone really think we were never going to see each other again?

The next morning, they left first. I hugged my granddad and kissed Anna, and John cried because she took her dog with her. That mutt and John had become good pals. I didn't know how I felt. I had been taken from my home and now I was saying goodbye to my sister and grandfather. We weren't leaving until the next day. Sal wanted to make love that night after the kids were asleep. I told him to forget it. All I could think about was what is going to happen to us and what a jerk he was for getting us into this mess.

A FRESH START

Sal, Angela, and their children, John and Marie, were met at the Rapid City, South Dakota, airport by a deputy who drove them downtown to a hotel.

N OT FAR FROM where we was staying, there were two white towers. I asked Sal, "What are those?" They didn't have windows so I knew they weren't apartments. Sal says maybe they're missile silos because he'd heard there was an Air Force base just outside town and the government had missiles hidden in silos all over the state. Sal asked someone and it turned out they were grain elevators. Right in the middle of the city—grain elevators! That's how out in the sticks we were! We went for a car ride and I said, "Hey, you know something, there's no subway here!" We both laughed. I mean, we'd seen the entire city in thirty minutes! Sal says to me: "I didn't see any Italian restaurants neither. How we going to eat?" There was a white-haired man standing in the hotel wearing cowboy boots and this big silver belt buckle. I said to Sal, "Sal, that's an Indian, a real Indian." He didn't believe me because the only Indians he'd seen was at the movies and they didn't look like that, but I asked the clerk and it was one.

The deputy told them a moving company would deliver their household belongings in six months. They could live in the hotel until they could find an apartment or a house to rent.

He arranged a telephone call through the Marshals Service's switchboard so that Angela could talk to her sister, Anna, and her grandfather. The Marshals Service wanted the women to tell the Captain that he had to sell his house in Brooklyn because it was against the rules for him to keep it.

Me and Anna knew there was deputies listening to our telephone conversation so we didn't say nothing about where we was. Anna says the Captain is really getting depressed. Someone had broke into his house in Brooklyn and spray-painted the word "snitch" on the front door in big red letters. When the Captain got on the phone, it was like he didn't care about nothing. He didn't even ask me about the kids. It was so sad. I told him he had to sell his house because the government wasn't going to help him buy another one unless he sold the first one first. "Angel," he says—that's what he always called me since when I was little—"I was born in my house. Your mother was born there, too. How can I sell it? It's got too many memories." He asked me if I thought he was going to be able to move back home after all this trouble with Tony blew over and I said, "Yeah, why not? I'm sure you can move home," and he seemed upbeat about that. I'm sure I made the deputies mad, but the Captain, he was almost eighty. I felt he needed something to look forward to, you know? It wasn't like they could put him in jail or toss him out into the street if he kept his house. Besides, it was their problem, not mine.

Two months later, the deputy told Angela that the Captain had suffered a stroke and died. His body was being taken to Brooklyn for a funeral and burial, but neither she nor her sister would be permitted to attend. The legal cases against Tony and the members of his mob crew were in the courts, and the prosecutors handling them were afraid it was too dangerous to allow either granddaughter to attend the funeral.

It killed me not to be able to be there. I felt all this relocation trauma caused the stroke and I blamed Sal. It was no different from putting a gun to the Captain's head and pulling the trigger. My last memory of him was him getting into a car with deputies at that lousy motel on the beach and me and the kids waving goodbye. He left everything he owned to me and Anna, but we had different last names now—all legally changed—so probate was complicated, especially since the deputies had to keep our new names a secret. The Captain left some certificates of deposit but we couldn't cash them because we couldn't prove we was related to him. Imagine, not being able to prove your grandfather is really your grandfather. The deputies didn't know what to do either. I did get my great-grandmother's wedding ring. Anna had it sent to me through the deputies and that meant a lot to me.

When Sal and Angela's furniture arrived, the box that contained the only photographs Angela had owned of her parents was missing.

I thought the deputies had destroyed the pictures because they told us we couldn't take anything from our past, you know, like my high school diploma. I was upset and cried. I had no pictures of my mom and dad but the deputy says, "Oh well, it's a good thing really. Someone might recognize them." I thought that was the stupidest comment I'd ever heard. Who in Rapid City, South Dakota, is going to see a picture of my two dead parents and recognize them? I wondered how he'd have felt if it was a picture of his parents.

In Brooklyn, we used only cash. Nobody in Tony's crew had a checking or savings account in a bank. The IRS could use those records to keep track of how much money you had. Sal kept cash in his pocket and I kept cash hidden around the house. Sal used to tell me not to bother hiding it because no one with any brains was going to rob us in Brooklyn. They knew what would happen to them. The deputy took us down to this bank in Rapid City and showed us how to use bank accounts. I was watching Sal and the whole time we was in this bank, he isn't paying any attention to the deputy. He is checking out the security. I thought he was going to rob the place right then. A judge had changed our names but we still didn't have new birth

certificates or any permanent identification or Social Security cards
with our new names, but this deputy talked to the bank manager and
took care of it somehow. I had trouble at first remembering my new
last name. Anytime anyone asked me a question about where I was
from or something personal, I would freeze and not know what to say.
Of course, it was easy for Sal. Oh, lying, it came easy to him.

*The deputy gave them cash each month for their living
expenses and said it was pointless for Sal to find a job
because federal prosecutors would soon call him to testify in
Brooklyn and he could be gone for weeks at a time.*

All Sal did was complain. I was used to being home with the kids,
okay, but he was useless. The kids got on his nerves. Back in Brooklyn,
Sal would go out every night to different clubs and restaurants to meet
with Tony and his crew. Every night except Sunday, usually. Sal didn't
know how to sit at home with his family watching TV. What bugged
him the most was no respect, you know, being a nobody. In Brooklyn,
if Sal walked into a restaurant, the owner came running up to say
hello. There was no standing in line for Sal, and Sal never ever made a
reservation. Not him. He was too important. Out in Rapid City, he was
a nobody. He hated it. I got him to go with me and the kids to this real
nice Catholic church once. There was a big air force base outside
town so it wasn't like the people in Rapid City had never met anyone
from New York or New Jersey. Even so, Sal really stuck out. He was
wearing gold chains and he liked to keep his shirt unbuttoned
because he had a big, strong, hairy chest. These people were
cowboys, you know, quiet and conservative. His entire personality
didn't fit with the place. Sal says to me one night: "If I had some of
Tony's crew here, we could run this city, but what would we have? Two
goddamn grain elevators." I laughed but I was having a tough time,
too. I missed Anna, and to be honest, I was bitter and angry at Sal. I
blamed him for busting up my family and he resented my attitude.
He'd say, "Hey, you knew who I was before you married me so don't
come crying to me now."
     One afternoon I decided it was time for me to get over it. I was

feeling bad for myself, I wasn't really there for the kids. I said to myself, "This can be an opportunity." I kept telling myself that. Me and Sal could live like ordinary people. I met this girl, Carol, at the grocery store. Our kids were the same ages. She and her husband, Dan, were good people. Dan liked to fish and he invites Sal and John to go with him. Now, Sal had never even held a fishing pole. They go up to this creek in the mountains and Sal can see the fish swimming around but he can't catch any. He gets so mad, he throws the pole at them! Dan falls down because he is laughing so much. Later, Sal catches one and he was like a little kid. He comes running in to show me this slimy, dead fish. Dan cleans it and we had this fish fry. It was a good time. I thought, "Hey, maybe this will work."

STARTING OVER AGAIN

THINGS GOT BETTER in Rapid City once Sal started flying back to Brooklyn to testify. He'd come home and tell me what he did. He'd say, "I looked them bastards right in the face when I was testifying. I didn't blink. When they bring Tony in, I'm going to point my middle finger at him and really get him good." Sal would tell me he was lying about some things he testified to in court but he wasn't worried at all about getting caught. For him, it was payback time and he wanted to please the prosecutors. He'd tell me how he and these FBI agents were making this case. It was "we" this and "we" that. All of his life he hated cops and now he's acting like one. I said, "Sal, there isn't any 'we.' These prosecutors and cops—you think one of them is going to give a damn about you once you finish talking? They ain't gonna remember your name." He got all pissed off. He says, "Why you trying to put me down?" Then he walked out the front door. I didn't know where he was going. He'd stay out all night. I didn't care. I'd call my sister, Anna. [The two had exchanged telephone numbers in violation of the WITSEC rules.] But she was very bitter about our grandfather dying and she sorta blamed me because I was married to Sal. She was doing okay without me. The deputies had gotten her into a beauty school in Philadelphia.

I began spending more time with my friend Carol, but she made me nervous, too. You don't realize how much you talk about your past until you don't have one to talk about. We'd be talking away about something, maybe guys we had dated, and I would have to catch myself because I was about to say something about Brooklyn. Like innocent things would throw you off, you know. I felt sure she knew I was lying sometimes. The deputy told us to say we were from Camden, New Jersey, because people out West wouldn't know the difference between it and Brooklyn. One day Carol says, "I've heard of Camden because they make Campbell's soup there." I didn't know. I had to go down to the library and read about Camden. We told everyone Sal was a warehouse foreman because no one knew what a warehouse foreman did. Sal could bullshit anyone anyway. It was our son, John, who scared me because he was too little to understand. When he turned five, Carol and her kids came over for a party and John and Carol's son begin wrestling and suddenly I hear John saying, "My daddy is going to kill your daddy. He's been in jail and a real sheriff comes to our house and gives us money." I grabbed him and made him say he was sorry and then I said something about how he was watching too much television.

Sal finished testifying two years after he and Angela were relocated. The deputy in Rapid City found Sal a job at Ellis Air Force Base as a civilian security guard.

Sal guarding government property—what a joke. He bought this big Cadillac with some cash he got as a reward for testifying. We fought a lot about money. Sal had never been any good with it. If he had cash, he spent it. If he needed more in Brooklyn, he just went out and took it. He couldn't do that now. We had a budget, or I had one. Our relationship was a mess. All we did was fight, but to tell you the truth, I didn't care. I didn't love him anymore. I hated him. Before we left Brooklyn, I thought he was a good husband. Now I'd seen how Dan treated Carol. I saw normal people who were happy, you know. Not that there weren't any normal people in Brooklyn—it's just we never hung around them.

One Saturday afternoon John, then age seven, rode his bike down a steep hill at the edge of town into a busy highway intersection. He was struck by a car.

No one could find Sal. I rushed to the emergency room. I could see John. The doctors and nurses were working on him and then everyone stopped and I knew he was dead. Carol and her husband were there with me but Sal never showed up. He comes home late that night and he doesn't even know what's happened. He told me he was at work but I knew he was lying. Those next few days were hell. I would have gone nuts if Anna hadn't flown out to be with me. We buried John in a cemetery in Rapid City. He didn't even have his real name on the monument. Anna stayed on for a while. Sal was useless. Our daughter, Marie, was too little to understand. She'd ask me why I was crying and then she'd keep saying, "Where's John?" Anna and I got real close again. She was out of the witness program and had gotten married to a really nice guy. She was working in a beauty parlor that she was buying. She told me she had gone back to Brooklyn without telling the marshals because one of her best friends was getting married. She said a cousin of Tony's was at the wedding and he told her Tony had gotten sent to prison for life because of Sal and Tony wanted revenge, but not against her or me or the kids. He tells her, "Tony ain't like that. He ain't gonna punish a man's family, but Sal, he's filth, garbage. Everybody in the neighborhood hates him for what he's done." Anna acted like she agreed and she played dumb when he asked where Sal was hiding. She got out of there because she was scared. As soon as Anna left Rapid City, I got real depressed again. I'd go into John's room and just sit there and cry. Somehow I felt responsible. I kept thinking, what if we hadn't left Brooklyn, what if I'd married a square, what if Sal had just toughed it out in jail?

Sal wasn't coming home at all. A week would go by and I'd not see him. I was spending a lot more time with Carol. We decided to start a preschool where other mothers could drop off their kids. It was her idea, I just helped. Carol was the teacher. But I had a real knack with kids and enjoyed reading them stories. It made me feel closer to John somehow. One afternoon me and Marie were coming home from Carol's house and the deputy's car is parked in front of my house. I thought Sal was dead or had stolen something. Then I got scared because I thought something had happened to Anna. Maybe Tony's crew had tracked her down. The deputy tells me Sal is gone. I said,

"What the hell are you talking about?" He says Sal had come to see him and told him about Anna's visit and how she had gone to the wedding in Brooklyn. Sal told the Marshals Service he didn't feel safe anymore in Rapid City because Anna knew where he was hiding and she hated him. He wanted to be relocated. The deputy said the government was required to move him because me and Anna had violated his security. He said Sal had taken all of our money out of the bank. He says, "I couldn't legally stop him because both of your names were on the accounts. Besides, this is all your fault for contacting your sister."

I was really angry at that creep. I looked in the house and Sal had left the furniture. By this point, the deputy is acting strange and then he tells me Sal is being relocated with another woman. I ask, "Who?" and he tells me the name of this bitch I knew back in Brooklyn. At first I couldn't understand how Sal got in touch with this girl and why him seeing her wasn't a security violation and then it falls into place. Back when we all lived in Brooklyn and Sal was part of Tony's crew, I'd heard Sal was messing around with this eighteen-year-old neighborhood slut named Rose. He'd been seen by a girlfriend of mine with her. I never said nothing but I was mad. Lots of Tony's crew had girlfriends. They would take us wives out on Friday night and then on Saturdays they'd take out their whores. Sal swore he didn't have no one like that.

The deputy tells me Rose was relocated with *us* when we was moved out to Rapid City! I said, "You moved her out here when you moved us?" He said they had to move her because they was afraid Tony would hurt her because she was Sal's girlfriend. They'd tried to put her somewhere else, but Sal and she insisted on being together. All the sudden, all these things begin making sense—like where Sal was going at night, why we was short of cash, even where Sal was when John was killed and no one could find him. I lost it. I screamed at this deputy. I said, "You knew that bitch was here the entire time and you never told me!" I freaked out. He said Sal and Rose had left that morning on a flight. I am boiling mad. It's like the government is giving them a honeymoon. I can't believe the deputies brought that woman to Rapid City and dumped me here with her, and now Sal and this whore are like a prince and princess and me and Marie are all alone. I screamed: "Where'd you send them?" and he says he can't say because Sal and Rose are getting new identities. I'm so angry I can't even talk.

He says I am going to be relocated. He doesn't ask if I want to. He tells me I have to move because the deputies don't want Sal to be able to find me. That's how they do it when there's a divorce. I start screaming again. I say, "How about Marie? Is Sal going to pay child support?" The deputy says he don't know. He tells me, "Look, I don't even know where Sal and Rose are being taken." I tell him, "I'm not changing my name or Marie's neither." Then I started crying and he says, "Isn't there someone you can call?" And that really puts me over the edge. I yell, "Like who? I'm not supposed to be talking to my sister, right? Just who in the hell am I supposed to talk to?"

I sold everything we owned. I didn't want to keep a damn thing that reminded me of Sal. Get this, Sal took my great-grandmother's ring—the one the Captain gave me. He stole it. Anyway, the deputy had me and Marie relocated. He said me and Marie could keep our names but he lied. We had to change our last names again. I didn't care anymore about Sal. It was saying goodbye to John that hurt. I hate he is buried there and don't even have the same name he was given. That wasn't right.

The night before we left, I went to see Carol and I told her everything. I didn't care anymore about the marshals and security and I figured I'd never see her again anyway. It was funny. She told me she thought something was weird about us, especially Sal, but they didn't know the government hid people like that. I think she was afraid of me because when I went to go, she didn't even want to give me a hug. I don't know why I told her. I just needed someone to listen to me, I guess. I just needed to tell someone the truth. It didn't change anything at all but I felt better.

MOVING ON

Angela and Marie were resettled in Phoenix, Arizona, with new last names that once again had been legally changed. Angela became a close friend of the deputy marshal helping her there and he frequently stopped by to visit.

I HAD TO EXPLAIN to Marie why we had a new last name. I said sometimes people change their names when their mommies got married or when they moved to new towns. She was only five and she believed me. She asked about Sal, but not as much as I thought she would. He had never spent much time with her but she knew he was her daddy. After a few months, I began telling her Sal was really her uncle and he had moved back east. One day I told her her real daddy had been a pilot in the air force and had been killed. I told her he had loved her a lot but she probably was too young to remember him. She remembered seeing all the big airplanes in Rapid City at the air force base there so this lie made sense to her. It was what I was telling people in Phoenix, too—that I was a widow whose husband had died. Marie seemed to me to believe it. She thought Sal was her uncle and her daddy was dead. I didn't feel bad about lying. Sal was a scumbag and I didn't want Marie to know anything about the mob and Brooklyn. That was behind me and her now.

We lived in an apartment and the deputy got me a job working in an office at the courthouse. I'd never really had a job and it was really,

really tough at first. But the other girls who worked there were great and they helped me a lot. I started trying to lose my Brooklyn accent and I tried to become more like everyone else. I dressed like they did. I avoided talking about my past. I'd say my husband was dead and it was too painful to talk about and no one would hassle me about it. There were a couple of good-looking guys at the courthouse but I didn't date any of them. I was afraid. I told them I still loved my husband. I remember when Marie was about ten, she was looking through old shoe boxes of photographs and there was a picture of Sal holding her and John in South Dakota. I'd kept it because of John. I couldn't bear to throw pictures of him away but I thought I had got rid of all the ones of Sal. Anyway, Marie asked me who Sal was! She had forgotten completely about him in the five years we'd been in Phoenix. I was happy about that. I thought, "If Uncle Sam can lie about stuff, why can't I?"

My sister, Anna, had a baby and me and Marie flew out east to visit them. I'd forgotten what big old cities are like. Anna said I should move back east to Philadelphia but I didn't want to. Marie was doing really good in school and she seemed happy. I liked my job at the courthouse, too. Besides, I had started buying a house. It was old and small but it was mine. I was feeling good about myself, you know? Before, I only did what Sal wanted to do but now, I was doing what me and Marie wanted. When we got back from visiting Anna, someone had burglarized my house. I was pissed. It was like a rape. You felt violated. These bastards took a big jar of pennies from Marie's room. Stealing from a kid. I was really fuming and then it hit me like a brick in the head: Sal used to be a thief. When he was a teenager, he broke into lots of houses and stole things. I'd never thought about none of those things before. I never thought about the people who he stole from or beat up or whatever. I was ashamed of what he'd done.

The cops came and had me write this long list of everything stolen and a few days later, they called me. Some neighborhood kids had my stuff. They was trying to pawn it. I went down to the police station and my heart almost stopped. There was this metal box me and Sal kept papers in. I had my birth certificate in there—the one my parents got when I was born—and the real birth certificates for John and Marie, not the new ones the deputies gave us. I had some stories from the newspaper in the box, too, about Sal and Tony and how Sal was testifying. Sal brought them back when we was in South Dakota. I don't know why I kept those stories but I had 'em in there. The burglars had broken open the box and I could see the birth certificates and articles were still in it. I thought: "Jesus Christ, the police got to be wondering why I got these certificates and articles." This officer says to me, "Lady, is this here your box of documents?" and I thought about lying but I thought maybe that's what they wanted me to do, you know, lie about it, so I said, "Yeah, it's mine" and he hands it to me. He hadn't looked inside. I decided to burn them—the articles—when I got home, but I kept the birth certificates. I put them in an envelope in my closet. Jesus, that was a close call.

I started dating Ted when Marie was about eleven. He had been watching me for several years at the courthouse. He's a lawyer but he was married back then so he didn't really say anything besides hello when he saw me. One day this lady who worked with me in the office said Ted's wife had died. She had a heart attack just like that even though she was young. This lady says to me, "You should help him out with advice," because everyone thought I was a widow. The next time I see him, I told him how sorry I was about his wife and he says, "Yeah, you know what it's like," and we started talking. In a way, I did know because Sal wasn't dead but he was not in my life anymore.

Sal was a show-off, really loud, macho, and stupid. Ted was quiet and very, very smart and that really scared me because I only finished high school and I didn't do good when I was a student. The first time Ted asked me out, I said, "Sorry, I don't date," and he says, "Let's just have coffee, like friends, not people on a date." I said okay. I remember thinking how kind he was when we talked. No one in Brooklyn I knew dated lawyers. He laughed a lot at my jokes. It was my way of throwing people off. I got a great memory for jokes and I tell jokes whenever I want to change the subject or if I start feeling uncomfortable around people. I started doing that in South Dakota. I used to answer questions by asking people questions back to throw them off. Another thing I did was ask people about their lives. Most people forget to ask about you once they start talking about themselves.

Me and Ted began going out and I was afraid he'd expect sex

right off but he was a perfect gentleman. He wasn't pushy like Sal and he sent me roses. Sal didn't send flowers and if he did that, I'd know he'd done something bad. Ted and Marie, they got along really, really good too. She'd wait for him to come over and ask him to help her do homework because I was never any good at helping her. Ted wanted to do lots of things. I think it was because his wife died so young. He said they had talked a lot about what they were going to do when they retired, and she died before they did anything. He decided we all needed to learn how to play golf, Marie too. He belonged to this country club and me and Marie and him went there for lessons. I liked how he wanted Marie with us. Me, I was terrible, but Marie and him were pretty good. I said, "Okay, I'll drive the cart." One day Ted says he wants to fly an airplane and he goes out and learns how to do it. He was ten years older than me. He would take me and Marie up on flights. Ted liked flying so he bought a part of an airplane with these other guys. They'd take turns.

Me and him began flying to Las Vegas on the weekends he got the airplane. We'd go to Caesars Palace because it was the best. Ted played blackjack and I'd hit the slots. One night I was on this machine when I hear: "Angela!" I turned around and there is a man there I knew from the old neighborhood. We'd gone to high school together. He wasn't in Tony's crew or nothing but I was terrified. I says, "You got the wrong girl, mister, my name is Irene," and then I ran up to our room. I told Ted I wanted to go home because I was sick but I really was scared we'd see this guy again. I thought about telling Ted the truth but I was really afraid because I had lied so much to him. He thought I was a widow from South Dakota and I knew he wouldn't want to be with some gangster's wife. Ted had big companies for clients. He didn't do criminal law. He told me he had started out wanting to be a Perry Mason type, proving the cops had the wrong guy, but then he discovered most people who get arrested are guilty. Don't kid yourself, it ain't because cops are smart. It's because criminals are stupid. He says to me once, "Angela, I would really get upset if I got someone off and he went out and hurt or killed someone." So I knew he'd be tough on me.

Here was another reason for me to keep my mouth shut. I didn't want Marie to ever know about Sal. I decided not to tell Ted anything, but living with a lie is scary because you become paranoid. Each time the phone rings, each time you go somewhere, each time you are in a restaurant, you're afraid you'll bump into someone who knows your secret. I wasn't afraid of Tony and the mob. That was too many years ago. I was afraid Ted wouldn't understand and would be embarrassed if people found out who I really was. I was happy with this new life of mine. I didn't want anything or anyone to change that. It was mine, but it wasn't mine, if you understand. It was pretend, but I wasn't really pretending. I knew, too, I knew in my heart, something terrible was going to happen because that is how life is. And it sure as hell did. Sal showed up.

WEAVING TANGLED WEBS

I STILL DON'T KNOW how Sal found me and Marie in Phoenix. Maybe some deputy told him. Maybe he found out through my sister, Anna—but she denied it. All I know for sure is one morning I opened the front door and there was Sal standing there. I was glad Marie wasn't home. She was at summer camp and was gone all week. I was supposed to be going on a trip with Ted. We was leaving later that day. I didn't want no one to see Sal so I let him into my house and he looks around and says to me, "Nice place you got here." I got right to the point. I asked him what he wanted from me. He says he wants a cup of coffee and goes and sits down like he lives there. He tells me he just got out of prison. That bitch he ran off with is long gone. He doesn't know what happened to her. He says her and him got relocated in Milwaukee after they left Rapid City and he started stealing cars and stripping them for parts. He'd gotten pinched and done time. He thought the deputies would save his ass but they didn't. He said he was in prison under a different name so no one knew about how he'd testified against Tony in Brooklyn. He tells me all these lies about how he spent all his time in prison thinking about me and how good we was together and how he screwed up things with me and how he thinks maybe we need to get back together. I told him there was no way in hell I'd be with him again or let him move in with me and Marie and he says, "Well, you know, we're still married. I never got a divorce and you never did neither." I thought, "Oh God, he's right." I couldn't divorce him because I didn't know what had happened to him. But I tried not to show anything. I says to him, "Yeah, but we got different names now so those people we were don't even exist no more." He reached over like he was going to slap me but he stopped himself. He starts telling me how he is Marie's daddy no matter what name he is using and he wants to make up for lost time and get to know her. I said, "Oh really? How old is she?" He didn't know. I said, "When's her birthday? You never sent her a gift." He says he didn't know where we were, and I said, "Well, you sure as hell are sitting here right now, aren't ya? Guess you could've found out earlier if you wanted." It was weird because I was glad he'd never talked to Marie or sent her stuff, but here I was busting his balls for not doing it.

He tells me he met this guy in the joint who is giving him a job as a mechanic down in Tucson so he'll be close enough now to see Marie even if I divorce him, which he knows I'm not going to do because I got a new life here and don't want anyone to know about my past. I looked at his hands because he says he learned how to fix cars in the joint and I knew he was lying. There wasn't any grease or oil on them. You ever meet a mechanic who didn't have grease-stained hands? I knew he didn't care nothing about Marie, either. He was trying to scare me so I'd give him money. I just came out and asked him how much it was going to cost me to get him to go away, and you know what he says? He says, "Ten grand and your pussy!" I said, "Sal, what the hell are you talking about?" and he tells me he wants to have sex with me, right there, right now. I'm so angry I'm about to explode. All I am thinking about is how much I hate his guts but I know if I don't handle this just right, he's going to make my life miserable so I said, "Sal, I'm in my period," and he says, "Hey, I don't care, where's your bedroom?" He took me back to my bedroom. He knew I was lying about my period. I never could lie to Sal very well. I just laid there and didn't move or say nothing but it didn't matter to him.

When he's done, he says, "So when can you get me the money?" I said it would take me a week and he says, "Okay, I'll be over tomorrow." He says he is going to claim his husband's right and I knew right then I was not going to get him out of my life ever. When he finally left, the phone rang and it was Ted. I told him I couldn't leave that afternoon on our trip. I forget what excuse I gave him but I told him I'd be ready to go the next day. Then I called the U.S. marshals' office and asked for the deputy who'd helped me when me and Marie first got to Phoenix. They told me he'd retired but I still remembered his home number and he was furious when I told him what Sal did. I lost it and began crying. He says Sal wasn't ever supposed to find me. He says I could charge Sal with rape but everybody in Phoenix would know about my past and the mob might come after Sal and me and Marie because it would make the papers. The deputy told me not to pay Sal but I felt trapped, because if I didn't pay him, he was going to talk to Marie and I didn't want him talking to her or to Ted. I didn't know if Ted would understand about how Sal forced me to have sex and all, and I knew Sal was right about us still being married and I didn't know what Ted would do if he found out about that and our past. Ted thought my husband was dead.

It was a big mess. No matter what I did, someone I loved was going to get their feelings hurt—either Marie or Ted.

I asked the deputy to help me, but he said there wasn't anything he could really do except ask the deputies to relocate me again and maybe hassle Sal when he showed up at my house tomorrow. He said Sal might be violating his parole by being in Arizona and he'd check to see if he could get Sal picked up by the cops when he showed up at my house. I told him I didn't trust no one but him, especially the cops. I figured they'd tell Ted. Anyway, it was a big, big mess. Finally, I said, "Me and Marie are going to disappear, will you help me?" He asked me to let the deputies help me relocate, but I was just too afraid. I packed up some bags after I hung up the phone and then I looked outside to make sure Sal was gone and then I got in my car and met him [the retired deputy] at this McDonald's. He begged me to reconsider, but I said, "Nope, this is the best way." I gave him my house keys and drove to the summer camp and took Marie out. I told her we were moving to California and she thought I was joking. Then she started yelling and crying and throwing a fit and threatening to run away. She says, "What about Ted?" She thought we were going to be a family and he was going to be her father and I started bawling and I said to her, "Honey, it's time you learned the truth." But, of course, I lied. I told her that her uncle Sal was in the Mafia and had testified against some gangsters in Brooklyn and now they were after us because of him. She didn't believe a word of it. I said, "Why do you think I changed our names when we left Rapid City?" and "Why do you think that deputy always was coming around to check on us when we first got to Phoenix?" That got her thinking.

I told her I loved Ted and wanted to marry him but if I did then the mob would be after him too, so we couldn't ever contact him again, but she could write him a goodbye letter and mail it before we got to California. She had a notebook from summer camp and she wrote him a letter while I was driving and then we stopped at this gasoline station and bought a stamp and envelope and mailed it to him. We were both just crying and crying. I made her promise never to tell anyone about what was happening. She was scared. I drove all the way to Los Angeles and checked us into a motel. I didn't know what else to do to get away from Sal. It was so strange, here I was running again, hiding again, only this time it wasn't from the mob, it was from my own husband.

CLOSURE

M Y DEPUTY FRIEND in Phoenix got Marie's school records for me and I decided to take a risky step. Sal knew our names in Phoenix and I didn't want him finding us in California. I knew I could change my name. All I had to do was tell people I had gotten married and changed my last name. The problem was Marie's school records. I thought a lot about how to do it and came up with this really swell idea. I drove to the school and showed the principal Marie's original birth certificate—not the one the deputies had made for us after we became witnesses—the one I got when she was born in Brooklyn. It had her real name on it. I told this principal I was moving to L.A. because I was getting a divorce from my second husband. I said Marie was my child from my first husband who was dead. I said Marie never was legally adopted by my second husband but we enrolled her in school under his last name because it was simpler and we didn't want her to feel like she wasn't part of the family. I said, "I know it wasn't right but no one in Phoenix ever checked, so her last name is all wrong on all the school records." I said, "Now I am getting a divorce so I want to get this cleared up and have Marie's real name on her records." I showed this principal her original birth certificate to show what I was saying was the truth. This principal was a man and when he started to ask me questions, I began to cry because I knew it would make him nervous. He changed Marie's last name on the records, so now her name was really her real last name. I went down and got her a Social Security card under her real last name too. She'd never had one before and I told Marie she was going to use that last name from now on. I didn't tell her it was her real last name, I just told her she needed to use it. Now, I know it sounds crazy—giving her her real last name back—but I figured Sal would never expect it so she would be safe. The only thing that worried me was Marie's birth certificate. Because it was real, it had Sal's name on it as her father and she still thought he was her uncle. Shit, things get complicated when you lie.

I was glad Marie had her real name back. It was like I was giving her back some of her past even if she didn't know it. I changed my last name to Smith—Angela Smith—because Smith is so common. I figured that would throw off Sal. I didn't think me or Marie was in any danger from Tony and his crew. We were about as far as you can get from Brooklyn. My sister had told me Tony was out of prison. I said, "I thought he got life," and she said a deputy told her life was the same as thirty years. All Tony had to serve was one-third, and with good behavior he was out in eight years. It really pissed me off. This guy was out walking the streets, free as a bird, and me and Marie are hiding out, looking over my shoulder. I mean, who really was sentenced here?

I got a job working with a tour packager. My boss bought blocks of tickets from airlines and hotels and put them together as tours. I learned fast and after about a year, I moved to a large travel agency. Marie was doing fine. I mean, it was tough at first. We both missed Ted, but me and Marie had been together and we are closer than most mothers and daughters. I had called the deputy in Phoenix after we got to L.A. and found a place to rent and he arranged for my furniture to be delivered. He had it in storage first, just like he did when he relocated someone. I had him call Anna, too, and tell her about Sal and how me and Marie had to move but he didn't tell her where and I didn't call her for a long time because I thought maybe she had told Sal about me and Marie being in Phoenix.

We did fine for several years and then one day when Marie was a senior in high school she came home really, really angry. She had figured out Sal was her daddy. She had gotten her birth certificate from my drawer without telling me because she needed to show it at school for some reason to be on this sports team and she had seen

Sal's name listed as her father. She knew I'd lied to her. Marie had gone to the school library because I'd told her that her uncle Sal was hiding from the mob and she looked through indexes for *The New York Times* on microfilm, and sure enough, she finds Sal's name and reads all about how he testified against Tony and his crew. She was a smart little detective. Well, she comes home and she tells me I had no right to lie to her about Sal. I told her he was no good and then I told her about how Sal had showed up in Phoenix and how that was the real reason we moved.

She exploded. She screams at me, "You're a liar. I had a dad and you lied to me. You should've let me decide if I wanted to know him. You had no right to make that choice for me. He's my father!" She called Anna and asked her about Sal. She wanted to find him. No one knew where he was. She wouldn't talk to me for a week. She slept over at her best friend's house. I didn't know what to say. She told me she used to have dreams about her father—not Sal, but the father I made up, the pilot who died in the air force. She used to dream about him coming to see her. She wondered what he looked like. She convinced herself he loved her. Now she knew he didn't exist and it was almost like a death to her. She was really, really angry. She felt cheated, confused. One night she asked me if I thought she was going to become a criminal—if that was why I never told her about Sal. She asked me, "Do you think it's in the blood?" She said she used to be afraid when we first moved to California of men coming after her, taking her away. She was so upset I took her to see a psychologist. He helped but it really bothered her that Sal was out there somewhere and she didn't know where and she didn't know if he wanted to find her or if he was even looking. She felt different from other kids, like she didn't really have any past.

Marie fussed so much I called my deputy friend in Phoenix and told him what was going on. He says, "I thought you knew. Sal's dead." He'd been shot in Queens a couple of years earlier. The cops didn't think Tony was involved but how could anyone be sure? Sal was stupid to go back but I wasn't surprised. I told Marie Sal was dead but she didn't believe me. She said, "You're lying again. You don't want me to talk to him. You're afraid I'll like him better than you." We had a big fight and I gave her the deputy's number and she called him and he told her, but she didn't believe him, either. She says, "You lied so much, you don't know what the truth is anymore."

I thought about moving back to Phoenix and contacting Ted after Marie graduated from high school and decided to go to college, but I was too scared. If Marie hated me for lying, how was he going to feel? I got my real estate license during Marie's freshman year in college. She lived on campus and was going to join a sorority so I was all alone now. I was selling real estate in the L.A. area. Funny, when the state checked into my background, they didn't find anything suspicious. This man was looking for a condo to buy and we didn't bother with condos because they weren't worth our time but he was a friend of my boss so I helped him out. He lived in New York but came out to L.A. all the time on business. He asked me out and during the next few months we got together whenever he was in town. He was my boyfriend. L.A. is a difficult place for any woman older than thirty. Everyone wants to date girls.

I was happy. Marie was doing great and I didn't have to worry about Sal anymore. I finally felt my life was falling into place and then I'm at work and I get this call. Marie is dead. She had been with another student in a small airplane. She loved to fly and wanted to get her pilot's license and something went wrong and the airplane crashed and she was gone—just like that. I had lost John in Rapid City and now Marie. Why did God take her? Why not me? I had to stop going into work. My boyfriend stuck with me. I lived for the days when he came into town. I needed to be with him all the time, so when he came to L.A., I said to him, "I'm going to tell you a story you aren't going to believe but I want you to know everything." I told him about Sal and Tony and the old neighborhood. I told him about Rapid City and John, and Phoenix and Ted, and how me and Marie moved to L.A. I told him every lie I had ever told. It was like a dam bursting open. The first thing he asked me was "Are you still in danger—are you still hiding?" I told him I was safe and I was happy he thought about me first. It felt good to finally be honest with someone. I felt this weight off my shoulders. I didn't have to worry about him finding a paper with my old name on it or me bumping into someone I knew from Phoenix or Rapid City or Brooklyn. I didn't have to worry every time the phone rang.

I clung to him. I wanted him to love me and I thought my

boyfriend could handle it because he had stuck by me when Marie was killed. But he started to back off. I could feel it. He didn't call me from New York as much as he had. I thought it was all just too much for him and I got really, really depressed. One day he called and said he was in town and he took me to lunch and he told me he needed to tell me something. I thought, "He's going to leave me." He says to me, "I'm married." He had a wife in New York and three grown kids. How could I have been so dumb? I told him I hoped his flight crashed on the way home. I said, "Don't ever call me again." Funny, huh? I was so busy trying to hide my own lies, I never thought about what lies other people were telling me. I should've been smarter. I had trusted him and he had lied to me.

I thought about killing myself. I missed Marie so much. Now I was really alone. I heard a man on the radio say, "When your parents die, you lose your past. When your children die, you lose your future." I had lost it all. I'd given up my past when I went into hiding, and without my children there was no future. None. For a long time I didn't care about anything. I went to see Anna in Philadelphia and one afternoon for no reason I got on the train and went to New York and rode out to Brooklyn by myself and visited the old neighborhood. In my mind, it always looked exactly like it had on the day when Mrs. Bonavolonta asked me to bring her salt from the store. But when I got there, whew, it was weird, because the buildings were pretty much the same but everything else was different. All the people I knew were gone. I walked up to my old apartment building. No one recognized me. The steps and front door were the same but I didn't know no one. I went to the building where the Captain had lived, where he was born and my mother, too. I knew what it looked like inside, every inch, but a young couple was living there now. I know this sounds melodramatic, but I felt like a ghost, only I was still alive.

Just when I was going to leave, I saw a man who had been in high school with me. He still lived in the neighborhood. When he walked by me on the sidewalk, I introduced myself. He remembered me. He had had a crush on Anna when we were little but was too shy to tell her. He told me everyone thought we were dead. There were rumors Tony had us murdered. We had been cut up and dumped at sea. We laughed about that and he told me about some of the people from the neighborhood and what had happened to them. Some had gotten into trouble, others had gotten sick. I hadn't thought about how their lives might have changed or their problems. I'd just thought about my own. But life had gone on for them, too. I didn't ask about Tony. I was afraid to. But he brought him up. It was funny, really, but Tony was dead, too. He'd been killed not that long after Sal. All this time, I had thought he was still out there.

When we said goodbye, I asked him not to mention seeing me. He says, "Why? Tony's dead." But I liked the idea that people thought we'd been dumped at sea. I went to the cemetery and visited the Captain's grave. The marshals did okay by him. I told him about what had happened. I had hit bottom and I knew it. I either was going to kill myself or pick myself up.

I went to see Marie at the cemetery when I got home and told her about the Captain. There was so much about her past she never knew. I told her about how it was for me when I was a little girl growing up. I know she is dead but I think she heard me. I changed jobs and began going to a therapist. I signed up for classes at a community college at night. One of the teachers was divorced and he asked me out for coffee. I started reading poetry and when I read Robert Frost's poem "The Road Not Taken," I sat down and cried. You know, Sal was looking at fifteen to twenty years when he got pinched, but now I know he'd have only done one-third of that. What if he had kept his mouth shut? Maybe John would still be alive, maybe Marie too. I used to think about it a lot—what me and Marie and John and Sal would be like—what would've happened to us.

It's been twenty-five years since deputies knocked on my door in Brooklyn. If there is anything I regret, it's all the lies. I don't care if people feel sorry for me when they read this. I told my story because of John and Marie. I wanted something in print about them. I used to feel there was a deputy following me with a broom sweeping up any evidence I was here. I hated that. Memories matter to me because in the end, memories are all any of us have. So I have told you my story for little John and my beautiful daughter, Marie. I've not forgotten them. They mattered.

PART FOUR

NEW FACES, OLD TRICKS

I t is as if everyone who came to the place were put into the witness protection program, furnished with a complete new public identity. . . . We are, most of us, much of the time in disguise. We present ourselves as we think we are meant to be.

—Meg Greenfield, Washington, D.C.

CHAPTER
EIGHTEEN

GERALD SHUR'S left leg felt as if it had a fifty-pound weight attached to it, and now a familiar feeling of fatigue began to sweep over him. He swore to himself, twisting in the cramped seat of the TACA international flight, trying unsuccessfully to get comfortable. "Not now, not here." The multiple sclerosis attack was beginning and there was nothing he could do to prevent it, no miracle medicines for him to swallow. He could feel bee stings. Hundreds of them, as if he had bumped into a hive and was under attack. He never knew how long the attack would last or how intense it would be. He glanced out the airplane's window and peered through the clouds at the green volcanic mountains passing below him. He tried to focus on his trip rather than the pain. He also tried to quiet the doubts that were now beginning to gnaw away at him, the voice in his head asking him whether a fifty-year-old attorney with MS should be leading six deputy U.S. marshals on a dangerous mission. They would feel obligated to stay with him and protect him if the pain became so overwhelming that he couldn't walk. He decided not to mention the attack to anyone. And then he wondered: "What am I doing here?"

Three weeks earlier, in late June 1983, Shur had been called into a deputy assistant attorney general's office and told the State Department needed help. It wanted a team of experts in courtroom security and witness protection to fly to El Salvador and help the government there prepare for a risky trial. "I'm not telling you it won't be dangerous," he had been told, "because it will—you could be murdered."

El Salvador was in the third year of a bloody civil war. The democratic government, which was being supported by the United States, was fighting the leftist Farabundo Martí National Liberation Front, known by its Spanish acronym FMLN. The Reagan administration and the CIA were afraid the country was going to fall into the hands of Marxists, just as nearby Nicaragua had fallen to the Sandinistas. But the Salvadoran military's and national guard's campaign against the FMLN had turned into a human rights nightmare. Military death squads roamed the tiny country arresting suspected rebel supporters and anyone else who dared to criticize the government. More than forty thousand Salvadorans had been abducted by soldiers and taken into the jungle, where they had simply "disappeared." Among those murdered was Monsignor Oscar Arnulfo Romero y Galdamez, the archbishop of San Salvador, who was assassinated in front of churchgoers while celebrating a mass in March 1980. It would later be revealed that his death had been ordered by a major in the national guard. Nine months after the archbishop was killed, four American nuns were stopped and forced from their car while traveling along a dirt road near the village of Santiago Nonualco. They were raped and then executed, their bodies kicked into a ditch. The Salvadoran government and its military at first refused to cooperate when the U.S. embassy investigated, and with good reason. The suspects turned out to be five national guardsmen, who had reportedly celebrated the sexual assaults and killings by passing around a cheap bottle of rum. Only after Congress voted to withhold $19 million in military aid to El Salvador were the five soldiers arrested. It had been nearly two years since then but not one of the men had been put on trial. El Salvador's prosecutors and judges were too afraid. Finally, a heroic judge named Bernardo Rauda Murcia agreed to schedule the case for trial in the city of Zacatecoluca. He was immediately threatened. The State Department was now sending Shur and the deputies to figure out how to protect the judge and his courtroom so the trial could finally begin.

Howard Safir had handpicked the deputies on the flight: William Brookhart, Paul Brinson, Alfred Miller Jr., Paul Moreno, James Tafoya, and Charles Almanza, who would double as Shur's interpreter. Along with their weapons, which included an Uzi submachine gun, they had packed survival equipment and maps in case they were forced to hide in the jungle. Also tucked inside the airplane's cargo hold was a brand-new magnetometer, a metal detector, which they planned to install outside the judge's courtroom. As the jet began its descent toward the capital city of San Salvador, the pain in Shur's legs became more intense, but he kept silent and grabbed his carry-on bag from the overhead compartment after the plane landed.

The State Department had warned them not to trust anyone except U.S. embassy personnel. The Salvadoran military didn't want the national guardsmen prosecuted, and killing Shur's squad would be an effective way to intimidate the judge and stop the trial. The FMLN might also try to harm Shur and the deputies and then blame the attack on the government to stir up trouble between their country's politicians and the U.S. Congress. As Shur entered the terminal, he spotted a tall American dressed in a business suit standing near the gate. "Justice Department security team!" the man called out, waving an arm in the air. "Anyone on board from the Justice Department security team?"

"Keep walking," Shur whispered to the deputies.

They passed the man and strolled around the terminal for several minutes until they felt confident no one was lurking nearby. Returning to the gate, Shur introduced himself.

"I'm here to drive you to the embassy," the man explained. "Whew! I thought I'd lost you."

"Another stupid move like this one and you *will* lose us, permanently," Shur thought.

The deputies discovered their magnetometer had been stolen during the trip. "How's that possible?" Shur asked. It was a heavy piece of equipment, and the only stop the jet had made after leaving the United States was a brief layover in Guatemala for refueling. Deputy Al Miller began making calls and learned the missing metal detector had been "confiscated" by Guatemalan customs officers when they rummaged through the plane's hold during re-fueling. It was already being used at a Guatemalan airport to screen passengers.

Shur and the deputies were driven to the El Presidente Hotel, where the U.S. embassy kept a block of rooms reserved. It wasn't going to be difficult for the national security forces or the rebels to find them here, Shur thought, since they were staying in the same hotel where the embassy usually boarded Americans. So much for security.

They asked for adjoining rooms so if one of them was at-tacked, the others could come to his aid. Once inside, they began looking for electronic bugs. They found plenty. It didn't matter. They'd already agreed they wouldn't discuss anything about their mission unless they were in the U.S. embassy or on the streets walking together. "We were doing what John Gotti and other gangsters did back home," Shur recalled later. "Gotti would walk up and down the sidewalk in front of his social club to avoid FBI bugs."

By now an exhausted Shur was ready for bed, but the pain in his legs kept him from sleeping. The MS attack had not yet sub-sided. Around 10:30 P.M. his room shook with a loud explosion. All six deputies came bursting in, guns drawn. The rebels had set off a bomb near the hotel, but the blast had nothing to do with their visit.

The embassy expected Shur and the deputies to spend their first day meeting various Salvadoran politicos and court officials, and although Shur was still feeling as if he were being stung by bees, he greeted each dignitary and questioned them about the na-tion's judiciary. He was told the government couldn't control its own national security force, and that corruption and threats were so widespread that only 5 percent of the defendants arrested for crimes were ever brought to trial. Having dispensed with the diplomatic and political formalities, Shur and his team planned to fly by helicopter the next morning to Zacatecoluca, where they would inspect the courtroom for the trial. Flying was safer than driving because of land mines along the jungle highway. That night Shur again had trouble sleeping, so just before dawn he took his camera and went outside to take a few snapshots. It was a clear, beautiful morning, and as he walked, his legs began to feel better. He noticed that men with guns were standing in the door-ways of downtown buildings. They were guards, and most of them were carrying weapons so ancient that Shur wondered if they would explode in their hands if fired. "I suddenly realized that these men were actually human alarms," he said later. "If anyone was going to attack, the guards would be the first ones shot, and when the persons inside heard the shot, they'd have time to grab their own guns or hide."

As he returned to the hotel, an older man carrying a World War I–vintage carbine stepped in front of him. "It's okay," said Shur. "I'm a guest here." But the guard refused to move, barking out a stern order in Spanish. Shur didn't understand. The guard nodded toward the camera and spoke again. Shur thought he might have inadvertently photographed some government build-ing in violation of the law, especially when the guard swung his rifle off his shoulder and cradled it in his arms as if he were prepar-ing to shoot it. Finally Shur understood. He snapped the guard's photograph as he stood at attention. Less than a month later, the man would be dead, the victim of a sniper.

Deputy Almanza greeted Shur with bad news. There were no helicopters available. The embassy was sending over two cars. "What about the land mines?" Shur asked. "The drivers are sup-posed to know how to miss them," Almanza replied.

Within an hour, they had left the city and were weaving through the lush mountain terrain along a rutty road when a tire on the lead car went flat. Shur and the deputies stepped from the two cars to stretch their legs while the driver began changing the tire. Suddenly Shur spotted someone moving in the brush. Then another. They were soldiers, but he couldn't tell if they were rebels or national guardsmen. The deputy marshals had seen those two and more hiding in the jungle. "Don't draw," Shur said. "Let's see if they are friendly." Almanza called out, and a soldier stepped from behind a tree. Instinctively the deputies formed a protective shield around Shur. The soldier asked what they were doing and where they were going. Almanza motioned to the flat tire and said they were U.S. health workers going to help some sick children up the highway. Shur glanced over at the car he had been riding in. The Uzi submachine gun was on the backseat. He didn't think health workers usually carried machine guns, and he knew the weapons would be prizes worth the soldiers' taking. Shur nodded toward the gun, and one of the deputies began easing toward the car to hide it. As Almanza continued talking to the soldier, the spare tire was quickly bolted into place.

"Got it," the driver called out as he tossed the flat tire into the car trunk. "Let's get out of here." The men eased into the cars. Almanza was the last. If the soldiers were going to attack, they would have to do it now. Shur felt like a sitting duck as Almanza slipped into the space next to him. The two cars moved forward. One of the soldiers waved from the bushes. Shur began to relax.

Before they reached Zacatecoluca, the delegation stopped in a village to inspect its courtroom. It was inside a building that had housed a grocery store. The floor was dirt, and there was no electricity. Because it was hard to see inside the building, the local judge sat near the building's huge front window. There was no glass, and anyone walking by could have reached through it and tapped the judge on the shoulder or, Shur thought, just as easily shot him in the head. With Almanza serving as an interpreter, Shur interviewed the local judge. He told them that soldiers in the area would often walk into the courtroom while a trial was in session and take a witness or a spectator away. Some were beaten; others never returned from the jungle. "They're watching you right now," he warned them, motioning down the street. Four soldiers were lingering outside a store about a block away. Noticing that the courtroom contained only a desk and a few wooden chairs, Shur asked the judge where he kept his court files and records. "The trunk of my car," he answered. "It has a lock." The delegation stopped at another village and found the courtroom there just as barren. Yet Shur was impressed by the commitment of the local magistrate. He said he didn't believe anyone could really protect him from the rebels or the national security force, yet he continued to hold court.

By the time Shur's squad reached the Zacatecoluca courtroom where the national guardsmen were going to be tried, he felt a sense of inspiration. "Those of us who stand up for justice are the true soldiers," he told Judge Bernardo Rauda Murcia. "We are the soldiers of truth." Later, he would say that he had become caught up in the moment. "My sermonizing and theatrics caught the deputies by surprise, but I was truly moved. It is much easier to dispense justice in some marble federal courthouse that is well guarded in a nation like ours, which has a history of respect for the judiciary and law and order, than it is in a barren store in an impoverished, war-torn country. It was clear during our brief mission that even though guns were more powerful than the law, they could not deter these judges."

When the judge asked Shur if he had any ideas about how to protect jurors, he replied: "Begin sequestering them." A look of horror formed on the judge's face. Almanza explained that the judge had interpreted the word *sequester* to mean "kidnap." Shur apologized. "Here I had been lecturing him about how we were soldiers of truth and then he thought I wanted him to begin kidnapping jurors. In a country where the national security forces were snatching up people every day, it had made him wonder just how concerned about justice I really was."

Rauda Murcia's courtroom was a large oblong room that had been divided into three sections. The judge sat behind a desk in front of a waist-high wooden railing. The defendants sat on a plain wooden bench behind the railing, which enclosed them like a box. Spectators sat closest to the door, behind the defendants.

"Where are the light switches?" Almanza asked.

There were none. "We don't need them because we don't hold court at night," the judge replied.

The deputies quickly decided the best way to protect the court was by having two armed men stationed next to the judge, two more stationed inside the railing with the defendants, and several more at the room's entrance. Now all they had to do was find guards brave enough to attend the trial. "When we returned to San Salvador, we asked officials from every component of the Salvadoran government whom they trusted most, and all said, without hesitation, the prison guards," Shur recalled, "so we recommended that they be used for the trial of the nuns' killers."

The next morning they headed back to the airport. Shur flashed his diplomatic passport at the gate but the guard there wouldn't let him pass without having him open his carry-on bag and step through a metal detector. Shur explained that he was carrying a gun—they all were—and they didn't want to surrender it. They'd already lost a magnetometer to Guatemalan customs officials, and Shur didn't want the weapons, especially the Uzi, to disappear. He also didn't want to be sitting in the gate area unarmed while waiting for the flight. Almanza and the security guard argued for several moments in Spanish, then the deputy told Shur that everyone could hang on to their weapons until it was time to board. Shur scanned the crowd. He was eager to get home to Miriam. Then Almanza had everyone put their guns into a bag, and with the security guard at his side, Almanza carried the bag onto the airplane and put it in the cockpit. After the airplane had pulled away from the terminal, he fetched it and walked through the cabin handing out pistols to his fellow deputies and Shur. He left the Uzi in the bag. Not a single passenger said a word.

"How'd you get that guard in the airport to let us keep the guns?" Shur asked.

"His bullets were old, so I gave him two of mine."

Shur had to work fast back in Washington. The trial was scheduled to begin in less than seven weeks. He spent hours on the telephone handling logistics. Sixty Salvadoran prison guards had been chosen in San Salvador and were waiting to hear from him. Shur arranged for the Federal Law Enforcement Training Center in Glynco, Georgia, to fit the guards into its packed training schedule and give them courses in basic courtroom security, automatic-weapons firing, and evasive driving techniques. None of the guards spoke English, so the center's training manuals had to be translated into Spanish. The deputies who had gone with Shur to El Salvador recommended the guards be given the best new equipment available so they could make a "show of force" that would cause national security forces and rebels to think twice before attacking the courtroom. The Marshals Service recommended they be provided with two dozen bulletproof vests, several cases of gas grenades, eighteen heavy-duty police cars, two bulletproof SUVs, and two nine-passenger vans specially equipped to transport prisoners, along with a number of firearms. Money wasn't a problem. The State Department and the Agency for International Development had set aside $800,000 for the purpose. The trouble was petty politics. While making arrangements, Shur learned there wasn't enough ammunition at the Georgia training center for the M-16 rifles the guards were going to be shooting, and the ammunition manufacturer couldn't deliver enough rounds in time for the training course. Shur was stymied until he learned the State Department had several crates of ammunition in a warehouse. Its security division didn't want to share their bullets, and it took Shur a day of infuriating telephone calls and finally the intervention of a senior State Department official to get the crates delivered. Then, just when it seemed everything was falling into place, Shur was told by an Agency for International Development (AID) officer that her budget chief was refusing to charter an airplane to fly the prison guards to Georgia. Shur lost his temper. "Everything was ready to go," he said later. "We had managed to do the impossible by getting the training center, which is booked months in advance, to find room for the guards. We had hired interpreters and found equipment, and now, because someone didn't want to sign an authorization form, we couldn't get the guards flown here." Shur telephoned an airline charter service and hired a pilot, crew, and airplane for the trip, charging the entire bill to his credit card. Two days later, an AID official sheepishly agreed to pay for the flight.

The Salvadoran guards finished their training one week before the trial was scheduled to begin. At their "graduation," Shur addressed them, saying they were about to embark on "a most important mission, for without an effective system of justice, no country can survive."

The national guardsmen's trial attracted international attention, and the newly christened Salvadoran Judicial Protection
Unit stood guard inside the courtroom in their American-made
uniforms, carrying their new automatic weapons. Despite their
presence, only seven of the twelve men and women chosen as jurors dared to show up. Still, the trial went off without a hitch. Defense attorneys accused the U.S. government of railroading the
five national guardsmen, but evidence showed that one of them
had left a fingerprint in the nuns' van. Another guardsman con-
fessed. They were found guilty and the judge sentenced all five to
serve thirty years in prison, the maximum sentence. Although the
guardsmen claimed they were carrying out orders when they
raped and murdered the nuns, none of the military officers who
oversaw them was ever charged. The civil war in El Salvador continued for nine more years, until December 1992, when the
United Nations negotiated a peace treaty between the government and the FMLN. Fighting between the two sides ended about
a year later.

"I was proud of the work we had done," Shur recalled. "I felt
the Salvadorans had proven they could protect a judge, a jury, and
prosecutors in a country where bribery, intimidation, and corruption were daily occurrences. Obviously, we hadn't solved all of the
judiciary's problems there, but we had helped them take that first
step and we had brought the nuns' murderers to justice. I remember thinking about how the mob had tried over the years to corrupt our judicial process. It reminded me of the obvious: There can
be no justice if there is intimidation."

CHAPTER
NINETEEN

ORGANIZED CRIME IN America was so bloodied that Justice Department officials announced on the front page of *The New York Times* in 1983 that the government was on the verge of winning its war against the mob. "In every city where there is a major organized crime family, we have indicted and/or convicted the top echelons of that family, and that's all within the past few years," Floyd Clarke, a deputy assistant director of the FBI's Criminal Investigative Division, proudly declared. David Margolis, chief of the Justice Department's Organized Crime and Racketeering Section, said the use of federal strike forces, the RICO Act, legal wiretaps, and WITSEC had effectively turned the tide. But the government had little time to celebrate. A new criminal element quickly filled the void, and Gerald Shur suddenly found himself the target of a twisted kidnap plot.

Less than $10 million worth of cocaine was smuggled into the United States during 1975. Nine years later, an estimated $1 billion worth was being dumped here. Eighty percent of it came from a single source: the Medellín cartel in Colombia, the richest and most deadly criminal gang in the world in the early 1980s. It was run by Pablo Escobar Gaviria, Carlos Ledher Rivas, and the Ochoa family, which included brothers Jorge Luis, Juan David, and Fabio. Their fingers reached across most of the Americas. Workers

harvested leaves and turned them into coca paste in Bolivia and
Peru, which was delivered by "mules" to secret laboratories in
Colombia, Nicaragua, and Panama. The final product was shipped
to warehouses in the Bahamas, Mexico, and the Turks and Caicos
Islands for delivery to the United States. Both the Reagan and
Bush administrations declared war on the so-called narco king-
pins. It proved a bloody campaign.

The cartel's most vicious leader was Pablo Escobar, whose
personal wealth in 1983 was estimated at $2 billion. Unlike the
Ochoa brothers, who were from the privileged class in Colombia
and viewed themselves as refined playboys, Escobar was a vicious,
poorly educated street thug. He first made a name for himself by
stealing cars but quickly graduated to the more lucrative crimes of
extortion, kidnapping, and murder, all committed before he became a cocaine trafficker. His trademark was *plata o plomo*—anyone he couldn't bribe with *plata* (silver), he killed with *plomo*
(lead).

The DEA got its first break in going after him and the cartel
when it arrested Adler "Barry" Seal, a three-hundred-pound
ex–Green Beret and self-proclaimed adventurer, in Miami during a
1982 sting operation code-named Screamer. Clever and brash, in
the 1970s Seal had been the youngest pilot ever to captain a 747
airplane, but he had gotten bored and had turned to gunrunning
and later dope smuggling, as much for the thrill as for the cash.
Now faced with a possible sixty-year prison sentence, Seal offered
to help the DEA go after the cartel if the charges filed against him
were put on hold. Overnight, he became the DEA's most prized informant.

Unaware that Seal had switched sides, the Ochoa family
hired him to smuggle three thousand pounds of cocaine into the
United States. But he ran into trouble after he flew to a concealed
airfield owned by the Ochoas in the Colombian jungle in June
1984 to pick up the first fifteen-hundred-pound installment. So
many pounds of cocaine were crammed into his airplane that it
couldn't clear the jungle, and crashed when taking off. Seal was
unhurt, and the Ochoas provided him with a second airplane filled
with cocaine. This time he got off the ground.

After a quick refueling stop in Managua, Seal was starting the last leg of his flight into the United States when one of the plane's engines caught on fire and he was forced to return to the Nicaraguan airport. Soldiers from Nicaragua's Sandinista army were waiting to arrest him. Seal spent three days in jail before he was taken back to his damaged airplane. The Ochoas had sprung him and arranged for the Sandinistas to unload and watch over his cargo. He was instructed to return to the United States in the damaged airplane. Meanwhile, the Ochoas were lining up a third airplane for him, this time a C-132 cargo plane, big and strong enough for him to retrieve the cocaine that he had been forced to stash in Nicaragua.

As soon as the DEA learned from Seal that the Sandinista army was protecting the Ochoas' cocaine, it contacted the CIA, which in turn notified the White House. President Reagan and CIA director William Casey were trying to whip up support in Congress for the contras, rebels trying to overthrow the Sandinista regime. Linking the Marxist Sandinistas to the Medellín drug lords would be a major public relations coup.

As promised, the Ochoas arranged for a C-132 cargo airplane to be delivered to Seal, and as soon as he took possession, the CIA hurried in and hid a camera inside it. Seal then returned to Nicaragua and secretly photographed several of the men who loaded the duffel-size bags of cocaine into the airplane's belly. When he returned to the United States, federal agents confiscated the drugs and developed the film. White House officials were ecstatic when they saw the snapshots. Not only had Seal photographed Sandinista soldiers, he had also caught a top Sandinista government official on film. But the real prize was a picture of Pablo Escobar himself, toting bags of cocaine into the airplane.

Reagan would later successfully use Seal's photographs to convince Congress to lift a ban that it had imposed on U.S. funding for the contras. The rebels would be sent another $100 million in aid. The Justice Department, meanwhile, issued indictments based on Seal's undercover work for the arrest of Escobar and the Ochoas. However, they were not arrested.

Although the United States and Colombia had signed an

extradition treaty in 1979, no one in the Colombian government wanted to risk handing over the drug lords to the United States. Everyone was afraid because Escobar had unleashed an unprecedented campaign of terror. Judges, politicians, and journalists who spoke out in favor of turning him over to the United States were assassinated. No one was safe, no matter how important. Colombia's justice minister, the equivalent of the U.S. attorney general, was gunned down by Escobar's assassins. More than thirty other judges were slaughtered. At one point Escobar paid a band of rebels to storm the Palace of Justice in Bogotá and hold the entire Colombian Supreme Court hostage. The guerrillas, who received a million dollars from Escobar, murdered eleven of the twenty-four justices. After a bloody fight, the Colombian military reclaimed the building and freed the remaining thirteen justices. But by then, Escobar's campaign had worked. The court declared the 1979 extradition treaty illegal, based on a technicality. At least for the moment, Escobar and the other cartel members were safe as long as they stayed in Colombia.

Escobar now turned his sights on revenge and Barry Seal.

In 1984, Seal was living with his wife in Baton Rouge, Louisiana. It was a city with few Latin residents, so Escobar was reluctant to send Colombian assassins after him because they would be conspicuous. Instead, the cartel offered a million dollars to a Miami man named Max Mermelstein to kidnap Seal and bring him to Colombia, or half that figure simply to murder him. Mermelstein ran the cartel's U.S. distribution operations from a series of pay telephones and dummy offices in Miami. He recruited smugglers, scheduled flights, kept track of inventory, repackaged drugs, and laundered cash.

Mermelstein had been introduced into the cocaine business six years earlier through his wife, a Colombian beauty named Cristina Jaramillo. At the time, he had been working as chief engineer at a Miami country club, a self-described Jewish kid from Brooklyn with no criminal record. One afternoon, Cristina arranged for him to meet Rafael Cardona Salazar, a Colombian with ties to Medellín smugglers. Cristina was pregnant, and Mermelstein's job didn't pay much. Cardona offered him some quick and easy money. A member of the country club where Mermelstein worked was a regular customer, so Cardona gave Mermelstein $1,500 to deliver a kilo of cocaine to him. Soon Mermelstein made two more deliveries. He would later claim that his fate had been sealed a few weeks later, on Christmas day in 1978, while he was riding in a van with Cardona. Both men had been at a party, and Cardona had gotten stoned on drugs. Without warning, he pulled out his handgun and blew out the brains of a third passenger riding with them in the van. "At that point," Mermelstein recalled, "I knew I was either in with Cardona or I was dead."

Cardona became a rising star in the Medellín cartel, and Mermelstein moved up with him. Unfamiliar with U.S. culture, the cartel depended on Mermelstein for advice about how best to exploit the booming cocaine trade in the states. Mermelstein would later brag that he was personally responsible for bringing some sixty-six tons of cocaine into the country during the early 1980s and sending $300 million in profits back to Medellín.

While Mermelstein didn't object to cocaine trafficking, he would later insist that he had no taste for bloodshed. So in December 1984, when he was given the Seal murder contract, he began to stall and look for some way to get out of the assignment. He soon got "lucky." The DEA, which had been watching him for months, arrested him under the RICO Act for "running a continuing criminal enterprise," a crime punishable by life in prison.

Barry Seal had had enough dealings with Escobar and the cartel to know he needed to keep quiet and lie low after his cover was blown. But his daring and ego proved to be even bigger than his waistline. Seal refused to enter WITSEC, saying he didn't want to disrupt his family, and then he did something even stupider. The DEA had not been the only law enforcement agency after Seal in 1982, when he was arrested as part of the Screamer sting. Federal and state agents in Louisiana also had been trying to catch him smuggling drugs. After Seal became a DEA informant, he assumed Louisiana investigators would ease off. But he was wrong.

In Baton Rouge, U.S. attorney Stanford Bardwell still considered Seal a menace and continued to search for ways to arrest him. An outraged Seal decided to take his fight public in late 1984 by calling a local television reporter and publicly attacking Bardwell in an hour-long special about drug smuggling and the government's practice of "targeting" suspects. Bardwell reacted by indicting Seal on a minor drug charge and for some banking irregularities. Their feud put the Justice Department in an awkward position. In Miami, where federal prosecutors were planning to call Seal as their star witness in several big drug cases, Seal was being portrayed as a heroic informant who had reformed. But in Baton Rouge, Bardwell was claiming he was still an unrepentant smuggler. Worried that the Baton Rouge charges might undermine Seal's reputation when he testified in Miami, the Justice Department ordered a truce.

In order to appease Bardwell, Seal pleaded guilty to the two minor charges filed against him in Louisiana. In return, Bardwell promised that Seal's sentence would "not exceed" whatever prison time he received in Florida, where the DEA was still holding the 1982 Screamer indictment over him. At first, it looked as if Bardwell had won. He told reporters that he expected Seal to be sentenced to ten years in prison. But when Seal appeared before a Miami judge, the DEA rushed in to defend him, and based on its recommendation, the judge put Seal on probation without requiring him to spend a single day in jail. It seemed as if Bardwell had been outfoxed, since he had promised to recommend that Seal receive the identical sentence in Baton Rouge as in Miami.

But when a confident Seal appeared in Louisiana for sentencing, Judge Frank Polozola added an unforeseen twist. Although he couldn't send Seal to jail, the judge said that as part of his probation, he was requiring Seal to report to a halfway house at six o'clock every afternoon for six months. Seal's lawyers immediately jumped to their feet to object. Their client would be an easy target for the Medellín cartel if assassins knew where he was going to be each night. But Polozola refused to budge. "You take your chances, Mr. Seal," he said.

Once again Seal was offered protection in WITSEC, and once again he refused. He told reporters, "Life isn't exciting unless you put yourself into life-threatening situations." Twenty-nine days later, on February 19, 1986, Seal drove into the parking lot at the Salvation Army halfway house at six o'clock, just as he had been doing religiously every day. But this time, two Colombian assassins were waiting. They rushed up to his white Cadillac and opened fire with Mac-10 machine guns before Seal could open the door. He was killed instantly. The assassins, who were caught within hours of the hit, both admitted that they had been sent by Escobar.

At a press conference the day after Seal was gunned down, Bardwell said his office had been trying to teach Seal a lesson by sending him to the halfway house but had not wanted to see him murdered. Judge Polozola refused comment.

Even though Max Mermelstein had known Escobar was determined to kill Seal, the murder scared him. He was now the only American alive who could testify about the inner workings of the cartel—if the United States ever succeeded in getting Colombia to extradite its leaders. Knowing how little Escobar valued others' lives, Mermelstein assumed it was only a matter of time before he too was murdered. He became even more spooked after his wife, Cristina, received a threatening telephone call from Rafael Cardona Salazar. "Max must not utter a word to the authorities or I will kill you and your whole family in Colombia," he warned.

From his prison cell, Mermelstein sent word to federal prosecutors that he wanted to cooperate. His first priority was getting Cristina and their children out of Miami and into WITSEC. He also wanted her relatives in Cali, Colombia, protected. Extracting them was going to be tricky. The Marshals Service suspected the cartel was watching them. A few days later, when an assistant

U.S. attorney accidentally leaked word that Mermelstein had become a government witness, WITSEC inspectors and Shur were forced into action. Working with the DEA, Shur secretly offered thirty-one of Mermelstein's in-laws protection; sixteen accepted. The DEA swooped them up at four different public spots in Cali and hurried them to a private airfield, where a U.S. military flight whisked them out of Colombia. They were the largest group ever to enter WITSEC at one time, and few spoke English.

Having already lost Barry Seal to Colombian assassins, the government hid Mermelstein in a cell known as the "submarine" because it was concealed in the basement of the federal courthouse in Miami. Ironically, one of the first prosecutors to interrogate him was Gerald Shur's son, Ronald, who had become a federal prosecutor in 1983 and was working in the Organized Crime Drug Enforcement Task Force in the U.S. attorney's Miami office. Mermelstein was now considered the United States' most important drug witness.

Within days, the ramifications of his arrest began to rock the Medellín cartel. Because he had overseen its American operations, the FBI and DEA were able to close down the cartel's distribution network and arrest several smugglers. Overnight, much of the cartel's cash flow stopped. In Colombia, Rafael Cardona Salazar, who had brought Mermelstein into the cartel's organization, was machine-gunned to death.

The cartel was in turmoil and seemed to be unraveling. In a move designed to win favor with Colombian officials, Escobar turned against fellow cartel member Carlos Ledher Rivas, perhaps the group's most eccentric member. Half German and a rabid admirer of Adolf Hitler, Ledher had once bragged about how he was using cocaine like a "Latin American atom bomb" to destroy the United States from within. On February 4, 1987, Escobar tipped off the Colombian police about a party that Ledher was hosting. He was arrested and handed over to the DEA, which flew him from Bogotá to Tampa on board a DEA plane.

The Marshals Service was responsible for protecting both Ledher and his main accuser, Mermelstein, when Ledher became the first cartel member to be put on trial. They hid Ledher, who was reportedly worth hundreds of millions of dollars, on a Florida military base and flew him into Tampa in a fully armed Blackhawk helicopter for the trial. A jury convicted him of drug smuggling and sentenced him to a prison term of life plus 135 years.

Furious that he had been betrayed by Escobar and the rest of the cartel, Ledher stewed in a prison cell and then contacted federal prosecutors. He announced that he was willing to testify against an even bigger fish in return for a reduction in his sentence and protection in a WITSEC unit.

The DEA had suspected for years that Manuel Noriega, known by his Latin enemies as "Pineapple Face," had been providing Colombian drug smugglers with safe passage in Panama and access to banks there to launder money. But it didn't have any direct evidence until Ledher began naming names. Working with Ledher and Mermelstein, DEA agents and federal prosecutors began putting together a case.

In December 1989 the U.S. military invaded the Panama Canal Zone and arrested the Panamanian president on money-laundering charges. Never before had the United States invaded a country and seized its leader on drug-related charges. The invasion alone cost taxpayers $164 million. The trial that followed lasted twenty-seven months. Some sixty-one witnesses testified against Noriega, and many of them were put under WITSEC protection. As always, defense attorneys accused the government of buying testimony because of the plea bargains that the Justice Department struck with some witnesses. Richardo Bilonick, who faced a sixty-year prison sentence for selling $400 million worth of cocaine, was allowed to keep all of his drug earnings in return for his testimony, defense attorneys claimed, and was given a new identity and relocated after serving four years in a WITSEC unit. Noriega was found guilty and sentenced to life in prison.

The fact that the United States would pluck a foreign leader from his own country outraged Escobar, who feared he might be next. Once again he began unleashing his assassins, trying as he had in the past to intimidate the Colombian courts and government. Three of the five candidates running for president were killed when they said they supported turning over narco kingpins to the United States. There were daily reports in the newspaper about bombings.

Still thirsty for revenge, Escobar also sent out word that he wanted Max Mermelstein dead.

By this point, Max Mermelstein was a free man. The DEA and federal prosecutors had recommended that he be treated leniently when he was taken before a judge for sentencing in June 1987, two years after he had first been arrested. The judge let him off with time already served. WITSEC inspectors had immediately reunited him with his wife, Cristina, and their children, who had been relocated under new names. But his bliss didn't last long.

"I used to bring a couple thousand keys [kilos] a week into Florida," Mermelstein recalled. "I was used to excitement, being on the move, not sitting around. My adrenaline would be pumping all the time when I smuggled drugs. Then, when I flipped over, I used to get just as excited bringing down those assholes who I was testifying against. Then suddenly I was vegetating, with absolutely nothing to do." He and Cristina began arguing. "No couple can be together twenty-four/seven without getting on each other's nerves." She was angry because she blamed him for ruining her family.

"Colombian families are extremely close," Mermelstein explained. "You don't separate them like Gerry Shur and the Marshals Service did, sending them to different cities in the United States and ordering them not to communicate with each other. I tried to explain this to Shur, but he refused to listen. He thought he knew what was best for everyone, and his refusal to be flexible cost my brother-in-law his life."

Arturo Jaramillo, Cristina's brother, was one of the family members spirited out of Cali and brought to the United States by the DEA and Shur. WITSEC inspectors had relocated him in Memphis, Tennessee, together with his wife and young son, but since none of them spoke English, they felt isolated. WITSEC inspectors arranged for Mermelstein and Cristina to talk to Jaramillo over the telephone because he was so depressed. Afterward, the Mermelsteins urged the WITSEC inspector handling Jaramillo to get him immediate psychiatric help. The deputy agreed but was scheduled to leave on vacation the next morning and couldn't find a Spanish-speaking therapist before leaving town. The next morning, Jaramillo hanged himself.

Family members learned about the suicide by calling each other through the WITSEC switchboard, since none of them was allowed to know where the others were located. At first WITSEC inspectors said the family couldn't attend Jaramillo's funeral, but when Mermelstein threatened to stop cooperating with prosecutors, they relented. The relatives were flown at WITSEC expense to Flushing, New York, for a private funeral. The church was patrolled by guards, and family members were driven to the cemetery in bulletproof limousines. As soon as the casket was lowered into the plot, they were whisked away. "We were all very bitter about what had happened," said Mermelstein, "especially Cristina."

The suicide, being cut off from her relatives, and having Mermelstein underfoot all day proved to be too much. Within a year, the couple separated, and each was relocated in different cities and given new names.

Lonely and bored, Mermelstein tried to find work, but he wasn't happy with the jobs that WITSEC found for him. "They want witnesses to become anonymous, so they offer you meaningless work like flipping burgers and scraping barnacles off the bottoms of boats in shipyards." He felt potential employers were afraid to hire him.

Mermelstein wasn't surprised when he was told that Escobar was trying to kill him. "Pablo was not the forgiving kind," he said. He went over all the steps the Marshals Service had taken to protect him, but "I was uneasy," he said. "After they fucked up with my brother-in-law, I was worried, but there were a couple of inspectors whom I had complete confidence in. I was glad to put my life in their hands." Just the same, he found himself glancing more and more over his shoulder.

In May 1991 Shur was asked to report to the Justice Department's command center, the most secure room in the majestic Constitution Avenue building. Heavily insulated and frequently swept for listening devices, the center is where a United States court meets to review sensitive requests by the FBI to use wiretaps in national security cases. Shur was greeted by a somber group of deputy marshals and FBI, DEA, and Justice Department officials.

"Gerry," said his boss and friend, deputy assistant attorney general Jack Keeney, "we have reason to believe you and Miriam are in danger."

A foreign criminal named Félix Bersago had been caught by Immigration and Naturalization service agents three weeks earlier as he tried to cross the Mexican border and enter Texas using a fake passport. He had once served time in prison for murder and was suspected of being a freelance hit man. When the border guards searched him, they found a spiral-bound address book that contained the names and telephone numbers of half a dozen Colombian drug traffickers, including members of the Ochoa family and business partners of Pablo Escobar. Near the back of it they'd also found these cryptic notes: "WITSEC—Gerald Shur, Arlington, Va.—Max Mermelstein."

At first, Bersago had refused to answer questions about why he was sneaking into the United States, but then he began offering bits and pieces in an effort to cut a deal. He wanted the INS to grant him asylum in return for telling them what they wanted to know. The agency had refused and turned his notebook over to the DEA. Its agents had gone through it with Bersago page by page, asking him questions about his Colombian contacts. When they finally got to the page that contained Shur's name, Bersago dropped a bombshell. The cartel had offered him $250,000 to abduct one of the Shurs in a plot to flush out Max Mermelstein. If Miriam was taken hostage, Shur would be told that she would be murdered unless he revealed where Mermelstein was hiding. If he was kidnapped, the cartel would send someone to torture him until he gave up Mermelstein's location.

"This guy might not be the only kidnapper the cartel has sent after you," Shur was warned. "The Colombians usually send more than one hit man when they put out a contract, so there's a good chance they've sent someone else to kidnap you or Miriam."

Shur's face betrayed no emotion. He had once been given a series of psychological tests as part of a federal management training program and the results had shown that whenever he was put under stress, he shoved his emotions aside and focused on gathering facts so he could make the best decision possible. "I had three thoughts," Shur said later. "I wished I had known about the threat earlier, since the suspect had already been in jail for three weeks before they asked why my name was in the book. But I still felt the odds of Miriam and me being found were slim as long as we stayed away from our home. I also knew the Marshals Service was very good at keeping people alive and its people would do whatever needed to be done to protect us."

Shur began asking questions: Where was Bersago now? Did the agents believe he was telling the truth? What did he know about him and his family? Did the DEA think the Medellín cartel knew Bersago had been detained?

Keeney was the first to suggest that Shur needed to leave town. "Why don't you take a vacation at government expense?" he offered, but Shur would have none of it. "I don't want protection. I think I can get around okay on my own, but I want Miriam protected." He wasn't trying to be macho or foolhardy. "One of my jobs, besides running WITSEC, was investigating threats made against U.S. attorneys and deciding whether or not they needed protection," he said later. "We didn't put U.S. attorneys into WITSEC, but we did send deputies to protect them whenever it was necessary. If my life was going to be on the line, I didn't want to turn over the investigation to anyone with less experience in the department. I wanted to be aware of everything that was being said and done."

Shur's first priority was Miriam, who was at that very moment teaching a first-grade class at Rockledge Elementary School in Bowie, Maryland. Shur asked Eugene L. Coon, who had been recently appointed by Howard Safir to be WITSEC chief, to send a WITSEC inspector to the school to protect her. Since it was a Friday afternoon, Coon ordered the inspector to stick close to Miriam and then, after she finished teaching for the day, drive her home so she could pack enough clothing for a weekend outing. The inspector was then to drive her to a hotel in Baltimore's Inner Harbor, where Shur would join her later that night.

Shur didn't think his children needed to be protected or told about the kidnap threat. His son, Ronald, had resigned from the U.S. attorney's office in Miami and was now working for a private law firm in another state. His daughter, Ilene, had married and taken her husband's last name.

Both Keeney and Coon wanted Shur to be protected by deputies, but he didn't think it necessary. No one could enter his office without passing through several security checkpoints and being buzzed into the WITSEC section. The only time he thought he would be vulnerable was when he was commuting in his car, so when he left work that night, two deputies followed him. After tailing him for fifteen minutes, one of the deputies called Shur on his cellular telephone and assured him that no one was tracking them. Nonetheless, Shur, who had a handgun within reach, decided to drive around for another hour before heading toward Baltimore. "I wanted to make certain I wasn't leading anyone to Miriam. I spent more time with my eyes on the rearview mirror than looking through the windshield." Finally, when he was absolutely convinced that it was safe, he turned north. An hour later, the port city's skyline came within his view, and he was struck by the irony of this moment. Shur had never gotten along well with Mermelstein, and he had been one of Shur's harshest critics. Now Shur and Miriam were going into hiding to protect him.

Mermelstein was told about the kidnap plot a few hours after Shur. He had never heard of a hit man named Bersago, he said. Nor was he particularly concerned about Shur. He and Shur had gotten into a bitter dispute a year earlier, when the CBS news show *60 Minutes* had wanted to broadcast a segment about Mermelstein's life as a cocaine cowboy. He had just written a book and was eager to promote it, but Shur had ordered him not to appear on the program. When sales of *The Man Who Made It Snow* were not as good as Mermelstein had hoped, he blamed Shur. Now the tables were turned. Gerald Shur was finally going to discover what it was like to be one of the hunted.

CHAPTER
TWENTY

MIRIAM SHUR had been told not to open the door to her hotel room unless her husband knocked two times and then quickly gave three more raps. It was a signal that no one was holding a gun to his back. As soon as she heard the secret knock, she opened the door and Shur hustled inside.

"An informant has told us he was hired to kidnap either you or me and torture us to get me to tell him where a witness is hidden," he explained. During the next several minutes, he told her everything he knew about the plot. Finally, he asked: "Do you want to leave town for a while?"

"Heavens, no!" she replied. "I have report cards to fill out."

He had expected as much. Miriam did not frighten easily. Once she had looked outside their house and spotted two men parked in a car, suspiciously eyeing a neighbor's home. Without thinking about the danger, she marched up and demanded to know what they were doing. "We're cops, lady," one replied gruffly, flashing a badge. "We're on a stakeout. Now get out of here." Miriam had always accepted the dangers that came with her husband's job. "It is part of being married to a man in law enforcement," she said. It was as simple as that.

Shur wondered sometimes if Miriam had gotten her grit from her great-grandmother, Sheema Heifetz, who had been forced to abandon her home in Russia and escape with her three grandchildren after their widowed father had been murdered during

Cossack pogroms against the Jews. En route, Great-grandma Heifetz had prevented drunken soldiers from raping her granddaughter, foiled a border crossing guard's attempt to hold one of the children hostage for ransom, survived a bubonic plague epidemic, and secured ship passage to America for the family even though she had almost no money. Miriam brought a deep steadiness to their marriage. She ran the home, reared the children, taught school, and accepted as part of the job the long hours that Shur spent at the Justice Department, his frequent trips, and the mysterious telephone calls at all hours from prosecutors and deputy marshals who demanded to speak to him immediately.

"Normally, we would have enjoyed spending a weekend sightseeing in Baltimore's Inner Harbor," Shur said later, "but knowing we were potential kidnap targets changed all that." They found themselves being unusually cautious whenever they stepped outside the hotel room. They were suspicious of people walking behind them, especially if they were there for a long time. They stood back from the sidewalk curbs in case a car zoomed up and someone leaped out and tried to grab them. They felt suspended in time. Everyone around them was going about their normal routines, but they were in hiding, their lives on hold.

Shur and Howard Safir had once discussed what they would want the Justice Department to do if one of them was kidnapped. They had agreed that they wouldn't want the government to negotiate for their release because if it did, it would encourage other kidnappings. But that had been when Shur was talking to Safir. It had been hypothetical. Now it was real. And now it was Miriam who was in jeopardy. She was a civilian, an innocent bystander. No one had asked her to put her life on the line to fight crime. The idea of losing her terrified him. He decided to ask her how she felt, what she would want him to do if she was kidnapped.

"I wouldn't want you to negotiate," she said. "I wouldn't want to be responsible for more kidnappings." Of course, she added jokingly, she hoped he would do whatever he could to save her. They laughed, and then Shur had told her that he didn't have a clue where Max Mermelstein had been relocated. "This is great," he said, trying, like her, to joke about the threat. "Me with a low pain threshold—and no useful information whatsoever for kidnappers. It's not a good combination."

Shur had lectured thousands of WITSEC witnesses in the past two decades about the sorts of problems they were likely to face once they entered the program. Now he was about to discover firsthand what it felt like to hide. Much to his surprise, he would learn that it was more difficult than even he had imagined.

On Sunday night, he called the hotel's front desk to ask for a wake-up call. "What's your name?" the desk clerk asked. Shur couldn't remember. The WITSEC inspector had checked them in under a pseudonym. It was such a simple thing, but he didn't have a clue. He began coughing, quickly covered the telephone receiver with his hand, and whispered to Miriam: "What's our name?"

"Parker," she whispered back. "Gerald Parker."

Neither of them wanted to continue staying in Baltimore. To them, living in such a nice hotel was a waste of taxpayers' money. Plus, it was inconvenient. But WITSEC chief Coon said it was too risky for them to return home, especially since home was not a house but a boat. It had been Miriam's idea to sell their Bowie home after their children had grown, and move onto a forty-two-foot trawler that they christened *Half-and-Half*. The name had come from the way Shur addressed Miriam in letters: "To one half from one half, together we make a whole." Both enjoyed living on water. Their trawler had teak-capped beams, a spacious master stateroom, two heads, and a spare bedroom. They liked the romance of it, the ability to pick up and cruise across the bay on a whim. They kept their trawler docked at a family-owned marina near Annapolis, Maryland, and liked the fact they were the only live-aboards docked there.

At first, Shur had thought living on a boat would give them an advantage in evading kidnappers. But it turned out that finding where *Half-and-Half* was docked was easy. WITSEC inspector John Cleveland had made a few telephone calls to the U.S. Coast Guard and Maryland licensing officials posing as a high school chum of Shur's, and they had not only told him where the trawler was docked, but offered him a floor plan of the craft when he asked what it looked like.

At Coon's insistence, the Shurs moved into an all-suite hotel in Bethesda, Maryland, where their room came equipped with a kitchen and was rented by the month. It was about thirty miles from the marina where they lived. Because this was seen as a temporary relocation, the Shurs didn't have to sever their contacts with their family and friends, but WITSEC arranged for Shur to get a driver's license under the name of Gerald Parker for identification, since that was how he had been registered at the hotel. They had to stop and think about what name to use when the phones in their new quarters rang. One phone was connected to the hotel, but WITSEC had arranged for calls made to their boat to be forwarded to a portable phone they kept in the hotel. On one line, they were the Parkers, on the other, the Shurs.

Coon insisted that Miriam be guarded at work. He assigned a young inspector named Wanda Watson Haynes to pick her up each morning at the hotel, drive her to school, and stay with her in the classroom until she finished and returned to their hotel quarters. Miriam told the school's principal, Arlene Verge, about the threat, and Haynes assured her that the chances of a kidnapper bursting into the school and snatching up Miriam were slim. She was most vulnerable when traveling to and from school. Still, no one wanted to take chances. With Verge's blessing, Miriam introduced Haynes to the other teachers as her new aide. Haynes told them she had just finished college and was trying to decide whether or not she really wanted to teach full time. "No one would have ever guessed, looking at her in that classroom, sitting on the floor reading a story to the children, that she had a handgun hidden under her jacket and was a tiger in sheep's clothing," said Shur.

Coon wanted to assign an inspector to watch over Shur, too, but he refused. Instead, two deputies met him each night when he was ready to leave the Justice Department and followed him until they were satisfied that he wasn't being followed by anyone else.

As soon as Shur had been told about the kidnap threat, he arranged for Félix Bersago to be moved into the BOP's Valachi Suite and for the FBI to give him a polygraph. The results showed he was "not being deceptive" about the kidnap plot. It was real. However, the examiner suspected from his answers that he was also holding back information. When the FBI bore down, Bersago revealed the cartel had given him a telephone number in Medellín to call after he sneaked into the United States. He was supposed to receive further instructions about how to go about finding and kidnapping Shur. The number seemed to be the FBI's best lead, so its agents dialed it and put Bersago on the line. But the man who answered claimed he had never heard of Shur, Mermelstein, or a kidnapping plot. He referred Bersago to an attorney in Miami known for representing drug dealers. The FBI called him, but that call, too, went nowhere. The attorney said he didn't have a clue who Bersago was or what he wanted. Obviously, the cartel had somehow figured out that Bersago had been caught. But how? The most likely explanation was that someone had been watching Bersago, perhaps another potential kidnapper. Shur was told to remain in hiding.

When the Shurs' trawler was moved to a nearby military base for safekeeping, no one paid much attention. After a few days of feeling uneasy, they tried to get back to their normal routines. They couldn't. When the hotel's fire alarm went off one night and the other tenants rushed outside, Shur suspected it might be a ruse to lure Miriam and him from their room. He held her back until they were fully dressed and he had stashed his pistol under his jacket. While everyone outside was watching the firefighters who came to the hotel, Shur nervously scanned the crowd. It turned out that another tenant had started a grease fire.

"I had told witnesses when they entered WITSEC that the best thing I could do was to relocate them someplace far away from their home so they didn't have to keep looking over their shoulders," Shur recalled. "But now I was someplace different and I was still looking."

Other lessons quickly followed. Their first weekend, they went grocery shopping at a store near the hotel and were about to push their cart into the checkout line when one of Miriam's cousins came inside. She lived miles away and had decided to stop there by chance. Neither of the Shurs wanted her to spot them and ask why they were shopping so far from their boat, so they abandoned the grocery cart and dashed down an aisle. They played keep-away from her until they could slip unnoticed out an exit. "I'd had witnesses tell me stories about running into persons from their pasts in completely unexpected places—during vacations, in elevators, walking through airports," said Shur. "I suddenly realized those stories weren't as odd as I had thought."

Shur was surprised how impatient he was becoming with the kidnapping case. There wasn't much Félix Bersago could add to his story. The FBI continued pressing him for facts, and it sent a daily progress report to one of Shur's top analysts, who had been assigned to monitor the case. But there were no new leads. The best the FBI could offer Shur was simply to keep hiding and be patient.

A frustrated Shur, meanwhile, was learning that one of the worst parts of hiding was lying. "After a while, you got used to the idea that someone might be watching you or be after you," he explained. "You convinced yourself that you were safe, that they couldn't find you. But the lying was something that neither of us ever got used to doing, especially to people we loved."

They had to beg off sitting with the family at their granddaughter Adena's high school graduation so they wouldn't endanger anyone else. They said Shur had to work late, then they rushed into the ceremony after it started, sat by themselves, and left early. They gave their children the same excuse on Father's Day, arranging for a picnic inside the Justice Department's courtyard, where guards were on duty, instead of gathering at home. Family events just weren't the same. The isolation was beginning to take a toll. The Shurs were being cheated out of memories.

About five weeks after they first went into hiding, Shur was scheduled to speak at a wardens' conference outside Philadelphia, and since he was going to be inspecting a WITSEC prison unit in Phoenix prior to it, he decided to fly directly to the Philadelphia airport from Arizona rather than returning home first. Miriam and Wanda Watson Haynes were supposed to meet him at the gate, but they were delayed in traffic and when they reached the terminal, they couldn't find a parking spot. Haynes double-parked, stuck the car's red police beacon on top of the roof, and telephoned the office to ask if the flight had already landed while Miriam dashed inside. Shur wasn't at the gate and Miriam became suspicious when a man who had been waiting there stood up suddenly and fell into step behind her. Thinking that she was overreacting, she stepped inside an airport souvenir shop and began surveying the magazines. A few seconds later, she glanced to her left and spotted the man again. He was watching her from outside the store's window. She turned back to the magazines and then glanced over again. He was gone. Hurrying to a pay phone, she dialed her husband's pager number. As she waited for him to return her call, she looked around. The man from the gate was watching her from some fifty feet away. Unsure what to do, Miriam left the phone and began walking toward the gate. If he followed, she would know for certain that he was stalking her.

Suddenly Shur appeared from nowhere, but her feeling of relief turned to fear when she saw there were two men walking next to him. "Oh God," she thought, "he's being kidnapped! It's really happening!" In that instant, she decided to ignore him when they passed. She would try to hurry outside and get Haynes.

"Miriam!" Shur called out. "We couldn't find you!"

The two men with him were deputy marshals. When he had landed and had not seen Haynes and Miriam, he telephoned the WITSEC office and by chance discovered that two deputies happened to be putting a witness on a flight near his gate. They had hurried over to protect him. Miriam looked around, but the man following her was gone. Although they would laugh about it later and decide the incident had been innocent, both of them had been frightened at the time. The line between caution and paranoia was easy to blur.

"I thought about all the times witnesses had told me how they had landed in an airport and were supposed to be met by deputies but no one was there," said Shur. "Once again, I was getting a taste of what it felt like to feel vulnerable."

They also realized they were becoming attached to Wanda Watson Haynes. She was becoming one of the family. She went with Miriam when she visited her mother or had to shop. Shur knew WITSEC inspectors were warned not to become too friendly with persons they guarded. Some inspectors called it "the Partington syndrome." But staying at arm's length was tough. "There was no doubt in my mind that Wanda would have taken a bullet for Miriam," Shur said later. "How could we not care about her?"

After two months they were sick of hiding. They ached for old routines, felt they had no privacy. When Shur's first boss, Henry Petersen, died unexpectedly, Shur had to be escorted to the funeral by WITSEC inspectors. "It was obvious that I was being protected, but not one of my colleagues asked why. They knew I couldn't talk about it, but it was strange. It was as if all of us accepted the idea that we could someday be targets."

After one more week, Shur had had enough of hotel life. It was beginning to affect his health. Three years earlier he had been diagnosed with a hiatal hernia. But when his condition didn't improve, he decided to get a second opinion. The doctor called in a cardiologist, who found a serious heart problem and immediately put him in the hospital. "I'm concerned that you may not live through the night," he warned. The next morning, Shur underwent double bypass surgery. He left the hospital determined to watch his diet, and he had shed forty pounds since then. "I got down to a weight of one-sixty, which was good for a five-foot ten-inch man," he said, "but I started gaining immediately after we moved into the hotel. I was totally out of my exercise and food routine. Before I knew it, I was back to two hundred. I told Miriam, 'We have to get home or this hiding out is going to kill me!'"

WITSEC chief Coon reluctantly agreed to let them move back aboard their trawler, but only after a night-vision video camera was installed on the topmast and monitors put in every room. They were thrilled to go home. Because of the kidnap threat, they had stopped going out at night and had canceled their vacation plans. The *Half-and-Half* gave them back their base.

There was one outing they refused to cancel. Each summer

they took members of a local multiple sclerosis support group on their trawler across the Chesapeake Bay to visit a maritime museum. They were scheduled to make two trips, one on a Saturday, another on a Sunday, taking twenty guests on each day trip. "Some of these people had been looking forward to this for months," said Shur. But there was more to it than that. They were tired of changing their plans because of the threat. Their decision to go ahead was a defiant gesture, a way to strike back at an unseen foe. Inspector Haynes and another WITSEC specialist, Joe Simon, volunteered to give up their weekend to protect them during the rides.

In late July the FBI finally got a break in its investigation. An informant in Florida told DEA agents that the Medellín cartel had hired a private detective in Miami to find Max Mermelstein. The FBI wanted to know if he also had been asked to find the Shurs. The cartel had used private detectives before to locate people it wanted to kill. It was a practice the FBI wanted to stop. It sent two agents to question the detective and warn him that if he helped the cartel locate Mermelstein and the witness was murdered, the government would arrest him as an accessory.

The detective admitted he had been hired to find Mermelstein, but claimed his clients were television reporters who wanted to interview Mermelstein, not drug dealers. When the agents asked for the reporters' names so they could verify the detective's story, he refused to say anything more, citing client privilege. He told them, however, that he had never heard of Gerald Shur.

Back in Maryland, the Shurs were beginning to relax. Then one night they were jarred awake by the sound of motorcycles entering the marina parking lot. From the trawler's master stateroom, Shur trained the night-vision video camera on the shoreline, and the image of six bikers appeared on the monitor. They were looking directly at *Half-and-Half*. Shur knew that drug dealers frequently used motorcycle gangs to do their hits. He prepared for the worst. He laid his Glock nine-millimeter automatic, a Ruger Mini-14 autoloading rifle, and a shotgun on a table next to him. "I took out several clips of ammunition and shotgun shells," he recalled later. "I wanted to make sure I had enough rounds to stop all six of them if they began boarding the trawler. I had the phone, too, and was ready to call the local police. Miriam and I watched the monitor and waited."

It was a surreal moment: the two of them sitting in the dark on their boat, surrounded by guns, their eyes glued to the black-and-white monitor, and the six bikers seated on their Harleys, calmly watching the trawler from the dock. It was like a twisted scene from *High Noon*. Shur had always been an outspoken critic of the death penalty. To him, life was sacred, all lives worth saving. But this was different. "I had never shot anyone, and you always wonder what you'd do in a situation like this one," he said later. As he sat there his doubts disappeared. "When it looks like it is going to finally happen to you, you don't wonder at all. I was ready to open fire if they came through that door."

Moments later, a biker reached into a saddlebag and began to pull something from it. Shur zoomed the camera in just as the biker removed a bottle of whiskey. They passed it around and then rode off. Neither of the Shurs slept that night.

It never ended. A few days later, Miriam spotted two men near her car over by the dock, and when one of them crawled underneath it, she dialed 911. The local police had been told about the kidnap threat and were there within minutes. Shur raced home. The pair turned out to be mechanics from a local garage who had been sent to pick up a car that a boat owner had asked them to service while he was out of town. He'd told them the keys would be behind a back wheel, which is why they had crawled under Miriam's car. They had mistaken it for his.

"I'd reached the limit. The investigation was going nowhere and there were no more leads," Shur said. Even though the FBI, DEA, and Marshals Service urged him not to do it, Shur flew to New Mexico to confront Félix Bersago face-to-face.

"I'm Gerald Shur," he declared when he stepped into the Valachi Suite. "I'm the man you were supposed to kidnap."

"No, you're not," said Bersago. "You're too old. Shur's in his forties."

Bersago had never seen a photograph of Shur, but he'd been given a description by the cartel and it didn't match. "I began interrogating him," Shur said, "and I began to suspect from his answers that the cartel had not been after me. It had been after Gene Coon, the WITSEC chief." Bersago's notebook had contained the words "Gerald Shur" and "WITSEC," but the address in the book had been Arlington, Virginia, which was where the Marshals Service WITSEC offices were headquartered and where Coon worked. "I decided the cartel had given Bersago the wrong name." Shur hurried from the cell and telephoned Coon's office, but he was out of the country on an assignment. A WITSEC inspector was sent to warn Coon's wife, Lynn. "The Marshals Service had insisted I be protected," Shur recalled, "but Gene was one of their own and the threat to him and his family was seen as an occupational hazard. I thought it was outrageous, but they refused to take any extra steps to protect him. None. The feeling was that he had been trained to deal with these threats."

Shur finally began to relax when he got back to Miriam and *Half-and-Half*. Not long after that, he received word that the Medellín cartel had finally crumbled. The Ochoa brothers had agreed to plead guilty in Colombia to cocaine smuggling charges to avoid being extradited to the United States. They were now cooperating with Colombian prosecutors, turning against the assassins and others in their own organization who had made them rich. Pablo Escobar had also surrendered to avoid being turned over to the United States. But he had not been sent to one of Colombia's overcrowded prisons. He was serving his sentence in a "prison" that he had built for himself in Medellín. When the United States investigated, it discovered the walled compound was actually a luxury villa, and it began pressuring the Colombians to move Escobar into a real prison. More than a hundred troops went to forcibly evict him one morning, but he had been tipped off and had escaped into the jungle. From there he launched yet another bloody campaign, killing fifteen persons. But this time his *plata o plomo* actions backfired. Vigilantes, who called themselves Los Pepes, an acronym for *perseguidos por Pablo Escobar*—

"people persecuted by Pablo Escobar"—burned and looted his mansion, broke into a warehouse and destroyed all his luxury cars, and began methodically killing bankers, money launderers, and lawyers who had helped him operate his cocaine empire. At one point, Los Pepes was killing as many as five people a day without interference from the police. When the assassinations grew to more than three hundred, including several of Escobar's relatives, he tried to send his wife and children to Europe, but no country would grant them visas. On December 2, 1993, a special team created specifically to hunt down Escobar traced a telephone call that he had made to a local radio station to protest how his family had been forced into hiding. His bodyguards were killed in the gun battle that followed, and he was wounded trying to escape. A team member stepped up to him as he lay bleeding on the roof of a building and shot him point-blank in the ear.

Max Mermelstein learned about Escobar's death on a newscast. He had voluntarily left WITSEC and moved to a new city, where he changed his name and found work completely on his own. Only a handful of federal agents knew how to reach him. While the death of Escobar meant an end to the cartel, Mermelstein still was listed as a potential witness in several unresolved drug prosecutions. Most of the accused had not been captured. "It's still not safe for me to surface," Mermelstein explained during a telephone call from an unknown location. "It may never be. I suspect I will be in hiding the rest of my life."

The INS, meanwhile, rejected Félix Bersago's request for asylum once the FBI decided it was pointless to continue questioning him about the kidnap plot. He was put on an international flight and expelled from the country. A few weeks later, he telephoned Shur to see if he would help him become an undercover operative for the DEA overseas. Shur said no. To this day, no one is certain whom Bersago was supposed to kidnap: Shur, Coon, or some other WITSEC official.

"Over the years, Howard Safir and I had warned witnesses that WITSEC was a program of last resort," said Shur. "Miriam and I had only been forced to hide for a few months—we did not have to endure the drastic changes most witnesses face—but I now knew firsthand that what we were saying was right on target. Being relocated was something I would not wish on anyone. The only reason to do it was if it was your only hope to stay alive."

CHAPTER
TWENTY-ONE

INSIDE THE MARSHALS SERVICE, they were known as Howard Safir's "black bag jobs"—special missions that usually involved WITSEC, were dangerous, and almost always had the potential for scandal. In December 1985, a delegation of DEA agents met secretly with Safir to discuss just such an operation. As soon as he heard why they needed his help, he agreed.

A month later, four deputies handpicked by Safir slipped across the U.S. border into Mexico, where they rendezvoused with six state judicial police officers the DEA had said they could trust. Safir's men had no legal authority in Mexico, a fact that was historically so well known it was often dramatized in old Wild West movies by having outlaws race across the Rio Grande on horseback and then thumb their noses at deputy marshals stuck on the American side. Officially, the deputies were advisers, there simply to watch what was happening, and for ten days that is exactly what they did. Then on January 24, the deputies and Mexican officers followed Rene Martin Verdugo Urquidez, a known drug dealer, and his family to a birthday party that he was hosting in the resort town of San Felipe for one of his sons. Midway through the festivities, Verdugo left the party to drive to a nearby liquor store to buy ice and beer. The deputies and Mexicans swooped down. Using three rental cars the deputies had driven into Mexico, the lawmen shot in front of and behind Verdugo, pinning in his vehicle. The Mexican policemen jerked him from his car,

handcuffed and blindfolded him, and pushed him into the backseat of one of their cars. With the Americans trailing them, the
Mexicans raced toward the border. Verdugo's wife, who had witnessed the abduction, telephoned his attorney and notified the
local police. Verdugo had several of them on his drug payroll, and
they immediately threw up roadblocks and began searching for
him. To avoid being caught, the deputies and Mexicans careened
off the highway, shooting across the desert. It was now night, but
they kept their headlights off, traveling blindly at eighty miles an
hour until they reached the chain-link fence that separated the
two countries. At that point, the car carrying the deputies shot
ahead, flipping on its headlights. "Here it is!" the driver declared,
slamming on his brakes, as he pulled toward a hole that had been
cut into the fence. The Mexicans dragged Verdugo from their car
and shoved him toward it. Deputy Tony Perez, who was in charge
of the operation, crawled through the opening. The Mexicans
shoved the still blindfolded Verdugo after him through the opening into Perez's waiting arms.

"You're under arrest," he declared.

The Mexican government was enraged when it learned what
had happened. The nation's top prosecutor said Verdugo had been
the victim of an illegal kidnapping and issued arrest warrants for
the six Mexican officers who had helped the deputies. But they
had already fled the country, along with twenty-four of their family members. Safir had arranged for them to enter the United
States, and Shur had accepted them into WITSEC. They would be
given new identities, relocated, and paid $32,000 in rewards.
Verdugo, meanwhile, was driven to a jail in Los Angeles to await
trial on marijuana trafficking charges. As expected, the Los Angeles defense attorneys hired to defend him said they were aghast at
the deputies' actions and argued that his arrest had been illegal.
"The U.S. Marshals Service has no right to storm into a sovereign
country and kidnap one of its citizens," Verdugo's attorneys
protested in a court motion demanding his immediate release. But
the Justice Department cited several long-standing court rulings
that said it did not matter how international fugitives ended up on

American soil, as long as their capture did not involve torture that "shocks the conscience." A judge concurred, and Verdugo remained locked up.

Although Verdugo was a major marijuana trafficker, that was not the main reason why Safir had agreed to help the DEA abduct him. He had taken part in the gruesome 1985 torture and murder of DEA agent Enrique Camarena Salazar, known to his friends as Kiki, and Safir and Shur were eager to do whatever they could to catch and punish Camarena's murderers. "I told my staff I would accept anyone into WITSEC who had any information about the Kiki murder, regardless of whether or not they would later be used as witnesses to testify," Shur recalled. "I was lowering our normal standards for admission because I was sickened by how he had been killed. In my eyes, the Camarena case had become the most important case in our office." As a former DEA agent himself, Safir had worried that other DEA agents would be slaughtered if the United States didn't act quickly to punish Camarena's killers. "Of course there was going to be political fallout," he said later. "But I felt what we did was justified. I was not going to stand by and watch a DEA agent's brutal murder go unavenged."

Camarena had been sent to Guadalajara, Mexico, in 1981 to help the local Mexican and state police combat an increase in drug smuggling there. He quickly ran afoul of two powerful drug lords. When their efforts to bribe him failed, they decided to abduct him. On February 7, 1985, Camarena left the U.S. consulate in Guadalajara, where the DEA had its office, to meet his wife for lunch. Five men forced him at gunpoint into a car. They drove him to a mansion less than ten minutes away and for the next thirty hours tortured him. Burning cigarettes were pressed against his flesh and he was struck repeatedly with a lead pipe. A nail was pounded into his head. At one point, his tormentors brought in a local doctor to inject him with lidocaine, to stabilize his heart rate and prolong his life so they could continue beating him. Incredibly, his kidnappers tape-recorded the torture, and Camarena would later be heard screaming in pain on the tapes. A Mexican airplane pilot, Alfredo Zavala, was being tortured at the same time in the same house. The drug lords were convinced Zavala was one of Camarena's sources and had been tipping him off whenever drug-laden flights took off or landed at the Guadalajara airport. Some thirty people visited the walled compound during the time the torture was being administered, but none did anything to help rescue the men. Their bodies were found a month later. They had been stripped to their shorts, eyes taped shut, and hands tied behind their backs. An autopsy showed Camarena had a broken jaw, two broken cheekbones, a broken nose, a crushed windpipe, and two skull fractures in addition to the nail driven into his head.

The Mexican government tried to downplay the murder. It dragged its feet in the investigation and then Mexican officials speculated that Camarena had been killed because he was accepting bribes. The United States reacted by ordering a trunk-by-trunk search of every northbound car crossing the Mexican border, paralyzing traffic and putting a chokehold on Mexico's $2 billion-per-year tourist business. Finally, the state police arrested nine small-time dope dealers, but the DEA knew the real culprits were going unpunished. Camarena had been overseeing Operation Padrino, which means "godfather" in Spanish, and its prime target had been Miguel Ángel Félix Gallardo. He and another godfather, Juan Ramón Matta Ballesteros, had transformed Mexico's drug trade from a cottage industry in the late 1970s into a billion-dollar conglomerate known as La Familia. Their ties reached into the highest offices in the Mexican government, and they were protected by Mexico's business community, where La Familia laundered millions of dollars in drug profits through three hundred different firms, including resort hotels, fancy restaurants, and large car dealerships. The DEA learned from informants that Gallardo had assigned one of his top lieutenants, Rafael Caro Quintero, to kidnap and interrogate Camarena. Caro had a personal grudge against him. A few months earlier, the DEA agent had overseen a police raid at a six-thousand-acre farm that Caro owned where some thirty-seven thousand laborers openly grew and harvested marijuana. The raid had cost him an estimated $50 million in lost profits.

When it became clear that Mexican officials were not going to help them go after the drug lords, the DEA decided to go after them on their own, starting at the bottom and working up, which is where Safir's black bag job had come into play. One of Caro's most trusted associates in the drug business was Verdugo, the smuggler shoved through the chain-link fence into the United States.

Worried that Safir would send his deputies after him next, Caro fled to Costa Rica, taking seven bodyguards and his seventeen-year-old girlfriend with him. There he bought a four-acre estate from an Iranian exile for $800,000 in cash, but three weeks later, acting on a tip from the DEA, Costa Rican commandos raided the villa and forced him to return to Mexico. He was arrested by Mexican authorities as soon as he crossed the border. They were worried that if they didn't put him in jail, Safir's deputies would snatch him up.

With two of Camarena's murderers now in custody, the DEA and Marshals Service moved up the ladder by going after La Familia's two godfathers. Juan Ramón Matta Ballesteros had returned to his native Honduras, where he was one of the wealthiest residents of Tegucigalpa, with a personal fortune estimated at a billion dollars. The Honduran constitution forbade extraditions of any kind, regardless of the crime, so the DEA and Safir began lobbying military and Honduran police officials to find some excuse to expel Matta. They refused at first but under increased pressure finally agreed to cooperate in one of Safir's black bag jobs.

On April 5, 1988, a team of deputy marshals led a hundred Honduran police and military soldiers to Matta's exclusive compound. They arrived at 5:30 A.M. and were poised to burst inside when someone pointed out that the Honduran constitution forbade the execution of search warrants before 6 A.M. Matta was not at home in any case. He had gone on his morning jog and was drinking coffee with his lawyer, who lived on the same street. Glancing outside, Matta's sister noticed the troops and telephoned him. Since Matta had not broken any laws in Honduras, his lawyer urged him to return home and investigate the commotion.

What happened next would later be hotly disputed. Matta would claim he was physically abducted, but Honduran police insisted that he had started swinging and kicking at them first. Under Honduran law, this gave them the right to arrest him and search his estate. The police would later claim they had found a bag of cocaine sitting in Matta's kitchen. This conveniently gave them the authority they needed to expel him from Honduras. With two of Safir's deputies riding in the car, Matta was whisked to the airport by two Honduran policemen. During the forty-minute ride, Matta offered the Hondurans a million dollars each if they would let him go and kill the deputies. When they didn't respond, he began upping the price; by the time the car reached the airport he was offering them $20 million each. The Hondurans didn't doubt Matta had the cash; they simply assumed that if they accepted it, he would kill them later without paying.

Matta was physically forced onto a flight headed to the Dominican Republic. By "chance," a deputy was sitting on either side of him. When the plane landed, Dominican customs officials refused to let him disembark because he didn't have a passport. The Dominicans, who had been tipped off by Safir, escorted Matta to another flight—the next one scheduled to leave their country. It "happened" to be an airplane bound for Puerto Rico, and now Matta found himself surrounded by four of Safir's deputies. Again, they "happened" to be sitting in the seats next to him. During the flight, he tried to bribe them, again offering as much as $20 million each, but they arrested him as soon as the flight entered U.S. airspace. When the flight touched down, he was taken immediately to a federal prison.

Now only one Mexican godfather was still at large. The DEA knew Miguel Ángel Félix Gallardo was living in a house in Guadalajara that was swarming with bodyguards. But when they staked out the compound, they noticed a curious fact: All the bodyguards left the house early in the morning to eat breakfast in a nearby cantina. It turned out that the drug lord's young wife refused to cook for them. The DEA and a squad of Mexico's state police pushed their way inside the house during breakfast and arrested him without firing a bullet. Inside his bedroom, the DEA found records showing that he owned fifty homes and two hundred ranches in Mexico, and was worth an estimated $3 billion.

For more than five years, the DEA and the Marshals Service continued to track down other Mexicans suspected of being involved in the Camarena torture and murder. Whenever they ran into a problem getting help from Mexican authorities, they found a way around them. For instance, in April 1990 Mexican bounty hunters burst into the medical office of gynecologist Humberto Alvarez Machain in Guadalajara and forced him across the border to where DEA agents were waiting. He was accused of being the physician who had kept Camarena alive with injections while he was being tortured. His arrest set off another round of angry protests. Abducting drug dealers was one thing; snatching a prominent physician was another. Mexico's president complained directly to the White House, and the nation's top prosecutor filed criminal charges in Mexico City against the DEA agents who had engineered the arrest. The prosecutor then suggested that the Mexican government hire U.S. bounty hunters to kidnap the DEA agents and deliver them to Mexico for trial. In Los Angeles, defense attorneys demanded the physician be released. This time a U.S. district judge agreed with them and ruled his capture was illegal. The Justice Department appealed, and the case reached the U.S. Supreme Court at the same time that marijuana smuggler Verdugo's appeal got there. Since both men were claiming they had been kidnapped, the court consolidated their petitions and issued its ruling in 1992. The justices said the U.S. Constitution did not prohibit federal agents from kidnapping fugitives living in foreign countries, nor did it prevent the government from paying or hiring others to kidnap them, even though the abductions might be "shocking" and violate international law. Ironically, when the physician was put on trial, a Los Angeles jury acquitted him, and he was sent back to Mexico after having spent three years in a U.S. prison.

In the end, more than twenty Mexican citizens were arrested in the Camarena case. Verdugo, who was shoved across through the fence, was sentenced to life in prison plus 240 years. His boss, Rafael Caro Quintero, was tried in Mexico and given a forty-year sentence. Honduran drug kingpin Juan Ramón Matta Ballesteros was sentenced in the United States to 225 years for drug trafficking, plus three life sentences for conspiracy in the death of Camarena. The last godfather captured, Miguel Ángel Félix Gallardo, was sentenced by Mexican authorities to a forty-year prison term.

The period between 1983 and 1989 would later be described by many as the U.S. Marshals Service's golden years. Safir would be credited with helping turn the service into a professional and highly specialized law enforcement operation. But much credit would also be given to Stanley E. Morris, who became the Marshals Service's director in 1983, replacing William Hall. Morris was not a cop. Instead, he was a skilled administrator who had served stints at the Office of Management and Budget and the Department of Health and Human Services. He understood how the Washington bureaucracy worked. Under his guidance, the Marshals Service was modernized and professionalized. It was Morris who established the National Asset Seizure and Forfeiture Program, which put deputies in charge of selling millions of dollars of property seized from drug dealers and other criminals under the RICO Act. He started a comprehensive Court Security Officers Program that trained deputies how to protect judges and federal courthouses. He began "Con Air," the service's private airline operation that shuttles some eighty thousand federal inmates each year across the country for court appearances or for prison transfers. He got Congress to increase his budget each year, and he used the extra funds to hire a third more deputies, purchase long-needed equipment, and build better facilities. He revamped the Marshals Service's pay structure, a move that gave deputies hefty raises and attracted better-qualified recruits. Under Morris, the Marshals Service adopted an unofficial slogan: "When a job needs to be done and you don't know who to give it to—give it to the U.S. Marshals."

The WITSEC branch thrived under Morris. It became one of the most envied assignments in the service. Its 160 inspectors were the top of the heap. In 1988, the Marshals Service opened a WITSEC Safesite and Orientation Center in a secret location in a Washington suburb. It was Howard Safir's brainchild, but it was Morris who had gotten the federal funds to build it. The center was created to operate as an Ellis Island for witnesses.

"The purpose of the center was to give WITSEC one voice," explained one WITSEC inspector who asked not to be named but who was responsible for designing it and oversaw its construction. "We were still having problems with consistency despite the use of MOUs [Memorandums of Understanding] that spelled out exactly what was going to be done for each witness. One inspector in the field might explain the program and MOU one way, another would highlight different things, and this led to some confusion. Mr. Safir thought if we brought every witness into one location and had a core of inspectors, who had been trained to say the exact same thing, explain to the witness what was going to happen, then we could be certain of consistency. The complaints dropped dramatically once we got the center operating."

Each witness and his family arrived at the center in an armored vehicle with blacked-out windows so they couldn't see where they were being taken. Once the vehicle had driven inside an underground garage, the witness and his family were directed down a hallway into hotel-like accommodations. "We had psychologists give them tests, and we had both psychologists and psychiatrists available to help them deal with the trauma of what, in effect, was being reborn. The fact that we had these professionals available showed the witnesses that we cared about them," the inspector said. "We also discovered that while many of these people had money from their criminal activities, they hadn't spent it on medical care, and many of them had medical problems that needed attention." During their stay at the center, they were given complete physical exams. "Many of them didn't really have the skills they needed to take care of a family in a normal society," the inspector recalled, "so we had people come in and help them learn how to take better care of their children. We were preparing them to go out into the legitimate world." The WITSEC analysts responsible for providing them with new documents also met with them. "One reason for past delays in getting new documents was mistakes that were made in filling out forms. If a paperwork mistake was made in the field, when that paperwork got to Washington it had to be sent back, and that meant delays." The analysts at the orientation center went over each form with the witnesses to ensure they were correctly and completely filled out. Inspectors also discussed job placement with each witness.

When all of the testing and various health exams were completed and paperwork done, each witness and his family were teamed with a WITSEC inspector who found them a suitable city to be relocated in. Before leaving the center, the witnesses would be shown videotapes of where they were being sent.

Movement inside the center was carefully controlled, much as it was in a prison. Doors were electronically bolted and could be opened only by inspectors in the center's control room. Hallways were monitored with video cameras and motion detectors. Inspectors were told about witnesses on a need-to-know basis, which meant that inspectors working with one witness would not know that another witness was in the center. "Witnesses never saw each other," the inspector said. The center could hold up to six families of five, and six prisoners in more-spartan rooms. It was designed to withstand an outside attack. Several fences kept the curious away. The center itself had an exterior wall and another completely separate interior wall to withstand bomb blasts. There were also vehicle barriers to prevent cars filled with explosives from being crashed into the building.

The typical orientation process lasted about two weeks. The witness and his family would then be driven in a vehicle with blacked-out windows to an airport and sent to where they were being resettled. A WITSEC field inspector would meet them at the airport and take them to an apartment, where they would live until they could move to a house and find a full-time job.

"You could often tell by the problems that you heard a witness or former witnesses complain about when they had been relocated in WITSEC," explained WITSEC chief Eugene Coon.

"There were the pre-Safir days, the Safir days, and the orientation center days."

Another veteran WITSEC inspector described it more bluntly. "In the early days of the program, witnesses were dumped in motels, given a hundred bucks, and told to wait there until the local U.S. marshal sent one of his deputies to 'help' them. There were a few improvements between 1970 and 1978, but not many. In truth, most of the witnesses whom we helped got minimal services, and most of them had valid complaints about how they were treated. They simply weren't a priority. After Safir arrived, things got significantly better, but there were still problems. We were struggling to fix the mistakes from the past and catch up. The number of complaints slowly dropped, but we still had a lot of problems in the field from 1978 until 1988. There were misunderstandings and there were still long delays in getting documents. But after 1988, we had the relocation process down pat. The program was running as smoothly as possible, given that it was a people program and that meant there would always be unusual circumstances and unforeseen issues and problems."

WITSEC's all-inclusive service wasn't cheap. In 1988 it cost $75,000 to relocate a family of four. But at the Safesite and Orientation Center's opening ceremony, Morris insisted the price was well worth it. The director cited a long list of sensational criminal cases that could not have been successfully prosecuted without protected witnesses. In cases where WITSEC witnesses testified, he added, prosecutors had almost an 80 percent conviction rate. Later, in a report to Congress, Morris cited examples of the defendants in 1988 alone who had been convicted in cases where WITSEC witnesses were used. They included:

- Seven corrupt Miami police officers charged with killing and stealing money from cocaine dealers in the so-called Miami River Cop case
- Nine members of the Outlaws, a motorcycle gang in Fort Lauderdale, accused of drug trafficking, white slavery, and contract murder

- Four members of the White Patriot Party, a white supremacy group in Raleigh, North Carolina, accused of stealing explosives from a military base
- Ten members of an extremely violent Irish gang in New York known as the Westies, whose specialty was chopping up their murder victims

Shur had developed an especially good working relationship with Eugene Coon after the latter took charge of the Marshals Service's WITSEC operations in 1985. "I felt Gene was simply a top-notch chief," Shur recalled. "When it comes to egos, on a scale of one to ten, Gene Coon clocked in at zero. He had none. His only interest was in doing the best possible job. He was imaginative and solid and solution-oriented."

Coon came from a law enforcement background. His father and grandfather had both been county sheriffs, and his uncle had been a top DEA official. He'd joined the Marshals Service in 1972, after a stint in Vietnam, and risen through the ranks, doing a variety of assignments. His first was escorting prisoners between the jail and courts in the District of Columbia, a job that often involved daily fistfights with angry prisoners. Like most deputies at the time, he received almost no special training. From there he had been sent to rural West Virginia, where he won praise by capturing a fugitive without firing a shot, even though the suspect had barricaded himself inside a trailer and bragged he would never be taken alive. Coon had surprised him by crashing through the front door and tackling him before he could grab his pistol. Coon was then sent to the Pine Ridge Indian Reservation in South Dakota, where he helped hunt for the murderers of two FBI agents. He also escorted nuclear missiles between military bases, another job done by federal marshals. At one point he was assigned to help protect Jimmy the Weasel Fratianno in the basement of a Cleveland courthouse, where the mobster was scheduled to testify. "Fratianno got out of his cot one morning," Coon said later, "and while he was eating his breakfast, he looks up and says to me, 'Hey kid, make up my bed, will ya?' I looked at him and said, 'Hey old man, make it yourself.' You had to let him know up front that he couldn't push you around, otherwise he'd never respect you." In 1978 Coon became a WITSEC inspector and was stationed in Connecticut, where he helped hide New York mobsters while they were waiting to testify.

Beginning in the 1980s, more than a dozen countries sent delegations to the United States to learn about WITSEC. They patterned their own programs after it. "We had reached the point," Shur said later, "where we had become the absolute best witness protection program in the world."

CHAPTER
TWENTY-TWO

O
N AN OCTOBER AFTERNOON in 1987, Arthur Kane walked into the local office of Merrill Lynch in Miami and began shooting. He critically wounded his stockbroker, Lloyd Kolokoff; murdered the office manager, Jose Argilagos; and then killed himself. Detectives said later he had recently lost $6 million in the stock market. Shur was stunned.

"If you had asked me to pick from the thousands of witnesses I knew, the most docile criminal I had ever encountered," he recalled, "I would have instantly named Arthur H. Kane. I would have sworn he was as safe a choice as I could have possibly made when it came to putting a criminal into the program."

Shur had personally persuaded Kane and his wife to enter WIT-SEC in 1977, and until the shooting he had considered their relocation a success story. He flew to Miami to meet with Kane's widow. "I asked her if she wanted to be relocated since her husband's past had been revealed," Shur recalled, "but she felt safe. I told her I just didn't understand what had happened. Neither did she."

When he returned to Washington, Shur combed though his records for some clue that would have warned him that Kane had a violent streak. There was none. "I had never seen anything but politeness and a calmness about him," said Shur. "The violence of the shooting was totally out of character."

Shur could still remember the Saturday afternoon when he had Kane and his wife brought from Kansas City to Washington to meet with him and his staff. On the surface, the Kanes appeared to have a wonderful life. Kane was a respected attorney; he and his wife lived in an exclusive Kansas City neighborhood, had healthy and talented children, and were socially prominent. But Kane had a secret. He was stealing more than $100,000 per year through his law firm by filing phony insurance claims and lawsuits. A Kansas City mobster was running the scam. He would arrange car accidents, file bogus medical claims, and have Kane file lawsuits on the victims' behalf. Eight doctors were also in on the ruse. Kane was so embarrassed when he was arrested that he immediately agreed to cooperate with prosecutors in order to avoid a trial.

"An excellent source had told me Kane was going to be murdered," Shur recalled, "but when I sent word to him, he was adamant about not wanting to enter WITSEC. He didn't want to disrupt his family or interfere with his wife's community and social activities." That's when Shur had arranged for the couple to come to his office on a weekend so he could personally explain the threat. But even then, they seemed oddly unconcerned. They cared more about returning home for an upcoming charitable event. "My God!" Shur erupted. "Don't you understand what I'm telling you? You are going to be *murdered*." Three days later the couple entered WITSEC.

Kane had refused to accept any WITSEC subsistence after he was relocated. Instead, he used his wife's money. They paid $400,000 in cash for an upscale six-bedroom house in Miami that shared a backyard with Congressman Dante Fascell. But he did let deputies find him a job as a claims inspector at the Social Security Administration, which paid him a salary of $30,000 per year. For the next ten years, Kane had been a model citizen—and then he had snapped.

Wanda Kolokoff, whose husband had been shot by Kane, accused Shur and other WITSEC officials in a civil lawsuit of gross negligence because no one had warned her husband that Kane had "homicidal tendencies," but a judge dismissed it.

Shur had spent much of his career trying to understand the criminal mind, and Kane simply didn't fit. He was better educated

than most criminals, was a devoted family man, and seemed to
have few vices. Yet he had become a murderer. "Kane had entered
the program before we were required to do risk assessments and
psychological testing of potential witnesses," said Shur, "but I
have little doubt he would have sailed through those evaluations
without anyone raising an eyebrow."

Shur asked the BOP psychologists if they knew of a foolproof
way to predict whether a potential WITSEC witness was going to
become violent after he was relocated. Based on their testing of
hundreds of WITSEC witnesses and thousands of other prisoners,
the psychologists sent him this answer: "There remains no consistent, reliable means by which to accurately predict an individual's future behavior."

"What this meant to me," Shur said later, "was exactly what
the Kane case demonstrated. Witnesses were unpredictable. People would tell me: 'You should have known this witness or that
witness was a walking time bomb.' But the truth is, every witness
who was a criminal was a gamble."

Shur then asked BOP psychologists if there was a difference
between the criminals who became government witnesses and
the criminals whom they testified against. He was told there
wasn't. Both came from the same damaged psychological bin.
While there were always exceptions, such as Kane, most had
"strong narcissistic personalities" and "severe antisocial tendencies." One BOP report described the "typical" WITSEC criminal
this way in a report prepared for Shur:

> WITSEC witnesses characteristically have superficial relation-
> ships with other people. Because of their shallow interpersonal
> skills and self-centered manner, they often experience serious dif-
> ficulty maintaining intimate, healthy relationships with others.
> Underneath their rough facade, these individuals are inwardly in-
> secure. Many feel inadequate and emotionally dependent. In addi-
> tion, they are often angry, belligerent, rebellious, and resentful of
> authority and rules. Their judgment is often poor and emotions,
> especially anger, tend to unduly color their assessment of disturb-
> ing personal events. When taken together, these tendencies fre-
> quently lead to acting out that includes violence.

Simply put: Criminals were criminals, and every one of them was equally capable of being a government witness or the defendant on trial. Circumstances had much more to do with who became a witness than any psychological traits. "In many cases, it's simply which rat is the first to jump off a sinking ship," a BOP psychologist explained. "The first one becomes the witness."

This was not the case, of course, when it came to the 6 percent of witnesses in the program with no criminal record. Many of them had simply been in the wrong place at the wrong time: a bookkeeper who discovered irregularities in a mob front company, a reporter who helped federal prosecutors by telling them about off-the-record conversations she had had with mobsters during a murder trial, a business owner who helped the FBI run a sting operation in New York after several local criminals mistook him for being in the LCN because his last name was the same as that of a New York City crime boss. These noncriminal witnesses usually paid a higher price than criminals in the WITSEC program.

"This was a terrible, terrible program for a noncriminal witness," Howard Safir recalled. "I told witnesses who were not criminals, 'Do not enter WITSEC unless you have absolutely no alternative, because it will be the toughest experience you will ever face.' "

While noncriminal witnesses would later voice the same complaints as others in WITSEC about long delays in getting new documents or other snafus they faced during relocation, they had to deal with a deeper problem. The psychologists described it as loss of identity, dignity, and self. "Without this program, my two daughters and I would be dead," a noncriminal WITSEC witness explained. "There is no question about it. But in giving up our pasts we paid a heavy price, because what you are as a person is based on where you came from and the people who love you. If you are honest, you suddenly find yourself being forced to live a lie, and you feel ashamed, even though you did the right thing in testifying, because you are now being forced to lie by your circumstances. You are not a criminal, but you are treated like one and made to act like one. I think they should have two programs: one for criminals and another for witnesses, with completely separate rules."

Although it had been more than fifteen years since Max Caulfield and his family entered WITSEC in August 1985, he was still bitter about the experience when he was interviewed for this book. His problems began in 1982, after he met Phil, the owner of several adult bookstores in Chicago. At the time, Caulfield was supporting his pregnant wife and their four-year-old daughter by training dogs, and when a police department changed its mind about buying one, he was left scrambling to find a way to pay his current bills. A friend had introduced him to Phil, who wanted a guard dog for his own personal protection, and he was so impressed by Caulfield that he not only bought the dog but hired him to work nights at one of his bookstores. A short time later, the store's manager went on a vacation, and Caulfield was responsible for collecting quarters from the store's video peep machines that showed X-rated movies. Caulfield bagged more than $6,000 worth of the coins during the week and reported that figure directly to Phil. "All of the sudden, Phil called me over to his house, and when I got there, he had this guy who was his enforcer standing right next to him," said Caulfield. "They both were angry and I was wondering what the hell I had done wrong." Phil demanded to know exactly how many quarters Caulfield had collected that week from the machines. Caulfield gave him an exact figure, which was over $6,000. "Then how do you explain this?" Phil demanded. "The guy who usually counts the coins has been giving me six hundred dollars a week for the past three years and that's all he says was ever in them. Now you count 'em for one week and there's more than six thousand." Without waiting for a reply, Phil continued, "Obviously, someone has been keeping some of the coins for himself."

Caulfield never saw the store manager again. He assumed Phil had fired him but didn't ask, and never knew whether something more sinister had happened. Phil promoted Caulfield, gave him a hefty pay raise, and began giving him gifts, including a newer car and clothes for his wife. He also arranged for him to move into a nicer apartment and began paying his rent. "I like to invest in people," he told him.

But when Caulfield objected to Phil bringing prostitutes into the bookstore, their relationship quickly soured. "I'm not going to be a keeper of a house of prostitution," Caulfield declared during a heated exchange. "Oh yeah?" Phil replied, pulling a ledger out of his desk.

"He handed me this ledger and it contained a list of every 'present' Phil had ever given me," Caulfield recalled. "If he bought me an ice cream cone, it was there." The list totaled more than $7,000, which Phil now said Caulfield owed him, plus $200 a week in unpaid interest.

"But you said those were gifts," Caulfield protested.

"I lied," Phil replied. "You want to be Mr. Clean, you got to pay up."

If Caulfield tried to quit his job at the store or didn't pay the debt, he and his family would be murdered, Phil warned. As soon as he could arrange it, Caulfield and his family fled town.

Chicago FBI agent Ivan Harris tracked him down a few months later. The FBI and the Chicago strike force had been watching Phil's adult bookstores for nearly five years and had noticed that Caulfield had disappeared. They also knew he did not have a criminal past. Caulfield agreed to testify against Phil, four of his employees, and three Chicago cops who had been accepting bribes. For seven months, the FBI hid him and his family in the Chicago area while it prepared its case. "They treated us really well," said Caulfield. "We felt safe." When Caulfield reported to the Marshals Service to undergo psychological testing so he could be approved to enter WITSEC, IRS agent Harris baby-sat his children. "Ivan took my daughter and newborn son to his daughter's birthday party—that's how much this guy was there for us."

But that special treatment ended, Caulfield said, as soon as the FBI turned him over to WITSEC. The WITSEC inspector in Roanoke, Virginia, where the family was first relocated, assumed he was a criminal. "I told him to read my file," Caulfield said. Even worse, when Caulfield pointed out that he wasn't a criminal, the inspector replied: "It doesn't really matter. We treat all witnesses the same."

"That meant he treated me like I was scum," Caulfield recalled.

Before they could settle in, the Caulfields' security was accidentally compromised. "They told us we would have to relocate and moved us into a motel temporarily," said Caulfield. "The night before we were scheduled to leave town, I went down to pay the long-distance portion of our telephone bill because I was responsible for all long-distance calls." Caulfield gave the night clerk $35 in cash. The next morning, that same clerk denied that Caulfield had paid him. "The WITSEC inspector automatically assumed I was lying. He told me to pay the clerk or I would be booted out of the program. I said, 'I am not a thief and I don't lie!' The desk clerk was lying but no one would believe me because I was in the program and suddenly I didn't have any credibility. Some night clerk, who knew WITSEC kept criminals in the motel and knew the marshals would believe his word over a criminal's, had pocketed my money. It was humiliating. I kept thinking: 'I didn't do anything wrong! Why am I being treated like a criminal?' "

With the inspector looking over his shoulder, Caulfield was forced to pay another $35.

Even though Caulfield warned deputies that his wife had relatives living in the Wilmington, Delaware area, WITSEC moved him there. "Once again, no one believed us. They just assumed we were lying to avoid being sent to Delaware. The marshals ended up sending a deputy to my wife's relative's house to knock on the door and ask if she was related to us." After living for nine weeks in a Wilmington hotel, they were flown to Bremerton, Washington, outside of Seattle, where the WITSEC inspector there greeted them with a stern warning: "You've been relocated twice, which means you've screwed up twice. Do it again and you'll be kicked out of the program!"

The stress of being relocated began to get to Caulfield. He broke into tears one night when he couldn't remember his alias while ordering pizza by phone. Meanwhile, his mother, Rose, became depressed about not being able to see her son and his family.

She pleaded in a letter to President Reagan for help. The White House sent the note to Safir, who ordered his inspectors to arrange a visit. Caulfield later claimed the inspectors who were given the assignment yelled at him because of the extra work it caused them.

Eight months later, Caulfield and his family met his parents in a Minneapolis, Minnesota, motel for a two-day visit. "Before my mother arrived, I told my kids the rules; 'You can't tell Grandma what your name is or where you live,' and during the visit we were not allowed to be together out of earshot of the marshals." At one point, Caulfield asked if he and his mother could talk privately. "They let us go into the bathroom, but said we had to keep the door open." Caulfield had wanted to hug his mom and tell her how much he missed her without the inspectors hovering over him. "I kept thinking, 'My God, we are adults here. I didn't do anything wrong. But they don't trust me to be alone with my own parents because they think I will tell them where we are hiding.' This is nuts."

On December 17, 1986, Caulfield was terminated from WITSEC because he had allowed a local police department to fingerprint him when he applied for a gun permit and because he had called FBI agent Ivan Harris to complain about how he was being treated in WITSEC. Since he still was waiting to testify against Phil and the others, Caulfield was terrified. He moved his family into a tiny camper and spent the next seven months hiding for short periods in state parks. His marriage collapsed, his wife sought psychiatric help, and his kids began having nightmares. When it came time for Phil's trial, the FBI arranged for Caulfield's safe return to Chicago. Phil and the other eight defendants were all subsequently convicted and sent to prison.

"Max was a very young man at the time," the FBI agent, Harris, recalled. "I have a lot of respect for him. He made a tremendous sacrifice."

After the trials, Caulfield went back into hiding. "I felt abandoned. I was scared. It took me years to recover. When my children asked me why their names were constantly changing, I told them there were bad people after them who wanted them dead. I wasn't going to lie to my kids." His son, Christopher, would later recall that his earliest childhood memories didn't make much sense. His father kept guns everywhere, even hidden behind the toilet. They lived in a series of motels, moving five or six times a year. "My family was paranoid," he later told a reporter at *New Times* magazine. "I remember seeing my father outside in a tree with a rifle waiting for a hit man to come. Other fathers didn't do that."

Caulfield changed his life around after he remarried. "My wife, Christine, saved my life. I was so haunted, I didn't know how to live in the real world anymore. I had no self-esteem until I met her." He blamed WITSEC. "These deputies treated us like garbage. They destroyed our sense of worth. I will never forgive them. They owe me and my family an apology."

Shur investigated several ways to make WITSEC easier for noncriminal witnesses, but none of them was adopted. "We thought about letting them keep their credit histories, for instance," Shur recalled, "but we discovered that would lead to a substantial increased risk of them being found. To replicate a credit history meant going to the credit reporting agencies—there was more than one—and getting them to change their records. This meant revealing to nongovernment agencies the new name, new location, and other identifying data of the relocated witness. One slipup by the credit agency and we could have a dead witness. I decided it simply wasn't worth the risk." In the end, noncriminal witnesses went through the identical relocation process. "The best we could do was be as forthcoming as possible when we explained the program to them so they would know it was not going to be easy."

Besides noncriminal witnesses, Shur found himself facing another unhappy group whose lives had been dramatically affected because of the program. These were the victims of relocated WITSEC witnesses, including relatives of murder victims and investors fleeced out of their life's savings.

"I always felt strongly that we needed to explain our actions to the public, especially when we made a mistake," said Shur. "I also thought we had a responsibility to listen, if for no other reason than to let someone who had been victimized say their piece. But I must admit, these were tough times for me, not because I felt we had done anything wrong, but because I could see their pain and understood that they were hurting, in part, because of a program that I had created."

One call in particular stuck in Shur's mind. A secretary told him that Pulitzer prize–winning journalist David Halberstam was on the telephone demanding to speak to a WITSEC official. She said he was so upset that Shur might not want to speak to him. Five years earlier, Halberstam's brother, Michael, a popular and well-respected cardiologist in Washington, D.C., had been murdered by a burglar. Halberstam and his wife, Elliott Jones, had returned home early one night and surprised Bernard C. Welch ransacking their house. Welch shot Halberstam and fled on foot. Although he was critically wounded, Halberstam got into his car and began driving to the hospital. En route, he spotted Welch running down a side street and ran him down. Moments later Halberstam blacked out and died. Police found $4 million in stolen gold, silver, jewelry, art objects, and furs in Welch's suburban house. They also identified him as an escaped convict who had broken out of prison in 1974 and had not been recaptured. A judge sentenced Welch to 143 years for the murder, and the Halberstam family hoped they had heard the last of him. But in 1985, Welch tipped off federal prosecutors to a prison escape plot, and Shur moved him into a WITSEC prison unit to protect him from other inmates.

Welch and another inmate escaped from the unit by using a weightlifter's barbell to knock a hole in a wall and then lowering themselves down to the sidewalk some six floors below with a seventy-five-foot extension cord.

"I felt Halberstam had a right to be angry and, if necessary, to scream at the person responsible for moving Welch," said Shur, "so I took the call, and when I got on the line, Halberstam asked me why someone such as Welch had been put into WITSEC. I explained why I had let him into a WITSEC prison unit. I assured him Welch was never going to be given a new identity or relocated. We had simply moved him from one prison to another to protect him from other inmates. Then I told him how sorry I was that Welch had escaped. He was angry at the loss of his brother and the escape, but polite. I felt awful afterward. I always did in these situations."

CBS correspondent Fred Graham had been a close friend of the murder victim, and he editorialized on the air about Welch's escape. "Gerald Shur . . . who accepted Welch into the Witness Protection Program . . . says it 'disgusted' him to accept Welch, but he did so because Welch gave important evidence to a grand jury," Graham told viewers. "But this is a flaw that has plagued the Witness Protection Program: Government lawyers seeking more convictions make deals with criminals who sometimes con the prosecutors in ways that produce more crimes and more heartbreak for innocent citizens. . . . Michael Halberstam's death has no meaning left at all."

When Welch was caught four months later, police found a million dollars' worth of stolen goods in his apartment and tied him to some forty burglaries, even though he had been on the loose for only four months. "I called David Halberstam and told him about Welch's capture. It was the only thing I could do," said Shur, "but while he thanked me, it clearly wasn't enough."

Shur knew from the statistical data available at the time that for every relocated witness who committed a new crime, there were three others who had not. He had testified so often about WITSEC that he could quote a slew of statistics that showed it had successfully removed thousands of criminals from the street, kept witnesses safe, and caused relatively little harm to the public. He could cite individual success stories—gangsters such as Pete "the Greek" Diapoulos, who had been Crazy Joe Gallo's bodyguard on April 7, 1972, when a lone gunman had walked into Umberto's Clam House in New York's Little Italy and opened fire. Gallo had been murdered, Diapoulos wounded. Few had thought the tough mobster would reform, but he had. "WITSEC gave me a new life," he recalled almost three decades after the shooting. "It gave me a chance to correct my life, and I never got into trouble again. Never."

But when Shur had to deal with the Halberstams of the world and the families of victims of witnesses such as Marion Pruett and Arthur Kane, all of his statistics and success stories seemed hollow. "I knew what I was doing was for a greater good, but that still didn't stop me from going home some nights heartbroken because of what had happened. I just didn't have all the answers. That was frustrating."

CHAPTER
TWENTY-THREE

B Y 1989, Shur was well-known inside the Justice Department as a problem solver who could maneuver through the bureaucracy and get complicated jobs done without bruising egos. Few were surprised when the Office of International Affairs (OIA) asked if he would take charge of the government's international prisoner transfer program. Shur looked into it and was shocked by what he discovered. Prior to the 1970s, few U.S. citizens had been arrested overseas and sentenced to long terms in foreign prisons. But the spread and use of illegal drugs changed this. Hundreds of American prisoners were now languishing in foreign prisons, often in inhumane conditions, and little was being done to help them because of red tape, confusion, and cultural misunderstandings. He jumped right in.

The Americans were not going to be turned loose after they were returned to the United States. They were going to be sent to federal prisons to complete their sentences. Still, life in the worst federal prison here was considered better than being locked up in most foreign prisons, especially in poor countries where living conditions were brutal. The State Department was especially concerned about thirty-four prisoners being held in Thailand, including several young women. According to a State Department report published in 1989, many of these women had been "seduced, lied to, or conned into transporting more than one kilo of heroin into Thailand."

Typically, a woman is approached overseas while traveling by a fast-talking man who offers her a free airplane ticket to anywhere she wants to go, in return for her delivering a package to "a friend" in Thailand. The man claims he can't make the trip himself because he can't get a visa or he comes up with some other believable excuse to appeal to her. Some women are told they will be carrying jewels. Others are told nothing and the illegal drugs are inserted in their luggage. They are stunned when the drugs are found and they are arrested.

The report warned that living conditions in Thai prisons were so harsh that few American women were expected to survive long sentences.

American women face numerous threats to their health. AIDS is rampant and is being passed along by male prison doctors, who routinely give gynecological examinations without ever changing their plastic gloves. Equally as dangerous is the . . . frequent non-availability of sanitary napkins for women during their menstrual cycle. . . . The women bleed on themselves and because of the extremely close sleeping quarters, frequently bleed on their neighbors.

"I had received letters from parents of several young people in Thai prisons for what I believed were often foolish mistakes, even though they were criminal acts," said Shur, "and when I thought about the heartbreak that these parents must have felt—first in learning that their daughter had been arrested and then discovering that she was receiving in their eyes the equivalent of a death sentence—I felt compelled to do what I could. I wasn't naive. I knew some of these women had known full well what they were doing. But I still didn't think anyone should have to die because of horrible living conditions, especially if I could get them back to the United States, where they would still be in prison, only a much safer and more sanitary one. The question was how was I going to help when I had been warned that Thai officials were very hesitant even to talk about this problem and were extremely sensitive about the criticism they were getting."

Shur mulled over the problem his first night in Bangkok. "I decided that I was not born to be a diplomat, that I couldn't dance around the issues, and that surely I could be direct without being offensive," he said. "I decided I had to be straightforward with the Thais."

He first went to meet personally with all the U.S. prisoners in Thai prisons. "The living conditions were appalling, even worse than I had read about. There were more flies than inmates in the prison kitchens. Sanitation didn't exist. But as I toured these prisons, I realized that U.S. prisoners were actually being treated better than Thai prisoners. The truth was that Thais just didn't like criminals."

In meetings with Thai officials, Shur spoke candidly. "Despite what I had been told, the Thais were just as candid with me. No one was offended. One official said to me, 'As with your government, our money is limited, and if we have a dollar to spend on a prisoner or a child, we are going to spend it on the child.' I discovered that criminals in Thailand are seen as outcasts, an affront to the Thais' gentle culture."

On May 11, 1990, as a result of Shur's trip, three American prisoners were released from the Bangkwang maximum-security prison and turned over to a federal Bureau of Prisons officer who escorted them back to United States. "It was the first transfer in the world of a foreign prisoner out of Thailand," Shur said later. During the next decade, Thailand would transfer 195 foreign prisoners back to their home countries, including forty-seven to the United States. But the problem of naive women being used as "mules" continued. In January 2000, there were eighty-eight U.S. prisoners being held in Thailand. Most were women, and only six were awaiting transfer.

In a 1993 memo, Shur noted that the number of Americans being held in foreign jails now totaled 2,500, most of them on drug-related charges. The biggest group—nearly 450—was in Mexico. Next, in order, were Germany, Canada, and Jamaica. "I was shocked when I discovered how many U.S. citizens were being beaten and tortured in Mexico," Shur later recalled, "so I met with

Mexican government officials to learn what could be done to stop this. They told me there wasn't much they could do. Nearly all the beatings and torture were taking place in local jails, and the officials said they didn't have any way to stop that. Once the Americans were sent to a regular prison, the torture ended. The officials assured me that it was not just Americans who were being tortured—the local Mexican police tortured everyone. It was easier getting a confession than investigating a case. But I didn't find that comforting."

After Janet Reno became U.S. attorney general, Shur was asked to oversee a large-scale prisoner transfer with Mexico, and in December 1993, one hundred Mexicans from United States prisons were swapped at the border for one hundred American prisoners. "Working on prisoner transfers appealed to my social-worker instincts," said Shur. "I felt having prisoners serve their time in prisons where they could speak the language, get visits from their family and friends, and understand the culture was much more rehabilitative than having them stuck in a foreign country."

A short time after Shur first began overseeing prisoner transfers, he was given yet another task that had nothing to do with WIT-SEC, and while he enjoyed his reputation for being a Justice Department pinch-hitter, this one turned his stomach.

In 1990, he was called before associate deputy attorney general Margaret Love and asked to draft a list of parole conditions for the release of Orlando Bosch, a militant anti-Castro activist who had become a hero to many Cuban-Americans. Bosch had been accused in the 1970s of helping plant a bomb on a Cuban-bound ship and of firing a bazooka at a freighter as part of an anti-Castro terrorism campaign. He had fled to Latin America but had been arrested in Venezuela and charged with masterminding the bombing of a Cuban airliner in October 1976 in which seventy-three people died. Bosch had spent eleven years in prison there while undergoing two trials, but he had been acquitted both times and finally released. When he returned to the United States in 1988, he was arrested by the INS and declared an undesirable alien since he was still a Cuban citizen. He was ordered deported. But no other country except Cuba would accept him, and the government was afraid that he would be executed if he was sent back. So Bosch had spent the last two years inside a federal prison.

"I didn't understand why we were suddenly going to release an airplane bomber who had killed so many people," Shur said later, "so I asked, 'Why? Why are we now going to release him?' Love told me that the White House had ordered the Justice Department to parole Bosch because President George Bush had received a call from his son Jeb, who had told his father that if he wanted to carry the Cuban vote in the next presidential election, he needed to release Orlando Bosch. I left that meeting *hot,* and on my way back to my office I thought about resigning. But then I decided that somebody else would just be given the job, so I decided I would draft the absolutely toughest rules possible for Bosch to follow. I was not going to make it easy on him."

Shur and a colleague drafted fourteen strict rules. If Bosch broke them, his parole could be revoked and he could be returned to prison. "One of them," Shur recalled, "was that he would be under house arrest." Not long after he submitted the restrictions to Love, Bosch was released. He received a hero's welcome from his supporters in Florida and held an immediate press conference in Coconut Grove, during which he condemned the restrictions that Shur had imposed. Even though he had been required by the restrictions to sever all connections with two militant anti-Castro groups, Bosch lauded both as "heroes of Cuba and heroes of mine" during his news conference and hinted that he would do whatever he could to support them.

Only one national newspaper saw politics at play. In an editorial, *The New York Times* questioned the timing of his release and speculated that Jeb Bush had pulled strings. It noted that the Justice Department, "under no legal compulsion, but conspicuous political pressure," had freed Bosch because of lobbying by "President Bush's son, Jeb," and it ended with this comment: "In the name of fighting terrorism, the U.S. sent the Air Force to bomb Libya . . . yet now the Bush administration coddles one of the hemisphere's most notorious terrorists. And for what reason? The only one evident is currying favor in South Florida."

Shur was angry for weeks. "Releasing a guy who was blowing up airplanes with innocent people aboard in exchange for winning the Cuban-American vote, and then having him bitch about the condition of his parole, was tough for me to swallow. I kept hoping for more of a public outcry, but there was none."

Shortly after Bosch was freed, several Cuban hotels were bombed and the Castro government blamed "the followers of activist Orlando Bosch" for the explosions. In Florida, Bosch denied it, but added that he was not unhappy it had happened.

The Justice Department had yet another prison-related assignment for Shur. He was asked to lead a delegation to the Bahamas to investigate complaints by U.S. prisoners who claimed the living conditions in the islands' Foxhill Penitentiary were barbaric. "Conditions there were worse than what I had seen in Thailand," he said later. "Prisoners who couldn't afford to bribe their guards were getting little food and not being allowed out of their cells to exercise."

When it came time for Shur to meet privately with American prisoners, he was led to a table and chair in a small dark room. A few minutes later, the door opened, but because there was a bright light behind the inmate standing there, Shur could see only his silhouette.

"Hello, Gerry," the inmate said. "What the hell did you do to get sent down to this hellhole?"

It was one of the very first Mafia witnesses whom he had put into the WITSEC program. Shur had not seen him for nearly twenty years and had no idea that he was in the Bahamian prison. "This is a frame-up," the prisoner said. "As soon as a new president is elected down here, I'll be released."

Shur returned home to file his report, and under U.S. pressure, the Bahamian government promised to improve conditions at the facility. A few months later, Shur learned the former WITSEC inmate had, in fact, talked his way out of prison after the presidential election. He was not surprised.

CHAPTER
TWENTY-FOUR

T HE FACE OF CRIME was changing once again in the early 1990s.

Having dealt with gangsters and drug traffickers, Shur faced two new enemies: inner-city gangs and international terrorists. Washington, D.C., was especially hard hit by gang violence, sparked largely by the spread of crack cocaine. It had a per capita murder rate three times higher than any other U.S. city. In 85 percent of all homicides, the police said they knew who the murderers were, but they could bring charges against only one-third of their suspects because witnesses were too scared to testify.

A gruesome example of the sort of intimidation the police were up against involved a Washington street gang that called itself the First Street Crew. The killing began after Arvell "Pork Chop" Williams, who was a friend of several gang members, volunteered to help police infiltrate an undercover narcotics officer into the gang. Word about his offer leaked out, and one afternoon while he was sitting in his parked car on a busy street, two gang members ran up next to the driver's window and began firing. They shot a total of eighteen times and then casually walked away. When the police arrived, they spotted several gang members mingling with onlookers. They were sipping sodas, munching on potato chips, and keeping track of whom the police were questioning. The first witness who agreed to testify was murdered two days after he was seen talking to the police. Three more were

killed a week later. Despite the danger, other eyewitnesses identified the killers, and police charged two gang members with murder. For the next ten months there were no killings. Then, during
a preliminary court hearing, a defense lawyer began grilling the
chief detective in the case about his witnesses. To protect them,
the detective referred to them only by numbers: W-2 and W-3.
Age, sex, and address were not revealed, but within hours, a forty-
one-year-old woman known to have information about the murder was shot as she walked home from a bus stop. As she lay
bleeding on the sidewalk, her killer put his gun into her mouth
and pulled the trigger again—a message to other potential witnesses. During the next four months, seven more witnesses were
murdered, bringing the total dead to twelve. The gang seemed to
be methodically eliminating potential witnesses within hours
after each was questioned. Suspicious, the police began looking for
possible leaks and discovered that a private detective had been
hired by the gang to shadow them. By the time the trial started,
forty witnesses were in hiding. Both of the murderers were found
guilty.

Federal prosecutors, the D.C. police, and gang experts told
Shur that the traditional WITSEC program was too harsh a solution for the witnesses in these cases. Many of them didn't want to
be permanently uprooted from their communities and cut off
from their family and friends. Inner-city gangs usually consisted of
only a few members and operated within a few blocks. They were
not huge organizations such as the LCN. Often, a witness's testimony would lead to everyone in the gang being convicted and sent
to prison, completely eliminating the threat. If the gang's leaders
were convicted, the gang itself often would disperse. Shur was told
that 85 percent of all violent crime in Washington happened
within six blocks of public-housing areas. "I was assured that we
could protect most witnesses simply by moving them away from
the housing projects until after they testified," said Shur. "They
could then return home and resume a normal life. I had my
doubts, but I was asked to put a short-term protection program to
the test."

Between 1991 and 1994, 78 witnesses and 150 of their relatives in Washington were temporarily relocated outside of housing projects until after they had testified. None of the witnesses was murdered. Meanwhile, more than a hundred gang members were convicted.

While the short-term program was considered a success, Shur remained skeptical. "I never really liked it," he said later. "I wanted as much certainty as possible that witnesses would be safe once we placed them in the program, and we could only get that if they entered the long-term program. The short-term program, in my opinion, allowed a higher-than-acceptable risk. We've been fortunate so far in that no one has been killed, but I've always felt it's only a matter of time." Despite Shur's reservations, other cities began copying the short-term program. In New York, the city's housing authority arranged for witnesses to be moved from one housing project to another to protect them temporarily while they were waiting to testify.

In dealing with international terrorists, Shur faced a different challenge: How do you make a witness from a foreign country and different culture blend into the American landscape? The Marshals Service had protected witnesses in terrorist cases before, including the 1988 Lockerbie, Scotland, airplane bombing and a 1989 bombing in Greece. But it was two attacks in New York that tested WITSEC. The February 26, 1993, bombing of New York's World Trade Center led to the arrest of four men, all followers of Ramzi Ahmed Yousef, an Islamic extremist who fled the country shortly after the blast killed six and tore a five-story hole in one of the twin towers. He was eventually caught in Pakistan and brought back for trial. Two years later, Sheik Omar Abdel-Rahman and nine of his followers were convicted of plotting to blow up several Manhattan landmarks.

WITSEC relocated more than a dozen foreign-born witnesses after they testified in the two trials. "They were going to stick out in Boise, Idaho," said Shur, "so just moving them out of Brooklyn wasn't going to be good enough. We were also worried because they had testified against religious sects that had ties to other militant Islamic groups. Some of these groups were well-organized paramilitary operations, with access to large sums of dollars."

WITSEC chief Eugene Coon brought in several experts in Middle Eastern culture to help his inspectors at the Safesite and Orientation Center prepare the witnesses for relocation. The FBI also provided him with intelligence reports about extremist groups and their supporters so WITSEC could make certain none of the witnesses was sent to a community where there were groups that supported the defendants and their sects. "It was unrealistic to have these people end all contact with their own culture," Shur said. "We couldn't expect them not to want to go to a mosque or a grocery store that catered to Middle Eastern customers." Instead, WITSEC chose cities where there were large numbers of immigrants, and Coon's inspectors helped the witnesses come up with logical explanations they could use if they were questioned about their pasts.

Besides gangs and terrorists, WITSEC was being used again to attack an old adversary. In 1987, eighteen Mafia figures were convicted in New York's infamous "Pizza Connection" trial of smuggling $1.6 billion of Turkish-bought and Sicilian-processed heroin into the United States. The mob used a string of pizza parlors throughout the East Coast and Midwest as fronts for its narcotics and money-laundering operations. While the seventeen-month trial put an end to the U.S. side of the case, more than two hundred Sicilian Mafia figures were still awaiting trial in Italy for supplying heroin to their New York counterparts. Several key witnesses, the most important a former Sicilian Mafioso named Tommaso Buscetta, were shuttled back and forth between Italy and the United States by WITSEC inspectors to testify. Buscetta was the first important mobster in Italy to break *omertà*. He would later be called the "most valuable Mafia informer on either side of the Atlantic" by federal and Italian prosecutors. He would spend eight years testifying in the United States and in Italy. In interviews, Buscetta said he would never have considered cooperating had it not been for WITSEC and the promise of a new identity and relocation in the United States. At the time he was recruited, he was hiding in Brazil, and he was offered WITSEC protection even though he was not a U.S. citizen and had not violated any U.S. laws. He was accepted into the program, and he died in April 2001 in an undisclosed location in the United States.

In the midst of handling these sensational cases, WITSEC came under attack within its own ranks. President Bush replaced Stanley J. Morris as director of the Marshals Service with a former federal prosecutor, Michael Moore, in 1989. Moore had aspirations of becoming a federal judge and early on locked horns with Howard Safir, whose performance had brought him kudos but whose ego had earned him a slew of enemies. Safir resigned. Morale dropped, especially in WITSEC. Moore served only fourteen months before he was appointed a judge. His replacement was another U.S. attorney, Henry Hudson, who also became a federal judge and so didn't stay long. President Clinton's pick in 1992 was Eduardo Gonzalez, the chief of police in Tampa, Florida. Although he had no federal law enforcement experience, he was initially welcomed because he saw the job as the pinnacle of his career, not a stepping-stone.

Gonzalez was told during briefings at the White House that the U.S. Marshals Service was a "troubled" organization that had grown too big for its mission. Some of Vice President Al Gore's aides, who were pushing his "Reinventing Government" program, complained that Safir's elite squads were duplicating jobs already being done by the FBI. When Gonzalez took control he began to streamline the service, and one of his first efforts was to combine its WITSEC operations with its court security program. It made sense to him because both protected people: WITSEC took care of witnesses and court security protected judges. Gonzalez told his underlings that WITSEC deputies were being "underutilized." The number of witnesses entering the program had dropped to around a hundred per year. Under Gonzalez, WITSEC was no longer the service's favored child; in fact, it fell to the bottom of the heap.

"I was baffled by his actions," Shur recalled. "If we had learned anything, it was that you needed a special type of deputy to work with witnesses. I felt Gonzalez was trying to turn back the clock." Shur warned Gonzalez privately and in memos that protecting federal judges and their families was "vastly different" from protecting and relocating witnesses and their families. "Judges do not need the panoply of additional services that criminal witnesses entering WITSEC require," he wrote in a memo. "It is therefore imperative that the Service maintain two specialized staffs." But Gonzalez was unconvinced. He told his aides that WITSEC inspectors were "crybabies" who thought they were better than other deputies and were "too secretive." In his eyes, the real heroes of the Marshals Service were the "PODs," the "poor old deputies" in the field, who didn't operate out of headquarters or belong to any of Safir's "alphabet special teams," such as WITSEC and FIST. "Despite Gene Coon's best efforts to keep everything going," said Shur, "this efficient and highly disciplined witness protection unit was slowly torn apart."

By 1994 Shur was beginning his thirty-fourth year as a Justice Department attorney and was about to turn sixty-one. He announced that he was going to retire at year's end. But he barely slowed down. He appeared before the Dutch parliament to describe how witness protection programs worked, met with Hong Kong officials who had asked him for permission to begin relocating their protected witnesses in the United States because their city was too small to hide them, and fought a 48 percent cut in the Marshals Service's budget request that had hit WITSEC especially hard. In one instance, WITSEC inspectors did not have enough money to purchase gasoline for their government cars because of cutbacks. But it was a call from an assistant U.S. attorney in the Eastern District of New York that brought his career full circle. "You can't leave yet. I'm going to get a court injunction against you leaving," she announced in jest, and then she turned serious. "We have a witness here who is reluctant to enter the program, and you're the only one I know who can reason with him and get him in. We simply can't afford to have him turn up dead. He's too important."

Shur had never before seen the security precautions put into place when "Sammy the Bull" Gravano was brought in to see him. "There were guards guarding guards guarding guards," he recalled. Gravano was already serving his prison sentence in a WITSEC unit, but he didn't want to enter the relocation phase of the program after he was paroled.

"I don't need you guys," he told Shur.

Shur talked about other Mafia tough guys who had thought they could take care of themselves. Gravano recognized most of them. All had been murdered. The problem was that he didn't want to be confined by Shur's rules. He was planning on writing a book, and he wanted to go on television and publicize it. Shur didn't argue with him. "What you have to consider is the long run and how we can help you," Shur explained. Where was Gravano going to live? What kind of work was he going to do? What about his family? In WITSEC, he could get a new name and a fresh start. If he really hated it, he could drop out voluntarily. That was something no one had told him before.

Shur fed Gravano's ego. There was a lot at stake here for the government. Gravano was being touted as the most important mob witness ever. He was historically important. The Justice Department couldn't afford to have him murdered. It would scare other witnesses. Suddenly Shur realized he was slipping into the same speech he had given Jimmy the Weasel nearly twenty years earlier. Knowing Gravano didn't give a damn if anyone else ever joined WITSEC, Shur emphasized how much the government needed him, wanted him, was eager to get him. He wanted not only to appeal to Gravano's vanity but to give him a sense of control. He also knew Gravano would be tempted to see how much he could get out of the deal. It was all part of the game. By the time the two men finished talking, Gravano was ready to sign the papers. He was Shur's last mafioso.

On July 18, 1994, attorney general Janet Reno presented Shur with one of the Justice Department's highest awards: the Attorney General's Award for Lifetime Achievement. She thanked him for creating WITSEC and being a pioneer when it came to introducing women into law enforcement as intelligence analysts and later helping them be promoted into jobs that historically had been held only by men. On a lesser note, she added that he had been the first to introduce fax machines at the Justice Department and had been in charge of such diverse jobs as deciding when U.S. attorneys could hypnotize federal witnesses.

The U.S. Marshals Service named Shur its Law Enforcement Officer of the Year and gave him a plaque with this inscription: "In recognition of your insight and dedication in developing WITSEC: a prosecutor's dream and a gangster's nightmare." At his retirement dinner in December 1994, he received accolades from a series of federal officials and foreign dignitaries. One admirer recalled that he had been a champion of civil rights. When a Mafia wiseguy in WITSEC had said, "Don't assign no niggers to protect me," Shur had delivered an antiracist sermon inches from the guy's nose. The next day, the mobster had several black deputies protecting him. Shur had ample accomplishments worth bragging about, but they weren't what he spoke about when he took the podium. Instead, he told the audience that the most satisfying moments of his career had been when he saw young people whom he had hired develop into highly skilled public servants.

Three years after Shur retired, Gonzalez asked him to review the Marshals Service's WITSEC operations. Shur was shocked because he had been openly critical of the new director's streamlining plans. For two months he interviewed WITSEC inspectors, reviewed cases, and talked to prosecutors, and in early 1999, he gave Gonzalez a grim nineteen-page report. Morale among WITSEC inspectors was as low as he had ever seen it, even worse than when the program began. The camaraderie that Safir and Coon had developed within the unit was gone. Shur wrote that WITSEC had fallen from being the most efficient witness protection program in the world to an operation that was stumbling along without direction, with no support from Gonzalez or other top administrators. Veteran inspectors were leaving the program, and many of those replacing them had not been carefully screened. Shur recommended a number of specific changes and urged immediate action, but Gonzalez left office in November 2000 without implementing any of the recommendations. He was succeeded by John Marshal Jr., who stayed less than two years. He too left WITSEC unchanged.

Sammy the Bull didn't stay straight long. He was arrested on drug-selling charges in February 2000 in Arizona, together with his wife, son, daughter, and son-in-law. He had undergone plastic surgery at his own expense and WITSEC had hidden him near Phoenix, where the government had helped him buy a half-million-dollar home and open a business called Creative Pools. But he had dropped out of WITSEC in 1997, hired a publicist, and started granting interviews on television and to newspapers and magazines. "For such a New York wiseguy, he was not so wise," an Arizona prosecutor told reporters. Even though his business built only two swimming pools in a yearlong period, he was seen driving expensive cars and flashing money around, causing authorities to suspect he was earning cash illegally. In May 2001, he was to plead guilty to running a drug ring, and was scheduled to be sentenced to fifteen years in prison.

Shur read about Gravano's arrest in the morning newspaper. The story described him as the latest in a long line of WITSEC witnesses who had escaped punishment by testifying and then disappearing with the government's help, only to get into trouble again. The names were all too familiar: Joseph Barboza, Vincent Teresa, Marion "Mad Dog" Pruett. Shur noted there was no mention in the article that the most recent study by the U.S. Marshals Service had found that less than 10 percent of the ninety relocated witnesses put into the program in one year had gotten in trouble.

Shur's friend Eugene Coon had recently retired, and one of the gifts that he had been given was a plaque that showed a phoenix rising from the ashes. It was the unofficial symbol of WITSEC. It represented witnesses being reborn, rising from their pasts to live honest lives. As Shur sat drinking a diet Coke and scanning the headlines, his thoughts turned to them.

EPILOGUE

Some Personal Observations by Gerald Shur

I AM A VERY LUCKY PERSON. I can honestly say that I couldn't have been happier going in to work each day at the U.S. Department of Justice. I felt privileged to be able to serve the public, and I enjoyed working in an office where we faced complex problems that had very real life-and-death consequences. It was a stressful environment, and decisions had to be made quickly; yet it was the pressure, the problem solving, the finding of the elusive successful solution that kept me going. When it came time for me to retire, I felt torn. Miriam was retiring after twenty-eight years of teaching first and second grade, and I wanted to spend the rest of my life full-time with her. At the same time, it was hard for me to walk away from a job that I had done for thirty-four years, and even more difficult to leave my co-workers and friends. It was seeing how well they performed that made it clear to me that although I was called the "father of WITSEC," it would function quite well without me.

I always liked the term "father" because WITSEC really had been like my child, and I liked to think, maybe sentimentally, that WITSEC was like a family. The program was fraught with problems in the early years. At times it seemed impossible to manage because of the number of different agencies involved and the huge number of witnesses coming into it. Like any parent, I took the brunt of criticism and attacks for its failings. But when it reached maturity, it had developed into an effective tool in our government's arsenal. The fact that WITSEC has never had one of its witnesses killed is a remarkable achievement that says much about the U.S. Marshals Service and the Federal Bureau of Prisons. Every single day WITSEC inspectors put their lives on the line protecting witnesses, knowing that the first shots fired will be at them. They do it because they are professionals. I admire, respect, and applaud that. They are brave and dedicated.

There are some concerns I have had over the years, and now seems a fitting time to address them. First, many people today don't realize just how powerful organized crime was in our country when I arrived at the Justice Department in 1961, and how behind we were in fighting it. As we have chronicled in this book, the first major investigation of La Cosa Nostra was done by Senator Estes Kefauver a decade earlier. I remember watching Frank Costello, known as the "prime minister of the underworld," testify. He had refused to allow his face to be shown on television, so cameras focused on his sweaty palms as he was questioned by chief counsel Rudolph Halley. Kefauver had discovered that every major city—*every one*—had been corrupted by the mob. In New York City, mobsters brazenly handed thousands of dollars' worth of bribes to Mayor William O'Dwyer in unmarked envelopes, and in New Orleans, the chief of detectives admitted spending $150,000 per year even though his salary was only $186 a month. Today's generation has become enamored with the mob, based on Hollywood's portrayal of it in movies such as *The Godfather* and television's *The Sopranos*. But believe me, there was nothing admirable about it when I was a kid listening to my father describe how people in the garment district were being cheated, threatened, and physically abused by mobsters.

Which brings me to another point. Under the highest counts I have ever seen, the Mafia has always numbered under five thousand members. That is a tiny, tiny, tiny fraction of the more than five million Italian immigrants who came to this country and helped make it what it is today. Yet even today anyone with an Italian name is still suspect. I find this prejudice repugnant. The mob was and is an evil and twisted criminal force run by a small element, and it is very important to remember this.

All of us who came in under Robert Kennedy to fight the mob were passionate about what we were doing. We didn't go to work for the Justice Department because of some desire for security or riches. I honestly believe we were answering John F. Kennedy's call. I remember my colleagues showing up to work on Saturdays and Sundays because they were committed to ridding the nation of organized crime. To all of us the mob was an enemy that had to be stopped but was untouchable because of *omertà*. WITSEC broke the code of silence, and once witnesses began talking, the mob's house of fear collapsed.

As horrible as the mob was, the gangsters I dealt with in the 1960s were in some ways a better breed of criminal than the thugs who took their places. In the early days, if Vinnie Teresa or Jimmy the Weasel made a promise to me, I could trust them to keep that promise. It was what they didn't say I had to worry about! I noticed that as the government began to have an effect on traditional organized crime, drug dealers, motorcycle gangs, and street gangs rushed in to fill the void. These were undisciplined and promiscuously violent groups that put the average citizen at greater personal risk. The mob had a criminal code of conduct, albeit a perverted one. The emerging groups had none—everyone was a potential target of their violence. I recall being taken aside by an elderly mobster who had spent years in prison and was in one of our WITSEC units. "Gerry, I have to warn you," he whispered to me. "You're not putting the same class of criminal into the program as you used to. These guys, they kill innocent people for no reason at all." He was right.

Some of the most interesting times in my career were spent talking to hundreds of criminals, almost all of whom were witnesses. I had no illusions why they were helping the government. Some had cut themselves a deal. Most knew it was their only chance to stay alive. Others wanted to take revenge on their former pals. They did not fool me, yet I genuinely felt there was some good in most of them, perhaps buried down deep, but still there. I recall going into a prison unit in which we kept the most difficult WITSEC inmates, only to find several of them sitting on the floor hooking rugs with designs of cartoon characters for kids in hospitals. Most of these men were killers, yet they took pride in their work for the kids. They had lived wasted lives and caused unbelievable pain to others. I often wondered what they could have accomplished if they had not chosen crime as a career.

There were many times while Pete and I were working on this book when I would become frustrated because it seemed that all we were doing was focusing on the failures, such as Marion

"Mad Dog" Pruett. WITSEC has, in fact, changed thousands of people's lives for the better. Criminals have given up crime. Children whose parents were murderers, thieves, or robbers have grown up in traditional law-abiding homes. WITSEC is a program that grew and changed because of its mistakes. After Pruett, we began giving witnesses psychological tests. Obviously, I wished we had done that before. I spent many sleepless nights tormented because of what he had done; I racked my brain trying to think of ways we could have stopped him. We didn't implement the change until Pruett showed us we needed new safeguards. The history of WITSEC is not a history of failures, however. It is a history of problems encountered and problems resolved. I also firmly believe that the thousands of witnesses and their families who have made a successful transition and are now leading ordinary lives should be allowed to maintain their privacy. I have often described a successful relocation as one in which the witness forgets he and his family have been relocated, forgets about us, and, most importantly, doesn't feel the need to look over his shoulder.

Studies undertaken during my tenure showed that WITSEC had a higher rehabilitation rate than any other government program. I believe there are several reasons why tough criminals changed after they were relocated. Obviously, many felt they would be killed, and the threat was such a deterrent that they gave up crime. But I also know from meeting thousands of witnesses that many of them jumped at the chance of a fresh start in a program that gave them a *real* opportunity to begin life over and improve themselves. They were moved into new surroundings, they were forced to cut their ties with their old associates, they were given comfortable housing and monthly subsistence, and we helped them find a job. We provided psychological support when needed, too. In short, we did all we could to help them succeed. Compare that to a convict who is released from prison. If he is lucky, he is sent to a halfway house. Because of his criminal record, his chances of finding a good job are slim. Worse, he has no money, may not have a home, and often ends up running with the same criminal friends that he left behind when he went to prison.

Not only did WITSEC help criminals change their lives, but

it helped remove more than ten thousand criminals from the streets. This is another aspect of the program that is often over-looked. Yes, Sammy Gravano killed nineteen people. Yes, he is a gangster who did horrible things, and I put him into WITSEC. But Gravano also was responsible for putting LCN crime boss John Gotti and thirty-six other gangsters in prison. How many people's lives were saved because Gotti and his crew were put behind bars?

When the program first started, some argued that it was okay to use mob witnesses but that the government shouldn't assist them by giving them new names and sending them into unaware communities. It should simply give them a sum of money and send them on their way. I've always felt this view was unrealistic. No witness is going to testify knowing that he or she will be mur-dered just before taking the witness stand or just after leaving it. Surely the witness is entitled to some form of protection—as is society. The best thing we could do for society was help this wit-ness to start a new, productive, honest life. As our recidivism stud-ies have shown, by helping a witness through the relocation process we were reducing the chances of his again committing crimes. I also remember that photo album the Bureau of Narcotics prepared early in my career, which contained eight-by-ten photo-graphs of government informants murdered in the most gruesome ways. I was determined never to see another album like that.

Is WITSEC perfect? Of course not. Have I made mistakes? You bet I have, plenty of them. One of my biggest regrets is that WITSEC was always most difficult for witnesses who were not criminals. Innocent bystanders who simply were in the wrong place at the wrong time paid a heavy price for doing the right thing. I wish there had been some way to make life easier for them.

I felt confident when I left the Justice Department's Office of Enforcement Operations that WITSEC was in extremely capable hands. Steve T'Kach, who took over my witness protection func-tions, was providing guidance as to policy. Sallie Saliba, who joined me just out of college, was now running WITSEC day to day and doing an extraordinary job. Cathy Breeden, who had worked with me since 1969, except for a short stint, was handling covert operations. But I soon discovered how fragile even a well-established government program can be. I have always felt that former director Gonzalez was well-meaning when he decided to combine court security with WITSEC, but that proved to be a disaster. When Gonzalez asked me to review the program three years later, I discovered morale was terrible. Old-timers were retiring and the service was finding it difficult to attract new blood.

Gonzalez didn't like specialists, but being a WITSEC inspector requires special skills—a real knack for dealing with people who are under tremendous stress and who often are not the nicest or easiest people in the world to get along with. Protecting federal judges is clearly one of the Marshals Service's most important functions. Consequently, the judges' needs are going to take priority. When I did my review, I found that after the merger of court security and WITSEC, resources that were supposed to be going to WITSEC were being diverted to meet the needs of the judges. The result was that WITSEC was understaffed. Much of what we accomplished during the years that I oversaw the program was and currently is in jeopardy. Dozens of Marshals Service employees pleaded with me for help. That is the reason I bring the problems up now: as a call to arms of sorts. This program is too important to law enforcement not to give it the support that it so desperately needs—especially now, after the terrorist attacks on September 11, 2001. Much as the Mafia was, terrorist groups are extremely difficult to penetrate. But WITSEC has proven it can help turn terrorists against each other. The key is demonstrating that we can protect those courageous enough to cooperate. This is another reason why we must restore WITSEC to the way it was before the changes, and give its specialists the resources they need.

The seeds for this book were sown shortly after I retired. Miriam encouraged me to put some of my experiences down on paper so my grandchildren would have the benefit of knowing a little more about their grandfather. I called it "Papa's Journal." As I worked, the book began to take on a life of its own, and when

Pete joined me, it became more than the recollections of a grand-father.

As I sit here writing these final pages and looking back on my career, I wonder where time has gone. I remember so clearly the first time that I entered the Justice Department and the awe I felt. I recall once reading a saying by St. Francis of Assisi that we have made this book's epigraph. He wrote, "Start by doing what's nec-essary, then what's possible, and suddenly you are doing the im-possible." I like that. It seems to fit WITSEC.

I also find myself thinking of my father, Abe. One night when I was a teenager, he took me with him to a tenement building on the Lower East Side where he was attending a community meet-ing held with members of a local teenage gang. As he was speak-ing, a gang member suddenly blurted out: "You don't know what it is like for us growing up here." My father's answer surprised me. "I know very much what it's like here," he said. "I grew up here. This was my ghetto, too." He described the poverty, the gangs, the lack of education, the anti-Semitism. Then he spoke about how he had improved himself by working hard during the day and at night studying Shakespeare and music. He said he now owned a busi-ness and lived in an apartment in an upscale part of Manhattan. "You can do the same," he insisted. During the ride home, my fa-ther talked to me, as he often did, about how important it was for a person to always remember his roots and to always, *always*, give something back to the community. "You owe a debt to society for what you have been given. You must give something back."

Dad, I tried.

ACKNOWLEDGMENTS

GERALD SHUR is deeply indebted to his colleagues in the Department of Justice with whom he worked from 1961 through 1995, especially those very dedicated public servants in the Office of Enforcement Operations. They consistently have served their country with integrity and dedication. Henry Petersen, John C. Keeney, and Phil Wilens deserve special recognition as mentors and friends. He thanks Fred Hess for allowing him to be his "partner" and for his support in OEO.

He is indebted to the original ten intelligence analysts: Peggy Alexander, Cathy Kimrey, Carol Cragg, Marcy Edelman, Pat Gerts, Andrea Grier, Patricia Harrison, Suzanne Hinson, Carolyn Prugh, Irene Rosenbloom, and to Linda Kuzmack, who soon followed them. Deep thanks to Hope Byrne and Sue Grimes, who became the first analysts solely dedicated to WITSEC, and to Betty Cleghorn, Dottie McElroy, and Janet Carter, his secretaries during WITSEC's formative years. They were succeeded by many others who faced equal challenges with the same dedication. He is especially grateful to his special assistant Diane Reid for her many years of valuable advice.

He was privileged to work for and with a succession of many chiefs of the Organized Crime and Racketeering Section, each of whom brought his own special talents and contributions to the war on organized crime: Edwyn Silberling, William G. Hundley, Henry Petersen, William S. Lynch, David Margolis, Kurt Muellenberg, and Paul Coffey. He is grateful for the efforts and cooperation of the federal investigators and the prosecutors who fought the real battles in the war on organized crime; they distinguished themselves every day. He is particularly grateful to G. Robert Blakey, the architect of the most significant laws used to fight organized crime, one of which was the foundation on which WITSEC was created. Had it not been for the imagination of Charles Rogovin,

Martin Danziger, Joseph Nardoza, and Henry Ruth, many organized crime efforts would not have come to fruition.

There are many who served in the United States Marshals Service to whom he is especially indebted for the success of the Witness Program: Wayne Colburn, Bill Hall, Stan Morris, John Twomey, Louis McKinney, Eugene Coon, Howard Safir, John Cleveland, Hugh McDonald, and the hundreds of inspectors, deputies, and specialists. In the Bureau of Prisons, he is grateful to Norm Carlson, Mike Quinlan, Kathy Hawk-Sawyer, J. D. Williams, Shirley Stutely Ritchie, and the other BOP employees for their extraordinary contributions to the success of WITSEC.

He is indebted to his agent, Ron Goldfarb, and the book's editor, Ann Harris, for making it a reality, and to his friend Joan Santelli for reading the manuscript and candidly sharing her views with him.

Gerry Shur is proud of the members of his family and grateful for the joy they bring to him: his wife, Miriam, who gives him her love and support always, and Ilene, Ronald, Jim, Leslie, Adena, Stephanie, David, Sam, Michael, Amanda, Evan, Walt, Ruth, Bob, Rick, Jim, Paulette, David, Cindy, Katie, Barbara, and Jeffrey. He is especially indebted to Abe and Emma Heifetz, who accepted him as their son from the moment Miriam and he married, and to Lillian Nissel, his aunt, who has always demonstrated faith and pride in whatever he does. He is thankful to his parents, Rose and Abe, who died much too young, for their love, warmth, and constant reassurance that he had worth. It was from them he learned the importance of integrity and the necessity that we all give back.

Finally, he thanks all of those who entered WITSEC, witnesses and family members, who because of their willingness to give up their current lives and testify, often under the fear of death, contributed so much to our system of justice. For it is they who have had to endure the hardships of relocation and changed lives.

Pete Earley would like to thank the following persons for their help with this book: Bernard Breslin, Don Campbell, Max

Caulfield, Pascal "Paddy" Calabrese, Peter Carlson, Norman Carlson, Lee Coppola, Paul Coffey, Eugene Coon, Monica D'antuono, Ronald Goldfarb, Fred Graham, Eduardo Gonzalez, Jesse Grider, William Hall, Wanda Watson Haynes, William G. Hundley, Eric Jurgensen, Reis R. Kash, Thomas Kennelly, John C. Keeney, Jerry Lyda, John S. Martel, Salvatore R. Martoche, Donald "Bud" McPherson, Max Mermelstein, Al Miller, Marilyn Mode, John Partington, Robert "Bob" Peloquin, Lynda Pinello, John Russell, Charles Rogovin, Howard Safir, Edward Schwarzer, John Twomey, Philip Wilens, and J. D. Williams. He would also like to personally thank Witness X for having the courage to share her personal story.

In addition, Pete would like to thank Nowathip Boulom; LeRue and Ellen Brown; Gloria Brown; James Brown; Phillip and Joanne Corn; Phillip M. Cowan; Donnie Davis and Dana Davis; George and Linda Earley; Mike Farrell; Toni Shaklee Focht; Carol Grudis; Keran Harrington; Marie Heffelfinger; Bill and Rosemary Luzi; John Martel; Richard and Joan Miles; Marvin Minoff; Mike Sager; C. T. "Tibbie" Shades; Charles and Donna Stackhouse; Dale and Judy Stewart; Lynn and LouAnn Smith; Elsie and Jay Strine; and Jennifer Unter. Special thanks go to fellow authors Walter Harrington and Nelson DeMille, as well as Robert Gottlieb at Trident Media Group and, at Bantam Books, Ann Harris, Matthew Martin, Irwyn Applebaum, Barb Burg, and Sue Warga.

Finally, Pete thanks Elmer and Jean Earley, who proofread the manuscript, offered advice, and provided moral support. Most of all, he would like to thank his wife, Patti Michele, for her unwavering encouragement, wisdom, and love, and their children, Stephen, Kevin, Tony, Kathy, Kyle, Evan, and Traci, for the blessings that they bring into his life every day.

INDEX